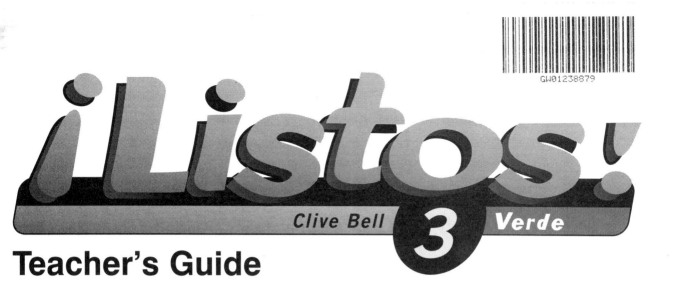

¡Listos!

Clive Bell

3 Verde

Teacher's Guide

Heinemann

Heinemann Educational Publishers, Halley Court, Jordan Hill,
Oxford OX2 8EJ.

A division of Harcourt Education Limited.

Heinemann is the registered trademark of Harcourt Education Limited.

First published 2002

07 06
10 9 8 7 6 5

A catalogue record is available for this book from the
British Library on request.

10-digit ISBN: 0 435430 33 5
13-digit ISBN: 978 0 435430 33 7

Produced by Ken Vail Graphic Design, Cambridge.

Cover photograph by Travel Ink/Simon Reddy (Kio Towers, Madrid)

Printed in the UK by Athenaeum Press Ltd.

Tel: 01865 888058 www.heinemann.co.uk

Contents

Introduction

¡Listos! is a three-stage Spanish course leading to examinations at 16+. It offers students of a wide range of ability a structured approach with plenty of variety and a clear progression. Stage 1 of *¡Listos!* is accompanied by differentiated workbooks (one for reinforcement and one for extension). In stages 2 and 3 there are separate Student's Books (*Rojo* and *Verde*) as well as separate workbooks, catering for the needs of students at different levels and preparing them for different examination tiers.

¡Listos! 3 can be used by students who have progressed from *¡Listos! 1* and *2* but is also suitable for those who have followed a different Spanish course in the earlier stages and are using *¡Listos! 3* to prepare for examinations at 16+. In GCSE terms, *¡Listos! 3 Verde* is for Foundation Tier and *¡Listos! 3 Rojo* for Higher Tier candidates; however, both books contain material suitable for potential C-grade candidates. The *Rojo* and *Verde* books also follow the same chapter and topic sequence, making it easy for students to move from one to the other if necessary.

The components

¡Listos! 3 Verde consists of:

- Student's Book
- 3 cassettes or CDs
- Teacher's Guide
- Foundation Workbook.

Also available to accompany both *¡Listos! 3 Rojo* and *Verde* are:

- Assessment Pack for AQA
- Assessment Pack for other examining bodies
- Colour OHT File.

Student's Book

The Student's Book includes all the language required to cover the 16+ exam syllabuses thoroughly and is expected to take students two years to complete. The material is divided into 10 chapters or modules (*módulos*). Each module begins with one or two double-page spreads of revision (*Repaso*), covering language presented in the preceding stages or in earlier modules of *¡Listos! 3*. The revision is followed by the core units (four or five spreads), which present and practise the new key language and structures.

At the end of each module there is a summary of the key vocabulary. This is arranged in topic areas, making it highly effective for revision purposes.

After every second module there is a speaking practice section (*Hablar*) designed to prepare students for the speaking test in their examination. Each *Hablar* section provides examination-style practice of the topics covered in the two modules, consisting of general conversation questions, role-plays and presentations. Useful tips on revision and exam technique are also given. (For further details, see the separate section of this introduction below.)

At the back of the Student's Book are four sections for further practice and reference. The *Trabajo de curso* pages are designed particularly for students who are taking the coursework option. However, as well as offering specific advice to those doing coursework, these pages are suitable for all students and can be used for additional practice in class or as homework. (For further details, see below.)

The *Leer y escribir* section offers further reading and writing practice for each module. (For further details, see below.)

The *Gramática* section, also at the back of the Student's Book, provides explanations of all the grammar introduced in *¡Listos! 3* and comprehensive coverage of the examination grammar syllabus. It also includes grammar practice exercises; answers to these can be found on pages 180–181 of this Teacher's Guide.

The Student's Book ends with a comprehensive Spanish–English and a shorter English–Spanish glossary *(Vocabulario)*.

Cassettes/CDs

There are 3 cassettes or CDs for *¡Listos! 3 Rojo*. They contain listening material for both presentation and practice, recorded by native speakers. The material is of varying length and complexity and will need to be presented in different ways to different groups of students. It is often helpful to get students to listen to a short passage or brief utterances with their pens down, so that they can concentrate on tuning in to the language and grasping the 'geography' of what they have to understand. If students try to write and listen at the same time, they can miss most of what is said. Differentiation can be achieved by asking for different (or additional) information, providing extra support (e.g. pre-listening activities, an extra hearing of the recording, vocabulary support) or pausing the recording after each utterance. However, stopping the recording too often can be unhelpful, as it interrupts the flow and can 'chop off' words or phrases.

Correction and feedback must be quick and focused. Correction might involve showing students the transcript, putting the answers on the OHP (especially if they take the form of a grid) and asking students what they got wrong and why, rather than simply asking for their scores. The emphasis should be on learning rather than testing. It is well known that listening can all too easily be turned into a test and that this can demotivate students.

Workbooks

The Foundation and Higher workbooks provide self-access practice material in reading and writing for use alongside the Student's Books. They are divided into 10 modules to match the Student's Books and, as well as offering a wide variety of reading and writing activities, each module in the workbooks ends with one page of grammar practice and one page of questions to prepare students for the general conversation section of the speaking test.

Miniature versions of the Higher workbook pages are reproduced at the end of each module in this Teacher's Guide, and answers to the closed exercises are given.

Teacher's Guide

The Teacher's Guide contains:

- a general overview of *¡Listos! 3 Rojo*
- UK examination mapping grids
- answers to grammar practice exercises

and for each module:

- an overview grid summarising the topics, grammar, skills and key language introduced
- teaching notes for all activities
- answers to closed Student's Book and workbook activities
- transcripts of recorded material.

Assessment

There are two assessment packs available to accompany *¡Listos! 3*: one for the AQA and one for the other examining bodies. The style of questions and rubrics reflects that of the relevant examination body and each pack contains test material at three levels: Foundation, Foundation/Higher and Higher.

There are five blocks of assessment material, each covering two modules, and a further cumulative assessment block for Modules 1–5, which could be used as a 'mock' examination at the end of the first year of examination study. Each assessment block comprises separate tests in listening, speaking, reading and writing. Transcripts for the listening tests and suggested teacher scripts for role-plays are included, and mark schemes are provided for all tests.

Covering a module

As mentioned above, each module begins with one or two *Repaso* spreads revising language that has already been presented. Able pupils might work quickly through these sections or do just a selection of the activities before moving on to the core units. As there is often a lot of language to cover, there are

many matching, ranking and multiple-choice activities, and blocks of text with the important language highlighted. All four skills are covered in the *Repaso* sections.

Each of the four or five double-page spreads comprising the core units of the module presents a different theme relating to the overall topic; hence a theme is covered in a single double-page spread, and again all four skills are practised. Students are given support in the form of *Gramática* and *¡Ojo!* boxes. The *Gramática* boxes highlight the main grammar points and refer students to the relevant pages of the grammar section at the back of the Student's Book. The *¡Ojo!* boxes alert students to particular problems or give advice on learning and examination techniques. In addition, extra vocabulary is provided for students to use where appropriate.

There is progression both within each unit and through the module as a whole. Simple activities lead on to more challenging ones, and the most difficult tasks or the most complex aspects of the theme are generally left to the end.

In the Repaso sections, instructions are given in Spanish and English, to help ease the students into the module. Thereafter the instructions are almost always given in the target language (the grammar section is an exception) and have been made as consistent as possible. One of the keys to effective use of the target language is exemplification: demonstrating to students what they have to do makes clear what is expected of them, so that recourse to the mother tongue generally becomes unnecessary.

Incorporating ICT into the *¡Listos!* classroom

Under the National Curriculum, students are entitled to have access to ICT to support their learning, and the richness of material, range of skills and benefits that students can derive from using ICT effectively and often are well known. The use of ICT is encouraged at many points in the Student's Book and Teacher's Guide.

Students are encouraged to use word processing to create a personal file (*fichero personal*) covering all the main topic areas. They can add to this as they cover a topic in more detail and at a more sophisticated level. The ability to draft and re-draft is crucial and, as an ICT expert pointed out some years ago, instead of writing being characterised by errors and often resulting in a sense of failure, the beauty of word processing is that success can be guaranteed.

Communication is covered by the inclusion of email messages as a common type of text in the Student's Book. Students should be encouraged to use email themselves, to communicate with Spanish speakers around the world and to improve their Spanish.

▣ Introduction

Finally, the Internet has dramatically improved access to the culture and language in recent years. It is just as easy to get a tourist guide or weather forecast for Mexico City as it is for Madrid. Hotel brochures, train timetables and online supermarket shopping are all at the students' fingertips, and the use of websites and search engines is suggested at appropriate points in this Teacher's Guide. Please consult www.Heinemann.co.uk/secondary/languages for the most up-to-date information and a selection of useful websites.

Any websites accessed must be previewed by the teacher to ensure that they are still active and contain appropriate material (and none that is inappropriate!). Accessing the web via the school or college Intranet is a safe way of ensuring that the material meets your needs. Should you discover that any of the website details listed are incorrect, please let us know so that we can update the information on our website.

Hablar

The *Hablar* sections (after Modules 2, 4, 6, 8 and 10) are designed to prepare students for the speaking test in their examination. They provide practice of and advice on general conversation questions, role-plays and presentations. In the role-plays, students are given cues (in Spanish or English) or open-ended/unscripted prompts (denoted by !). Students must be encouraged from the start to take responsibility for their own learning and to provide reciprocal help for their partner. A useful technique is to insist that both partners play both roles and that (unless they have genuine difficulties) they only ask the teacher to come and hear them once they are sure that they can perform both roles satisfactorily. This ensures that teacher time is spent mostly on moderating their best performance and that the students evaluate critically both their own and their partner's performance. Tape-recording role-plays, presentations and conversations, either in class or for homework, allows students to review their work and discuss it with their teacher or an assistant (if available). It is a particularly good way of identifying common mistakes in pronunciation and exploring ways of enriching spoken language or incorporating good communication strategies. Over time, students can build up a bank of such recordings that will help them with revision (and, incidentally, constitute a record of progress).

Trabajo de curso

The coursework section at the back of the Student's Book provides material to support five of the most popular coursework assignments and is linked to five of the modules, as follows:

Módulo 2: *En el cole*	Assignment: *Tu uniforme escolar ideal*
Módulo 3: *De vacaciones*	Assignment: *Unas vacaciones pasadas*
Módulo 5: *¿Qué te ha pasado?*	Assignment: *Tu ciudad/región*
Módulo 6: *En casa y en el trabajo*	Assignment: *Tus prácticas o un trabajo a tiempo parcial*
Módulo 8: *De juerga*	Assignment: *Una película o una novela interesante*

As mentioned above, this section provides useful practice material regardless of whether students are taking the coursework option and, indeed, whether they choose to do these particular assignments or different ones. Model texts are followed by comprehension tasks, additional grammar support and a range of tips and advice to enhance students' writing.

Teachers may choose to use the relevant coursework pages either as an extension of the module students are working on or later, when students are due to start work on a coursework assignment.

Answers to closed exercises in the *Trabajo de curso* are provided at the end of the relevant modules in the teaching notes.

Leer y escribir

In the *Leer y escribir* section at the back of the Student's Book there is a double-page spread of extra self-access reading and writing material for each module of the course. This can be used for classwork, homework or cover lessons. The wide variety of text types includes emails, letters, magazine articles, recipes and advertisements, and is exploited by an equally varied range of comprehension tasks. In most cases, the texts provide a model for the writing tasks that follow. Both the reading and the writing tasks reflect those that students are likely to encounter in examinations.

There is some differentiation in this section: generally speaking, the texts and/or tasks on the left-hand page of each spread are more straightforward than those on the right-hand page. However, the *Leer y escribir* section aims above all to stretch the most able students and ensure that they reach their full examination potential.

Answers to the closed reading comprehension tasks are provided at the end of each module in the teaching notes.

Coverage of AQA Themes/Modules in ¡Listos! 3 Verde (for Specifications A and B)

M = *Módulo* (Chapter)

Theme/Module 1: My World

Subtopic	Page references
1A Self, Family and Friends	
• Self, family and pets:	M1, pp. 6–11; M9 pp. 112–113
• Jobs:	M10, pp. 122–123
• Opinions, feelings about family members:	M9, pp. 114–115.
1B Interests and Hobbies	
• Hobbies, interests, opinions, preferences:	M6, pp. 70–71; M8, p. 100, pp.104–105
• Invitation to participate:	M8, pp. 98–101
1C Home and Local Environment	
• Describing your home and bedroom:	M1, pp. 12–13
• Home town, local environment, opinions:	M1, pp. 14–15
• Climate, comparisons:	M3, p.33
1D Daily Routine	
• Weekday routine:	M2, pp. 26–27
• Mealtimes:	M6, p. 71
1E School and Future Plans	
• Classroom requests and instructions:	M2, p. 20
• Subjects, opinions, timetable:	M2, pp. 18, p. 21; M10, p. 123
• School size, location, facilities:	M2, pp. 23
• Extra curricular activities:	M2, pp. 24–25
• School uniform, rules:	M2, p. 22
• Future plans in coming months:	***

Theme/Module 2: Holiday Time and Travel

Subtopic	Page references
2A Travel, Transport and Finding the way	
• Exchange information about location:	M4, pp. 44–45
• Maps, timetables:	M4, pp. 45, 49
• Buy tickets:	M4, pp. 48–49
• Means of transport, time, cost, problems:	M4 pp. 46–47, pp. 50–51
2B Tourism	
• Information about town, area:	M3, pp. 38–39
• Weather conditions:	M3, pp. 32–33
• Holidays, details and opinions:	M3, pp. 40–41
• Local customs, festivals:	***

Coverage of AQA Themes/Modules in *¡Listos! 3 Verde*

Subtopic	Page references
2C Accommodation	
• Exchanging information about accommodation:	M5, pp. 64–66
• Making complaints:	M5, pp. 67
2D Holiday Activities	
• Signs about restaurants:	M3, p. 35–36
• Reserving a table, ordering, paying:	M3 pp. 36–37
• Making complaints:	M3, p. 37
2E Services	
• Postal services, changing money:	***
• Loss or theft:	***
• Doctor, dentist, chemist, common ailments:	M5, pp. 58–63
• Accident or breakdown:	M4, pp. 50–53

Theme/Module 3: Work and Lifestyle

Subtopic	Page references
3A Home life	
• Eating habits, meals and mealtimes:	M6, p. 71
• Help around the house:	M6, pp. 72–73
3B Healthy Living	
• Eating habits, healthy eating and lifestyles:	M6, pp. 76–77
3C Part-time Jobs and Work Experience	
• Telephone calls and messages:	M8, p. 101
• Weekend jobs and work experience:	M6, pp. 74–75
3D Leisure	
• TV programmes, radio, films:	M6, pp. 70
• Facilities, times, prices:	M8, pp. 98–99
• Arrangements to go out:	M8, pp. 98–101
• Publicity about leisure events:	***
• Sporting events:	***
• Narrating a film:	M6, p. 79; *Trabajo de curso* (8 – De juerga (A))
3E Shopping	
• Signs and announcements:	M7, pp. 84–85, p. 92, p. 90
• Exchange information about goods:	M7, pp. 84–85, pp. 87, 89, 90–91
• Shopping experiences, preferences:	M7, pp. 86–87, p. 90
• Complaints about unsatisfactory goods:	M7, p. 91

Theme/Module 4: The Young Person in Society

Subtopic	Page references
4A Character and Personal Relationships	
• Character and personality, self and famous people:	M9, pp. 110–113; M8, p. 102; *Leer y escribir* (1 – Me presento)
• Feelings, problems and relationships:	M9, pp. 114–115
• Marriage and children:	***
4B The Environment	
• Transport issues:	M4, p. 47
• Pollution, recycling, improving the environment:	M9, pp. 118–119
4C Education	
• Types of school, further education and training:	M10, pp. 124–125
• Issues at school:	***
4D Careers and Future Plans	
• Advantages/disadvantages of occupations, career plans:	M10, p. 126
• Working abroad:	***
• Future plans, marriage, children:	M10, pp. 126–127
4E Social Issues, Choices and Responsibilities	
• Seeking a job, advertisements:	M10, pp. 128–129
• Smoking, alcohol, drugs:	M9, pp. 116–117; *Leer y escribir* (9 – Yo)

Coverage of Edexcel topic areas in ¡Listos! 3 Verde

M = *Módulo* (Chapter)

At Home and Abroad

Subtopic	Page references
• Things to see and do:	M1, pp. 14–15; M3, p. 39; M8, pp. 100–101
• Life in the town, countryside, seaside:	M1, pp. 14–15
• Weather and climate:	M3, p. 33, M1, p.32
• Travel, transport and directions:	M4, pp. 44–51
• Holidays, tourist information and accommodation:	M3, pp. 38–39, 40–41; M5, pp. 64–65
• Services and shopping abroad:	M7, pp. 84–93
• Customs, everyday life and traditions in target-language countries and communities:	M2, p.27

Education, Training and Employment

Subtopic	Page references
• School life and routine:	M2, pp. 18–27
• Different types of jobs:	M10, pp. 126–127, pp. 140–141
• Job advertisements, applications and interviews:	M10, pp. 126–129, p.131; *Leer y escribir* (10 – El futuro)
• Future plans and work experience:	M6, pp. 74–75; M10, pp. 123–129

House, Home and Daily Routine

Subtopic	Page references
• Types of home, rooms, furniture and garden:	M1, pp. 12–13
• Information about self, family and friends:	M1, pp. 6–11; M9, pp. 110–113
• Helping around the house:	M6, pp. 72–73
• Food and drink:	M3, pp. 36–37; M6, p. 76–77; M7, pp. 88–89

Media, Entertainment and Youth Culture

Subtopic	Page references
• Sport, entertainment and fashion:	M8, pp. 96–101
• Famous personalities:	M8, p. 102; M9, p. 111; *Leer y escribir* (1 – Me presento)
• The media:	M6, pp. 78–79
• Current affairs, social and environmental issues:	M4, p. 47; M9, pp. 118–119

Social Activities, Fitness and Health

Subtopic	Page references
• Free time (evenings, weekends, meeting people):	M8, pp. 96–101
• Special occasions: ***	
• Hobbies, interests, sports and exercise:	M6, p. 76; M8, pp. 104–105
• Shopping and money matters:	M7, pp. 84–93
• Accidents, injuries, common ailments and health issues (smoking, drugs):	M5, pp. 58–63; M6, pp. 76–77; M9, pp. 116–117; *Leer y escribir* (9 – Yo)

▞ Coverage of OCR contexts in ¡Listos! 3 Verde

M = *Módulo* (Chapter)

1 Everyday Activities

Subtopic	Page references
a Home life	
• Information about homes, rooms, features:	M1, pp. 12–13
• Routine:	M2, pp. 26–27, M6, p. 71
b School life	
• General information about schools:	M2, p. 20
• Subjects, like and dislikes:	M2, pp. 21–22
• Views and opinions:	M2, pp. 21, 24; M10, p. 123
c Eating and drinking	
• Expressing requirements in restaurants:	M3, p. 35, pp. 36–37
• Problems in a restaurant:	M3, p. 37
• Health and diet:	M6, pp. 76–77
d Health and fitness	
• Symptoms and injuries:	M5, pp. 59–63
• Keeping healthy:	M6, pp. 76–77
• Instructions for medicines or remedies	***
• Account of injury:	M5, p. 62

2 Personal and Social Life

Subtopic	Page references
a People – the family and new contacts	
• Give information about and describe family members:	M1, pp. 6–11; M9, pp. 110–112
• Invitations and responses:	M8, pp. 100–101
• Family life:	***
b Free time	
• Interests, pastimes, leisure activities:	M6, p. 70; M8, pp. 96–101, 104–105
• Describe activity, event or performance:	M6, p. 79; M8, p. 105
c Making appointments	
• Where and when to meet:	M8, p. 98, p. 100–101
• Accepting, rejecting, modifying:	M8, p. 100
d Special occasions	
• Festivals and special events:	***

Coverage of OCR contexts in *¡Listos! 3 Verde*

3 The World Around Us

Subtopic	Page references
a The local and other areas	
• Local area and opinions:	M1, pp. 14–15
• Account of an area visited:	M3, p. 40
b Shopping and public services	
• Specify requirements, rejecting, choosing:	M7, pp. 88–91, 85–87
• Account of period of time in the shops:	***
• Money exchanges:	***
• Explain that something has been lost:	***
• Problems or complaints in a shop:	M7, pp. 87, 91
c The environment	
• Weather and forecasts:	M3, pp. 32–33, p. 40
• Problems affecting the environment, conservation:	M9, pp. 118–119, *Leer y escribir* (10 – El futuro); *Trabajo de curso* (9 – Yo)
d Going places	
• Give and seek directions:	M4, pp. 44–45
• Information about best way to reach destination:	M4, p. 46
• Times and timetables:	M4, p. 49
• Traffic and transport bulletins:	M4, p. 49
• Buying tickets:	M4, pp. 48–49
• Account of a journey:	M4, p. 53
• Mechanical problems with a car:	M4, p. 50–51
• Advantages and disadvantages of different transport:	M4, p. 47
• Account of an accident:	M4, pp. 52–53

4 The World of Work

Subtopic	Page references
a Jobs and work experience	
• Jobs done by candidate:	M6, pp. 74–75
• Information about and applying for a job:	M10, pp. 127–131; *Leer y escribir* (10 – El futuro)
• Spending money:	M6, p. 74
• Opinions about a job:	M6, p. 75; M10, p. 126
b Careers and life-long learning	
• Preferences and opinions about further study, work, jobs:	M10, pp. 124–126

5 The International World

Subtopic	Page references
a The media	
• Listening and viewing habits:	M6, pp. 78–79
• Opinions about the media:	M6, p. 79
• Preferences for magazines:	***
b World issues, events and people	
• Famous people:	M8, p. 102; M9, p. 111, *Leer y escribir* (1 – Me presento)
c Tourism and holidays	
• Information about tourist possibilities:	M3, pp. 38–39; Leer y escribir (5 – ¿Qué te ha pasado?)
• Account of holiday, in past or planned, opinions:	M3, p. 39, pp. 40–41; *Trabajo de curso* (3 – De vacaciones); *Leer y Escribir* (5 – ¿Qué te ha pasado?)
d Tourist and holiday accommodation	
• Seek and give information about requirements:	M5, pp. 64–66
• Problems during the stay:	M5, p. 67
• Describe past holiday accommodation:	M5, p. 67

■■ Coverage of WJEC topics ■ in ¡Listos! 3 Verde

M = *Módulo* (Chapter)

Topic A

Subtopic	Page references
a The language of the classroom	M2, p. 20
b Home life and school	
(i) Home life	
• Home and garden:	M1, pp. 12–13
• Daily routines:	M2, pp. 26–27
• Meals at home:	M6, p. 71
• Household tasks:	M6, pp. 72–73
• Spending money:	M6, p. 74
(ii) School	
• School size and facilities:	M2, p. 23
• Arrival and departure, routine times:	M2, pp. 26–27
• School uniform:	M2, p. 22
• School activities, clubs:	M2, pp. 24–25
• Subjects, likes and dislikes:	M2, p. 18, p. 21
c Food, health and fitness	
(i) Food	
• Restaurants, requirements, menus, bill, prices:	M3, p. 35, pp. 36–37
• Make complaints:	M3, p. 37
• Recipes:	*Leer y escribir* (3 – De vacaciones)
(ii) Health and fitness	
• Describe symptoms, personal accident, advice from chemist:	M5, pp. 58–62
• Instructions concerning medicines:	M5, p. 61
• Say whether anyone is hurt:	M4, pp. 52–53

Topic B

Subtopic	Page references
a Self, family and personal relationships	
• Name, age, date of birth, pets, nationality:	M1, pp. 8–9; M9, pp. 110–113
• Describe themselves and others:	M1, pp. 6–7, 10–11
• Likes and dislikes in radio, TV, clothes:	M6, pp. 78; M7, p. 90
• Comment on personality traits and relationships:	M9, pp. 110–115
b Free time and social activities	
• Buy food, drink, clothes, souvenirs:	M7, pp. 84–91
• Locations and facilities in department stores:	M7, p. 92
• Return items, give reasons:	M7, p. 91
• Make bookings (cinema, etc.):	M8, pp. 99

Subtopic	Page references
• Opinions on event (e.g. film, concert):	M8, p. 105
c Holidays and special occasions	
• Procedures at bank, information office:	M3, p. 38
• Say where they want to go:	M4, pp. 44, 46
• Distances, public transport:	M1, p. 15; M4, p. 46–47
• Buy tickets:	M4, pp. 48
• Read timetables, understand times of arrival and departure:	M4, p. 49
• Obtain help at a garage:	M4, p. 51
• Understand travel announcements, information:	M4, pp. 48–49

Topic C

Subtopic	Page references
a Home town and local area	
• Where they live, local area and amenities:	M1, pp. 14–15
b Natural and made environment	
• Describe climate:	***
c People, places and customs	
• Aspects of life in other countries:	M2, p.27; M3, p. 40

Topic D

Subtopic	Page references
a Further education and training	
• Subjects, likes and dislikes:	M2, p. 18, p. 21; M10, p. 123
b Careers and employment	
• Discuss work experience:	M6, pp. 74–75; *Trabajo de curso* (6 – En casa y en el trabajo)
• Describe part-time job:	M6, pp. 74–75
• Future aspirations and career plans:	M10, pp. 124–129
c Language and communication in the workplace	
• Request special services (e.g. fax):	***

Topic E

Subtopic	Page references
a Tourism at home and abroad	
• Discuss holidays:	M3, pp. 32–33, pp. 39–41
• Vacancies and facilities at youth hostels, hotels, campsites:	M5, pp. 64–65
• Understand notices:	M5, p. 66

Coverage of WJEC topics in *¡Listos! 3 Verde*

Subtopic	Page references
• Enquire about lost property:	***
• Report accident, breakdown:	M4, pp. 51–53
• Complain about accommodation:	M5, p. 67
• Ask for and give directions:	M4, pp. 44–45
• Discuss advantages and disadvantages of different transport:	M4, p. 47
b Life in other countries and communities	
• Comment on aspects of interest:	M3, p. 40
c World events and issues	
• Comment on matters of environmental interest:	M9, pp. 118–119

Coverage of CCEA topics in ¡Listos! 3 Verde

M = *Módulo* (Chapter)

1 Everyday Activities

Subtopic	Page references
(a) Home and school life	
• Home routine:	M2, pp. 26–27; M6, p. 80
• Helping at home:	M6, pp. 72–73
• School building, facilities, number of teachers/pupils:	M2, p. 23
• School day:	M2, pp. 22–23, 27
• Timetable, subjects:	M2, pp. 21–22
(b) Food and drink	
• Likes, dislikes, preferences:	M3, pp. 34–35, pp. 36–37
• Recipes:	*Leer y escribir* (3 – De vacaciones)
(c) Shopping	
• Location of shopping facilities/department/item:	M7, p. 92
• Types of items, availability, cost, number/quantity/ colour/size, trying something on:	M7, pp. 84–91
• Shopping announcements, special offers:	M7, pp. 96–98
• Exchanging an item, refund:	M7, p. 91
(d) Eating out	
• Reservation, menu, ordering food/drinks, settling bill:	M3, pp. 34–35, pp. 36–37
• Problems and complaints:	M3, p. 37

2 Personal Life and Social Relationships

Subtopic	Page references
(a) Self, family and friends	
• Name, date of birth, age, family, pets:	M1, pp. 6–7
• Physical features, nationality, marital status:	M1, pp. 8–11
(b) Health	
• Condition, needs, pain, illnesses, doctor/dentist/ chemist:	M5, pp. 58 62
• Medicines, treatments, instructions:	M5, p. 61
(c) Leisure activities	
• Hobbies/interests/pastimes:	M6, pp. 70, 78–79; M8, pp.96–97, pp. 98–101, 104–105
• Times, dates, tickets:	M8, pp. 99–100
• Making arrangements to go out:	M8, pp. 98, 100–101
• Merits of performances, events:	M6, p.79; M8, p. 104; *Trabajo de curso* (8 – De juerga)
(d) Celebrations and special occasions	
• Festivals:	***
• Making arrangements for a party:	***

Coverage of CCEA topics in ¡Listos! 3 Verde

3 The World Around Us

Subtopic	Page references
(a) House and home	
• Type of house/flat, rooms, furniture:	M1, pp. 12–13
(b) Town and countryside	
• Places in the town:	M4, pp. 44–45
• District/region:	M1, pp. 14–15
• Town and countryside:	M1, p. 14
(c) Getting around	
• Directions:	M4, pp. 44–45
• Means of transport, distances:	M1, p. 15; M4, pp. 46–47
(d) Weather	
• Seasons, types of weather:	M3, p. 32–33
• Weather forecasts:	***

4 The World of Work

Subtopic	Page references
(a) Services to the Public	
• Bank:	***
• Reporting/describing lost property:	***
• Services in garage:	M4, pp. 50–51
(b) Occupations and places of work	
• Full time and part time jobs:	M6, pp. 74–75; M10, pp. 124–127
(c) Future plans and careers	
• Type of job they would like to do, reasons:	M10, pp. 126, 128
• Plans for immediate future:	M10, p.124–126
• Opportunities for work in target country:	M10, p.128

5 The International World

Subtopic	Page references
(a) Travel and Tourism	
• Planning to go on holiday:	M3, p. 32
• Hostel, campsite, hotel, etc:	M5, pp. 64–67
• What you did on holiday:	M3, pp. 40–41; *Trabajo de curso* (3 – De vacaciones)
• Travel problems:	M4, p. 47, 53
(b) Life in countries or communities in which the target language is spoken	
• Nationalities:	M1, p. 10
• Main cities/towns, national dishes, regions;	M3, p. 32, p. 35, pp. 39–40; *Leer y escribir* (3 – De vacaciones)
(c) Caring for the environment	
• Pollution matters, conservation measures:	M9, pp. 118–119; *Trabajo de curso* (9 – Yo)

Coverage of Standard Grade topics and topic development in ¡Listos! 3 Verde

M = *Módulo* (Chapter)

Basic topics	Page references	Topic development	Page references
• Name, age, domicile, nationality, cardinal points, spelling:	M1, pp. 6–7, p. 10–12	• Personal information given/asked for in polite language:	M10, pp. 129–131
• Members of family, friends, physical description:	M1, pp. 6–10	• Members of family, friends and friendship, physical and character description, interpersonal problems and relationships:	M1, pp. 6–11; M9 pp. 114–115, 110–113
• Parts of body, illness/accidents:	M5, pp. 55–63; M4, pp. 52–53	• Parts of body, illness/accidents, making appointments:	M5, pp. 58–63; M4, pp. 52–53
• Own house/rooms:	M1, pp. 12–13	• Houses/rooms and ideal house:	M1, pp. 12–13
• Routine:	M2, pp. 26–27; M6, p. 71	• Comparison of routine and lifestyles in Scotland and in the other country/countries:	M2, pp. 27
• Birthdays, days, dates:	M1, pp. 6–7	• Life in future, past and future events (in routine):	M2, pp. 26–27; M6, p. 71
• School subjects, time:	M2, pp. 18–19, pp. 21–22	• Comparison of education system with that of the other country/countries	***
• Leisure, sports:	M6, pp. 70, 78–79; M8, pp. 96–101, 104–105	• Leisure, sports and health issues: healthy eating, exercise, drugs; TV, film and music:	M6, pp. 76–77, 78–79; M8, pp. 96–101, 104–105; M9, pp. 116–117
• Foods/drinks:	M3, pp. 34–35; M6, p. 71; M7, p. 85, pp. 88–89	• Other food issues:	M6, pp. 76–77
• Snack food:	M3, p. 35	• Restaurants/menus, making arrangements:	M3, p. 35, pp. 36–37; M8, pp. 98–101
• Simple directions:	M4, pp. 44–45	• Giving simple and complex directions:	M4, pp. 44–45
• Buildings:	M4, pp. 44–45	• Tourist information, comparison town/country, helping the environment:	M3, pp. 38–39; M1, p. 14; M9, pp. 118–119
• Pocket money:	***	• Changing money:	***
• Simple transactions, e.g. souvenirs, gifts, clothes, accommodation, snacks, transport:	M7, pp. 84–87, pp. 88–91; M5, pp. 64–65; M3, p. 37; M4, pp. 46, 48	• Negotiating transactional problems: • Jobs/working and studying: • Relative merits of jobs: • Work experience: • Future employment:	M7, p. 87, 89, 91 M10, pp. 114–129 M10, p. 126 M6, pp. 74–75 M10, pp. 126–129
• Countries/place:	M1, p. 10–11, pp. 14–15; M3, pp. 32, 38–40	• Travel information: • Travel plans: • Relative merits of different means of transport: • Comparisons between different countries: ***	M4, pp. 46, 48–49 M3, p. 39 M4, p. 47
• Weather:	M3, p. 32–33	• Weather: • Future holidays: • Ideal holidays: • Past holidays:	M3, pp. 32–33 M3, pp. 32–33, 39 M3, p. 40 M3, pp. 40–41

módulo 1 · Me Presento

(Student's Book pages 6–17)

Main topics and objectives	Grammar	Skills
Repaso 1 (pp. 6–7) Giving personal details Using the Spanish alphabet	Present tense, first person singular	
Repaso 2 (pp. 8–9) Talking about family members Describing your own and other people's physical appearance	Adjective endings	
1 Te presento a mi familia (pp. 10–11) Introducing family members Talking about nationality	*Éste/ésta/éstos/éstas* Soy de (España)./Soy español(a). Present tense of *ser* and *tener*	
2 Mi casa (pp. 12–13) Describing your house or flat Describing your bedroom	*(No) Me gusta(n) /Me encanta(n)* Use of *hay*	Giving reasons for opinions Use adjectives and *y* and *pero* in descriptions
3 ¿Cómo es tu barrio? (pp. 14–15) Describing the area where you live Talking about transport and distances	Adjectives Adverbial expressions	Giving opinions Using *afortunadamente* and *desafortunadamente*

Key language

Buenos días/¡Hola!
¿Qué tal? ¿Cómo estás? (Estoy) fenomenal/muy bien/regular/fatal.
¿Cómo te llamas? Me llamo …/Soy …
¿Dónde vives? Soy de …/Vivo en …
¿Cómo se escribe? (Spanish alphabet)
¿Cuántos años tienes? Tengo … años.
¿Cuándo es tu cumpleaños? Es el … de …
¿Tienes animales en casa?
Sí, tengo un perro (dos perros, etc.)/un gato/un conejo/un pez/un caballo/un periquito/un ratón.
No, no tengo animales.

¿Cuántas personas hay en tu familia? Hay … personas.
¿Tienes hermanos? Sí, tengo…/ No, soy hijo/a único/a.
¿Cómo se llama tu madre/padre/ hermano/hermana/madrastra/
padrastro/hermanastro/hermanastra/abuelo/abuela/tío/tía/primo/a?
Mi … se llama …
¿Cómo eres/es …?
Tengo/tiene los ojos azules/marrones/grises/verdes
y el pelo corto/largo/rizado/liso/moreno/negro.
Tengo/tiene bigote. Llevo/lleva gafas.
Soy/es (bastante) alto/a /bajo/a /delgado/a /gordo/a /guapo/a /feo/a/rubio/a /moreno/a /viejo/a/joven.

Éste/ésta es mi… Éstos/éstas son mis…
¿De dónde eres? Soy de España/ México/ Los Estados Unidos/ Soy español/a/ inglés/a/ escocés/a/ irlandés/a/ galés/a/
australiano/a/ brasileño/a/ portugués/a/ alemán/a

Vivo en un piso/un chalet/una casa …
… en el campo/centro de la ciudad/la costa/un pueblo/las afueras/un barrio residencial.
¿Cómo es tu casa/tu dormitorio?
Es (muy/bastante/demasiado) grande/pequeño/a /moderno/a /antiguo/a /bonito/a.
Hay/Tiene cuatro dormitorios/una cocina/un comedor/salón/cuarto de baño/garaje/balcón.
En mi dormitorio (no) hay …
Mi dormitorio (no) tiene un espejo/radiador/ordenador/vídeo/una televisión/una cama/alfombra/lámpara/moqueta/
silla/mesa/ventana/muchos libros/pósters de …
(No) Me gusta(n)/me encanta(n) mi casa/mi dormitorio/los cantantes de Rap, porque …

Mi barrio es …
(No) Me gusta mi barrio porque … (No) Hay mucho que hacer.
Hay mucho/a contaminación/desempleo/turismo.
Es (muy/bastante/demasiado) antiguo/moderno/precioso/ruidoso/ sucio/tranquilo/turístico.
En mi pueblo/barrio (no) hay un/una …
Mi casa/piso está cerca del/de la/de los/de las…
… hospital/castillo/río/centro comercial/museo/polideportivo/ ayuntamiento/supermercado/ discoteca/biblioteca/playa/
estación de trenes/tiendas.
¿Dónde está el/la… /están los/las …?
Está(n) (muy/bastante) lejos/cerca
Está(n) a (unos/sólo) … kilómetros (de aquí).
¿Cómo se va allí? En tren/coche/autobús/metro/ bicicleta/a pie

Repaso 1

(Student's Book pages 6–7)

Main topics and objectives

Giving personal details
Using the Spanish alphabet

Grammar

Present tense, first person singular

Key language

Buenos días/¡Hola!
*¿Qué tal?/Cómo estás? (Estoy) fenomenal/muy bien/
regular/fatal.*
¿Cómo te llamas? Me llamo …/Soy …
¿Dónde vives? Soy de …/Vivo en …

¿Cómo se escribe? (Spanish alphabet)
¿Cuántos años tienes? Tengo … años.
¿Cuándo es tu cumpleaños? Es el … de …
¿Tienes animales en casa?
*Sí, tengo un perro (dos perros, etc.)/un gato/un
conejo/un pez/un caballo/un periquito/ un ratón.*
No, no tengo animales.

Resources

Cassette A, side 1
CD 1, track 2
Cuaderno pages 2–7
Gramática 7.2, page 171

Suggestions

Module 1 of *¡Listos! 3* and a number of subsequent
modules cover a range of themes and topics which
pupils will be expected to talk (and possibly write)
about in their GCSE/Standard Grade examination.
Students should be encouraged to build up a *fichero
personal* of likely questions and their answers, for
revision purposes. This could be done either on
paper, or keyed in and stored on a floppy disk, which
can then be updated on a regular basis.

The aim of the *Repaso* sections is to provide quick
revision of language covered in earlier stages, without
pupils becoming bored, and to demonstrate to them
how much they already know. Depending on pupils'
ability and time available, teachers can either work
through the *Repaso* quickly in class, or use the
material for homework.

1a Lee y rellena los espacios.

Reading. Personal details. Students read two short
texts and complete statements in Spanish.

Answers

1 María vive en *Colombia*.
2 Carlos es de *España*.
3 María tiene dos *hermanos*.
4 El cumpleaños de Carlos es el veintidós de *marzo*.
5 El perro de María se llama *Fidel*.
6 Carlos vive con sus *padres*.

1b Anota el nombre, la edad y el cumpleaños. (1–6)

Listening. Name, age and birthdays. Students note
down the details. The Spanish names used and all
months of the year are given on the page, for support
with spelling.

Tapescript

1 – *¡Hola! Me llamo Juan. Tengo 18 años y mi cumpleaños
es el 15 de agosto.*

2 – *¡Hola! ¿Qué tal? Soy Anita. Tengo 15 años. Mi
cumpleaños es el 2 de mayo.*
3 – *Me presento. Soy Manolo. Mi cumpleaños es el 17 de
junio. Tengo 16 años.*
4 – *Me llamo Susana y tengo 14 años. Mi cumpleaños es el
26 de febrero.*
5 – *¡Hola! ¿Qué hay? Me llamo Pablo. Tengo 19 años y
celebro mi cumpleaños el 7 de noviembre.*
6 – *Soy Nuria. Mi cumpleaños es el primero de marzo.
Tengo 20 años.*

Answers

1 Juan/18 años/15 de agosto
2 Anita/15 años/2 de mayo
3 Manolo/16 años/17 de junio
4 Susana/14 años/26 de febrero
5 Pablo/19 años/7 de noviembre
6 Nuria/20 años/primero de marzo

1c Escribe las letras correctas. (1–5)

Listening. Pets. Pupils match up what they hear with
the correct picture.

Tapescript

1 – *Tengo un gato bonito.*
2 – *Tengo dos ratones pequeños.*
3 – *Tengo un conejo grande.*
4 – *Tengo un pez y un periquito en casa.*
5 – *Tengo un caballo que se llama Pancho y dos
perros también.*

Answers

| 1 A | 2 D | 3 C | 4 E | 5 B |

1d Túrnate con tu compañero/a.

Speaking. Pairwork on personal details. Pupils greet
each other and ask and answer questions about how
they are, their name, where they live, their age,
birthday and pets. All the key questions are given,
and support for answers is provided in the form of

brief prompts and the beginnings of sentences in Spanish. The *¡Ojo!* feature also reminds pupils that most present tense verbs end in 'o' in the first person singular and in 's' in the second person singular. Teachers may wish to revise numbers in Spanish and refer students to the language support for giving dates and month of the year, on page 6, to help students say when their birthday is.

1e ¡Preséntate!

Speaking. Personal details. Students introduce themselves, giving as many personal details as possible. They can refer to the texts in 1a as good models and, where appropriate, should be encouraged to use conjunctions (e.g. *y, pero, con*), simple clauses (e.g. *que se llama(n)*) and give reasons (*porque …*). Getting students into the habit of using such enhancements from the beginning will stand them in good stead later on in their GCSE/Standard Grade examination.

2a ¿Cómo se escriben los nombres de estas ciudades? (1–5)

Listening. Spelling the names of towns in Spain and Latin America. Pupils listen to people being asked the name of the town where they live and how it is spelled, then write down the name of the town. The key language support on the page gives students a phonetic version of how each letter of the alphabet is said in Spanish. Teachers may want to give students practice of understanding and saying the alphabet, before tackling the listening task.

Tapescript

1 – ¿Dónde vives?
 – Vivo en Medellín.
 – ¿Cómo se escribe?
 – M-e-d-e-l-l-í-n.
2 – ¿Dónde vives?
 – Vivo en Granada.
 – ¿Cómo se escribe?
 – G-r-a-n-a-d-a.
3 ¿Dónde vives?
 – Vivo en Guadalajara.
 – ¿Cómo se escribe?
 – G-u-a-d-a-l-a-j-a-r-a.
4 – ¿Dónde vives?
 – Vivo en Lérida.
 – ¿Cómo se escribe?
 – L-é-r-i-d-a.
5 – ¿Dónde vives?
 – Vivo en Caracas.
 – ¿Cómo se escribe?
 – C-a-r-a-c-a-s.

Answers

As tapescript

2b

En secreto escoge tres equipos de fútbol y deletrea cada uno. Tu compañero/a escribe el equipo correcto.

Speaking. Spanish alphabet/spelling. A list of Spanish football teams is provided. Students work in pairs. One student closes or covers his/her book and their partner spells out the name of one of the teams, in Spanish. The first student writes down the name, then checks their spelling against the book. Students take turns to do the spelling and the writing.

2c Rellena los espacios de los apellidos. (1–4)

Listening. Spelling your name. Students listen to people being asked to spell their name and fill in gaps, to complete the names. Teachers can follow this with oral practice of the question *¿Cómo se escribe?* and encourage students to spell out their name and/or the name of the place where they live, in Spanish.

Tapescript

1 – Buenas tardes. Me llamo Señor Ramírez.
 – ¿Cómo se escribe?
 – R-a-m-í-r-e-z.
2 – Buenos días. Me llamo Señora Martín.
 – ¿Cómo se escribe?
 – M-a-r-t-í-n.
3 – Buenas noches. Me llamo Señora Aguilera.
 – ¿Cómo se escribe?
 – A-g-u-i-l-e-r-a.
4 – Hola. Me llamo Señor Sayavera.
 – ¿Cómo se escribe?
 – S-a-y-a-v-e-r-a.

Answers

As tapescript

Repaso 2

(Student's Book pages 8–9)

Main topics and objectives

Talking about family members
Describing your own and other people's physical appearance

Grammar

Adjective endings

Key language

¿Cuántas personas hay en tu familia?
Hay … personas.
¿Tienes hermanos? Sí, tengo … /No, soy hijo/a único/a.
¿Cómo se llama tu madre/padre/hermano/hermana/
madrastra/padrastro/hermanastro/hermanastra/

abuelo /abuela/tío/tía/primo/a (etc)?
Mi … se llama …
¿Cómo eres/es …?
Tengo/tiene los ojos azules/marrones/grises/verdes
y el pelo corto/largo/rizado/liso/moreno/negro.
Tengo/tiene bigote.
Llevo/lleva gafas.
Soy/es (bastante) alto/a /bajo/a /delgado/a /gordo/a
/guapo/a /feo/a /rubio/a /moreno/a /viejo/a /joven.

Resources

Cassette A, side 1
CD 1, track 2
Cuaderno pages 2–7
Gramática 3, pages 167–168

1a Escribe la letra correcta.

Reading. Vocabulary for family members. Pupils look at the family tree and match the words for family members to the pictures.

Answers

1 D	**2** E	**3** C	**4** I	**5** H
6 F	**7** G	**8** J	**9** A	**10** B

1b Escucha a Antonio y escribe los nombres de cinco miembros de su familia.

Listening. Introducing family members. Pupils listen and write down the names of Antonio's family members.

Tapescript

Hola, me llamo Antonio. Te presento a mi familia. Es una familia bastante grande: ésta es mi madre, Juanita, y éste es mi padre, Miguel. Tengo un hermanastro, un hermano y una hermana. Ésta es mi hermana que se llama Isabel y éste es mi hermanastro; se llama David, y aquí está mi hermano; se llama Carlos.

Answers

1 madre – Juanita **2** padre – Miguel **3** hermana – Isabel
4 hermanastro – David **5** hermano – Carlos

1c Lee y contesta a las preguntas.

Reading. Giving information about family members. Students read the text and complete answers to questions in Spanish.

Answers

1 – Se llama Pedro.
2 – Vive en Barcelona.
3 – Son seis (en su familia).
4 – Vive en Sitges.
5 – Vive con su marido y sus (dos) hijos.
6 – Sí, tienen dos gatos y un perro.

1d Túrnate con tu compañero/a.
Escribe las respuestas.

Speaking. Pairwork on talking about your family. The questions are given on the page, with short prompts to support students with their answers. Students note down their partner's replies.

2a Empareja las descripciones con las personas.

Reading. Describing your hair and eyes. Students match each sentence to the correct picture. They could brainstorm vocabulary for eye colour and adjectives used to describe hair, before beginning the reading task.

Answers

1 C	**2** A	**3** D	**4** B

Gramática

This gives students a brief reminder of masculine and feminine singular and plural adjective endings in Spanish. Further explanation and a practice exercise can be found in the grammar section at the back of the Student's Book.

2b ¿Qué significan estos adjectivos? Escucha y rellena el cuadro.

Listening. Describing physical appearance. Pupils find out the meaning of a list of adjectives, by looking them up in the back of the Student's Book or in a dictionary. They then copy out a grid and listen to family members being described. Students fill in who is being described and tick the relevant columns in the grid.

➕ As extension, more able students could note down any other details given, such as age, eye colour, hair style and length, etc.

Tapescript

Hola, me llamo Zaida y voy a describir a los miembros de mi familia para ti. Mi madre es bastante alta y delgada. Tiene el pelo negro y los ojos verdes y es morena. Es vieja – tiene cuarenta y cuatro años. Mi padre es rubio y tiene el pelo corto. Es bajo y delgado. También es viejo. Mi hermana es baja y morena. Es joven – sólo tiene 10 años. ¡Ay, sí! También es gorda. Finalmente, mi abuelo es viejo con el pelo gris. Es alto y gordo. ¡Todos somos muy diferentes!

Answers

Who?	Tall	Short	Fat	Slim	Blond	Dark	Old	Young
madre	✓			✓		✓	✓	
padre		✓		✓	✓		✓	
hermana		✓	✓			✓		✓
abuelo	✓		✓				✓	

2c Escoge tres personas famosas y pregunta a tu compañero/a '¿Cómo es …?'

Speaking. Describing famous people. Students work in pairs. They take it in turns to ask their partner to describe three famous people. The example on the page provides a model for students to follow.

2d Descríbete a ti mismo y a otro miembro de tu familia. ¿Cómo eres? ¿Cómo es otro miembro de tu familia?

Writing. Describing yourself and family members. Pupils write a physical description of themselves and of a family member.

1 Te presento a mi familia

(Student's Book pages 10–11)

Main topics and objectives

Introducing family members
Talking about nationality

Grammar

Éste/ésta/éstos/éstas
Soy de (España)/Soy español(a).
Present tense of *ser* and *tener*

Key language

Éste/ésta es mi ...

Éstos/éstas son mis ...
¿De dónde eres?
Soy de España/México/Los Estados Unidos /Soy español/a/ inglés/a/ escocés/a/ irlandés/a/ galés/a/ australiano/a /brasileño/a /portugués/a /alemán/a

Resources

Cassette A, side 1
CD 1, track 3
Cuaderno pages 2–7
Gramática 3.4, page 169

1 Empareja las imágenes con las frases correctas.

Reading. Introducing family members. Students match each sentence to the correct picture.

Answers

1 d	2 c	3 e	4 b	5 g	6 f	7 a

Gramática

This gives a brief explanation of the four forms of *éste*, which is also explained in the grammar section at the back of the Student's Book, with a practice exercise.

2a Empareja las banderas con las frases correctas.

Reading. Understanding nationalities. Students match statements about nationality with the countries' flags. The flags are labelled with the first three letters of the name of each country, for support. All but one of the nationalities used are cognates or near-cognates of English and students should therefore recognise them. The last one (*alemán*) may be familiar to students as the name of a school subject in Spanish.

Answers

1 E	2 C	3 F	4 A	5 D	6 B

2b Escucha estas nacionalidades y escribe la letra de la bandera correcta (1–6).

Listening. Nationalities. Students listen and identify each speaker's nationality, by noting down the letter of the flags used in **2a**, above.

Tapescript

1 – ¡Hola!, me llamo João y soy brasileño.
2 – Me llamo Juanita y soy de los Estados Unidos.
3 – Soy alemán y vivo en Alemania con mis padres.
4 – Me presento: me llamo Ana y soy portuguesa.
5 – ¡Hola!, ¿qué tal? Me llamo Pepe y soy mexicano.
6 – Vivo en Galicia y soy español.

Answers

1 E	2 C	3 B	4 A	5 D	6 F

Gramática

This explains and demonstrates two ways of describing nationality: one using *ser de ...* (and hence avoiding the use of adjectives and their endings), the other using adjectives of nationality. Further explanation of adjectives and their endings and a practice exercise are given in the grammar section at the back of the Student's Book.

2c Copia el cuadro e incluye las otras nacionalidades.

Writing. Adjectives of nationality. Students copy out a grid, giving the masculine and feminine singular and plural of four adjectives, then use this model to write out the different forms of four other adjectives.

➕ Teachers may wish to use this as an extension activity for more able pupils only.

Answers

1 galés/galesa/galeses/galesas
2 australiano/australiana/australianos/australianas
3 inglés/inglesa/ingleses/inglesas
4 irlandés/irlandesa/irlandeses/irlandesas

2d Túrnate con tu compañero/a.

Speaking. Pairwork practice of name, nationality and where you live.

Gramática

The complete paradigm of the verbs *ser* and *tener* in the present tense. There is further explanation and practice of the present tense in the grammar section, at the back of the Student's Book. *Ser* and *tener* are also included in the irregular verb tables, on pages 182–183.

2e (a) Describe a alguien de tu clase (nombre, nacionalidad, aspecto físico y dónde vive). (b) Encuentra una foto de un miembro de tu familia y escribe una descripción.

Writing. Describing people. Students write two descriptions, one of a member of their class, the other of a family member. They should be encouraged to include as much information as possible, building on what has been covered in the module so far, in particular name, nationality, physical description, where the people live and their family. ✚ More able students could be encouraged to add further details, such as age and birthday.

Main topics and objectives

Describing your house or flat
Describing your bedroom

Grammar

(No) Me gusta(n)/Me encanta(n) …
Use of hay

Skills

Giving reasons for opinions
Use adjectives and y and pero in descriptions

Key language

Vivo en un piso/un chalet/una casa …
… en el campo/centro de la ciudad/la costa/un pueblo/las afueras/un barrio residencial.

¿Cómo es tu casa/tu dormitorio?
Es (muy/bastante/demasiado) grande/pequeño/a / moderno/a /antiguo/a /bonito/a.
Hay/Tiene cuatro dormitorios/una cocina/un comedor/salón/cuarto de baño/garaje/balcón.
En mi dormitorio (no) hay …
Mi dormitorio (no) tiene un espejo/radiador/ ordenador/vídeo/una televisión/cama/alfombra/ lámpara/moqueta/silla/mesa/ventana/muchos libros/pósters de …
(No) Me gusta(n)/Me encanta(n) mi casa/ dormitorio/los cantantes de Rap, porque …

Resources

Cassette A, side 1
CD 1, track 4
Cuaderno pages 2–7
Gramática 7.13, page 176

1a ¿Dónde viven estas personas? (1–5)
Toma notas breves.

Listening. Saying where you live. Students listen and note down in Spanish the type of dwelling people say they live in and its location. Students are supported with key vocabulary for the dwellings and locations, on the page. Depending on pupils' ability, teachers may wish to pre-teach and practise this key vocabulary, before tackling the listening activity.

Tapescript

1 – *Vivo en una casa en un pueblo.*
2 – *Vivo en un chalet en el campo.*
3 – *Vivimos en un piso en el centro de la ciudad.*
4 – *Mi amiga vive en una casa en la costa.*
5 – *Mis padres viven en un piso en una ciudad. Me gusta el piso porque es moderno.*

Answers

1 casa/pueblo	2 chalet/campo	3 piso/ciudad
4 casa/costa	5 piso/ciudad	

1b Túrnate con tu compañero/a.

Speaking. Role-play on saying where you live. Students work in pairs to ask and answer questions about where they live, the type of dwelling they live in, its location, its size and whether they like it. The *¡Ojo!* feature encourages students to support their opinion with a reason. Students need to develop, early on, the habit of volunteering opinions and reasons, which will earn them marks in their examination. Students are supported by a key language grid on the page.

1c Lee y rellena los espacios.

Reading. Describing your home. Students read the text and complete the sentences in Spanish. The text includes key language for saying what rooms there are in your house or flat. Either before or after students have undertaken the sentence-completion task, teachers may wish to draw out and practise this key language orally, by asking students (e.g.) *¿Cómo se dice 'There are four bedrooms in the flat', 'I don't share my bedroom', 'I've got a stereo system'?* (etc.)

Answers

1 Conchita vive en *Santander*.
2 Su familia vive en un *piso*.
3 Hay *cuatro* dormitorios.
4 No hay *garaje*.
5 Le gusta el piso porque *es grande y porque no comparte su dormitorio.*
6 En su dormitorio hay *un equipo de música, y muchos pósters de sus cantantes favoritos.*

Gramática

This draws attention briefly to the singular and plural versions of *me gusta(n)* and *me encanta(n)*. Further explanation is given in the grammar section at the back of the Student's Book.

2a Describe tu casa: cambia el mensaje de Conchita.

Writing. Describing your house or flat. Students adapt the model text in **1c** to write a description of their own home. They should be encouraged to use the key language, give opinions and reasons and use conjunctions, as appropriate. Once it has been corrected, teachers may wish students to add this to their *fichero personal*, for later revision and examination preparation.

2b ¿Qué cosa falta en cada habitación? (1–3)

Listening. Furniture and household equipment. Students listen and note down the items of furniture or equipment which are not mentioned but are shown in the pictures. Teachers may wish to precede the listening task with aural practice of the names of the rooms and the furniture/equipment listed on the page, then follow it with oral practice of this key vocabulary.

Tapescript

1 – En la cocina hay la lavadora, el lavaplatos, el congelador y la cocina.

2 – En el salón hay el sofá, el equipo de música, los estantes, la televisión y las butacas.

3 – En el cuarto de baño hay la ducha, el lavabo, la alfombra y el espejo.

Answers

1 la nevera	**2** la lámpara	**3** la bañera

2c Haz el juego. Describe lo que hay en …

Speaking. Rooms of the house, furniture and equipment. Students work in pairs to play a cumulative speaking game. They take it in turns to add the name of another room or piece of furniture/equipment to what their partner has said. Their attention should be drawn to the key language grid at the bottom of the page, which includes many items of vocabulary that could be used in the game.

2d Describe tu dormitorio.

Writing. Describing your bedroom. Students write their answers to four questions, describing their bedroom and giving an opinion. The *¡Ojo!* feature encourages them to avoid simply making lists of furniture vocabulary, by using conjunctions. This will be important advice in helping students to achieve the best grade in their GCSE/Standard Grade writing test. Teachers may wish students to add their corrected piece of writing to their *fichero personal*, to be used later for revision and exam preparation.

3 ¿Cómo es tu barrio?

(Student's Book pages 14–15)

Main topics and objectives

Describing the area where you live
Talking about transport and distances

Grammar

Adjectives
Adverbial expressions

Skills

Giving opinions
Using *afortunadamente* and *desafortunadamente*

Key language

Mi barrio es …
(No) Me gusta mi barrio porque …
(No) Hay mucho que hacer.
Hay mucho/a contaminación/desempleo/turismo.
Es (muy/bastante/demasiado) antiguo/moderno/
precioso/ruidoso/sucio/tranquilo/turístico.
En mi pueblo/barrio (no) hay un/una …
Mi casa/piso está cerca del/de la/de los/de las …
… hospital/castillo/río/centro comercial/museo/
polideportivo/ayuntamiento/ supermercado/
discoteca/biblioteca/playa/estación de trenes/tiendas.
¿Dónde está el/la … /están los/las …?
Está(n) (muy/bastante) lejos/cerca
Está(n) a (unos/sólo) … kilómetros (de aquí).
¿Cómo se va allí?
En tren/coche/autobús/metro/bicicleta/a pie

Resources

Cassette A, side 1
CD 1, track 5
Cuaderno pages 2–7
Gramática 3, page 167 and 5.1, page 170

1a Empareja las descripciones con
las imágenes correctas.

Reading. Describing the area where you live. Students
read three short texts and match them to the pictures.
Students should be encouraged to use the vocabulary
support given, as well as their reading skills (spotting
known language, cognates and near-cognates,
inferring, etc.) to complete the task. It might be
valuable to ask students, afterwards, to share with the
class what clues and skills they used to complete the
task. Teachers may wish to give students aural
practice of the key language, after the reading and
before moving on to the listening task which follows.

Answers

1 C	2 A	3 B

1b Escucha y decide si a la persona le gusta
o no le gusta. (1–5)

Listening. Describing the area where you live.
Students listen and use verbal clues to determine
whether each speaker likes or dislikes the area where
s/he lives. They then draw a heart or a crossed-out
heart next to the number of each speaker. As with the
preceding reading task, teachers may wish to ask
students to explain how they arrived at their answers.

Tapescript

1 – Mi pueblo es bonito y muy tranquilo. Para mí es
      perfecto.
2 – Mi barrio es feo. Hay mucha contaminación.
3 – Odio mi ciudad – es demasiado industrial.
4 – Mi pueblo es muy turístico y muy moderno.
      ¡Me gusta mucho!
5 – Mi barrio es excelente – tiene un ambiente agradable y
      hay muchos lugares antiguos.

Answers

1 Likes	2 Dislikes	3 Dislikes	4 Likes	5 Likes

1c Túrnate con tu compañero/a.

Speaking. Role-play on describing your area. Students
work in pairs to ask and answer questions about what
their area is like, whether they like it or not and give
reasons. They should use the key language given with
the activity and above, for support. Teachers may
wish to have students practise these words and
phrases orally, before they tackle the pairwork task.

2a ¿Qué hay en cada lugar? Escucha y escribe
la letra correcta (1–6).

Listening. Saying what there is in your area. Students
note down the letter of each place mentioned.
Students could brainstorm the names of the places
shown in the pictures, most of which should be
familiar to them from previous years' study, before
tackling the listening task.

Tapescript

1 – En mi pueblo hay un castillo grande.
2 – Mi casa está cerca de la discoteca.
3 – Mi piso está cerca del hospital.
4 – Vivo en el campo – hay un río grande en mi jardín.
5 – Me gusta ir de compras al centro comercial.
6 – El ayuntamiento está lejos de mi casa.

Answers

1 D	2 E	3 A	4 H	5 J	6 K

2b Escribe sobre el lugar donde vives.

Writing. Describing the area where you live. Students write a description of their area, including what it is like and what facilities there are. The *¡Ojo!* feature reminds students that using the adjectival phrases given will help to gain them extra marks in the exam and of the importance of giving opinions and reasons. This written piece, once corrected, could be added to the student's *fichero personal*.

3a Copia y rellena el cuadro con la información necesaria (1–5).

Listening. Places, distances and transport. Students listen to dialogues in which people ask where places are, give distances and discuss the best means of getting there. They then fill in a grid. Students should be reminded of key vocabulary for the places in question, means of transport and how distances are given in Spanish, before tackling the listening.

Tapescript

1 – ¿Dónde está la playa?
– Está lejos – a unos 9 kilómetros.
– ¿Cómo se va allí?
– En tren o en coche.
2 – ¿Dónde está la estación de trenes?
– Está lejos – a 6 kilómetros.
– ¿Cómo se va allí?
– En autobús.
3 – ¿Dónde está el centro de la ciudad?
– Está bastante lejos, a 4 kilómetros.
– ¿Cómo se va allí?
– En metro o en autobús.
4 – ¿Dónde están las tiendas?
– Están cerca – 200 metros de aquí.
– ¿Puedo tomar el autobús?
– No, es más fácil ir a pie.
5 – ¿Dónde está tu colegio?
– Está cerca, a sólo 2 kilómetros.
– ¿Cómo vas allí?
– Voy en bicicleta.

Answers

	Lugar	Distancia	Transporte
1	Playa	Lejos – 9 km	Tren/coche
2	Estación de trenes	Lejos – 6 km	Autobús
3	Centro de la ciudad	Lejos – 4 km	Metro/autobús
4	Tiendas	Cerca – 200 m	A pie
5	Colegio	Cerca – 2 km	Bicicleta

3b Túrnate con tu compañero/a.

Speaking. Pairwork on places, distances and transport. Students take it in turns to ask and answer questions, based on the pictures on the page. A model dialogue, with options/variations, is provided.

➕ More able students could be encouraged to create their own version of the dialogue and as many students as possible should be encouraged to eventually reproduce dialogues from memory/without support.

Leer y escribir

(Student's Book pages 146–147)

Leer 1a Copia y completa para Brad Pitt.

An 'identity card' profile of the actor Brad Pitt, followed by a multiple-choice comprehension exercise.

Answers (in bold)

> Brad Pitt nació en **Oklahoma** y su **cumpleaños** es el
> 18 de diciembre. Es de **los Estados Unidos**. Su **madre** se
> llama Jane y su **padre** se llama Bill. Tiene **un hermano** y
> **una hermana**. Le gustan **los animales**: tiene cinco **perros**.
> Brad tiene los ojos **azules** y el pelo **rubio**. A veces tiene
> **barba**. Uno de sus vicios es que bebe **café**. Algo que le
> **interesa** es la arquitectura. **Le gusta** practicar el ciclismo
> y el tenis. **Le gusta** la música.

Escribir 1b Escribe una ficha de identidad
sobre ti mismo.

Students use the model text in Leer 1a to write a
similar identity card profile of themselves.

Escribir 1c Escribe un párrafo sobre ti mismo.

A follow-up task in which students write up the
information from their own identity card as a
paragraph about themselves.

Escribir 1d Usa el internet para buscar
información sobre un/a español/a famoso/a
como Penélope Cruz o Enrique Iglesias. Luego
escribe su carta de identidad.

Students create an identity card profile of a famous
Spanish-speaking person, by looking up information
on the Internet or in magazines.

Teachers looking for further material on writing
profiles of famous Spanish-speaking people may wish
to refer to the coursework section material for
Module 8, which offers a model text about the
Spanish film-maker Pedro Almodóvar, with follow-up
comprehension exercises and guidance to students
on writing a similar piece of their own.

Leer 2a and **2b** Lee el mensaje electrónico de
Cristina. ¿Verdad o mentira?

A text in which a girl describes her home town of
Córdoba, followed by a true/false exercise.

Answers

1 mentira	**2** mentira	**3** verdad	**4** mentira
5 mentira	**6** verdad	**7** verdad	

Escribir 2c Escríbele a Cristina. Contesta a sus
preguntas sobre tu pueblo/ciudad.

An examination-style writing task, replying to
Cristina's questions.

módulo 1 · Cuaderno

(Workbook pages 2–7)

page 2

1a

Answers

1 f	**2** e	**3** a	**4** d	**5** b	**6** c

1b

Answers

1 Ascensión **2** Ana Isabel **3** Michele **4** Jorge
5 abuelo **6** Nuria y Elena

page 3

2a

Answers

1 Me, vivo
2 Padre, años
3 Me, cuarenta
4 Hermano, tengo

2b

Answers

Divorciado/a
Hijo, mujer
Casado/a
Hijos

3

Answers

1 Tengo un perro blanco y negro.
2 Mi conejo blanco se llama Bugsie.
3 Mi hermana tiene un gato gris.
4 Tenemos tres caballos morenos.
5 Mis abuelos tienen muchos periquitos amarillos.

page 4

4a

Answers

Opiniones positivas	Opiniones negativas
El barrio donde vivo está cerca del centro comercial.	Es demasiado pequeño, no hay cines.
Lo bueno es que hay un polideportivo muy cerca.	Vivimos en una gran ciudad industrial – es muy ruidosa.
Hay mucho que hacer para los jóvenes.	Vivir en este pueblo no me gusta nada.

4b

Answers

1 d	**2** c	**3** a	**4** b	**5** e

Cuaderno

(Workbook pages 2–7)

page 5

5a

Answers

1 b	2 c	3 a	4 a	5 b	6 b	7 b	8 a

page 6

Gramática

1a

Answers

a escocesa   **b** divorciados   **c** antigua, pequeña **d** delgados, guapos   **e** azules, moreno   **f** mexicana

2a

Answers

1 tengo, soy   **2** tiene   **3** tienes   **4** tiene   **5** tiene **6** son, tienen

2b

Answers

a esta, este   **b** estos   **c** estas   **d** este   **e** esta **f** esta   **g** estos   **h** estas

En el cole

(Student's Book pages 18–31)

Main topics and objectives	Grammar	Skills
Repaso 1 (pp. 18–19) Talking about school subjects Telling the time	*(No) Me gusta(n)/Me encanta(n) …* *Es la …/Son las …* (+ time)	
Repaso 2 (pp. 20–21) Classroom equipment and language Reasons for liking or disliking school subjects	Adjective endings	
1 Mi colegio (pp. 22–23) Talking about your school timetable Describing your school uniform Describing your school	*Tener* *Tener que* + infinitive Question forms Time	Including opinions and reasons Question words
2 ¿Qué se puede hacer en el colegio? (pp. 24–25) Talking about after-school clubs and activities Saying what you do at break and lunchtimes	Present tense Preterite tense of regular verbs and *ser* Expressions of time and frequency	Adding time indicators to spoken answers (siempre, a veces/de vez en cuando, nunca)
3 Mi rutina diaria (pp. 26–27) Describing your daily routine Saying how you travel to school and why	Present tense of reflexive verbs Comparatives	Questions and answers in Spanish and English

Key language

¿Te gusta(n) el/la/los/las … (+ school subject)?
(No) Me gusta(n)/Me encanta(n) … Odio/Detesto …
… el alemán/comercio/deporte/ dibujo/diseño/español/francés/inglés/teatro
… la biología/cocina/educación física/geografía/historia/informática/música/religión/
… los trabajos manuales/
…las ciencias/matemáticas
¿Qué hora es?
Es la una/Son las dos (etc.) y media /y cuarto/menos cuarto/y veinte (etc.)

Necesito un(a)…, por favor.
No tengo un(a) …
He olvidado mi … … bolígrafo/cuaderno/libro/lápiz/regla/goma.
¿Cómo se dice … en español/inglés?
No entiendo.
Más despacio, por favor.
Lo siento, no lo sé.
… es/son (muy/bastante) divertido/a/os/as/aburrido/a/os/as/difícil(es)/fácil(es)/interesante(s)
El profesor/La profesora es simpático/a/(muy) estricto/a.
Nos mandan demasiados deberes.
¿Cuál asignatura te gusta más/menos?

¿Qué tienes el lunes? (etc.)
El lunes/martes (etc.) tengo (matemáticas).
Tengo recreo/comida a la/las + time.
(No) Tengo que llevar uniforme.
Tengo que llevar …
Llevo … … un vestido/jersey negro (etc.)
… una corbata/falda/camisa/gorra negra (etc.)
… unos vaqueros/unas zapatillas deportivas negros/as (etc.)
(No) Me gusta (mucho) mi uniforme porque es cómodo/moderno/feo.
¿Cómo se llama tu colegio? Se llama …
¿Qué tipo de colegio es? Es un colegio mixto/femenino/masculino.
¿Es grande o pequeño? Es (muy/ bastante) grande/pequeño.
¿Cuántos alumnos/profesores hay?/Hay (mil) alumnos y (ochenta) profesores.
¿Cómo es el edificio? Es (muy/ bastante) moderno/antiguo/feo.
(No) Hay un gimnasio/una biblioteca/una sala/una sala de teatro/una sala de informática/una sala de profesores/(muchos) laboratorios/(ciento) aulas.

Hay un club de lectura/atletismo/teatro/deportes/idiomas (etc.) en mi colegio.
¿Eres miembro de algún club?
Soy miembro del club de fútbol/natación/idiomas/ajedrez (etc.)
¿Qué haces durante el recreo/en la hora de comer/después del colegio?
Siempre/a veces/de vez en cuando/nunca/el martes …
… canto en el coro/toco el piano (en la orquesta)/practico deporte/como en el comedor/voy al club/taller de … /estudio en la biblioteca
… juego en el patio/en un equipo de …
Ayer/la semana pasada/el lunes pasado …
… fui al/a la… /canté …/toqué …/ jugué …/practiqué …

¿A qué hora te despiertas/levantas/ duchas/lavas los dientes/relajas/acuestas?
Me despierto/levanto/ducho/lavo los dientes/relajo/acuesto a …
Tomo el desayuno/Salgo de casa/ Vuelvo a casa/Ceno/Hago los deberes a …
¿Cómo vas al colegio? Voy en autobús/a pie/en tren/en coche/en metro/en bicicleta porque …
…. es más fácil/rápido/barato/ divertido/interesante (que …)

Repaso 1

(Student's Book pages 18–19)

Main topics and objectives

Talking about school subjects
Telling the time

Grammar

(No) Me gusta(n)/Me encanta(n)
Es la …/Son las … (+ time)

Key language

¿Te gusta(n) el/la/los/las (+ school subject)?
(No) Me gusta(n)/Me encanta(n) …
Odio/Detesto …
… el alemán/comercio/deporte/dibujo/diseño/
español/ francés/inglés/teatro
… la biología/cocina/educación física/geografía/
historia/informática/música/religión/
los trabajos manuales/las ciencias/matemáticas
¿Qué hora es?
Es la una/Son las dos (etc.) y media/y cuarto/menos
cuarto/y veinte/menos veinte (etc.)

Resources

Cassette A, side 2
CD 1, track 6
Cuaderno pages 8–13
Gramática 7.13, page 176 and 11.3, page 179

1a Empareja las frases con las imágenes correctas.

Reading. Likes and dislikes with school subjects. Students match each sentence to the correct picture. Students could brainstorm the school subjects before tackling the reading. A complete list of the subjects is provided in the language support on the page.

Answers

1 A	2 E	3 G	4 C	5 H	6 D	7 B	8 F

Gramática

A brief reminder of the singular and plural variations of *me gusta(n)* and *me encanta(n)* in relation to school subjects. Further explanation is provided in the grammar section, at the back of the Student's Book.

1b Escucha e identifica las asignaturas y las opiniones (1–6).

Listening. Likes and dislikes with school subjects. Students copy and complete the grid. Students demonstrate their comprehension by putting a tick under the appropriate face in the grid. The key language grid provides spelling support for the school subjects and pupils should be encouraged to use the article, as well as the noun as they complete the grid.

➕ The *¡Extra!* column of the grid offers extension for more able students, who are encouraged to listen for additional information, such as why the speakers like or dislike certain subjects.

Tapescript

1 – *Me encantan los trabajos manuales porque el profesor es simpático.*
2 – *Detesto el inglés porque es difícil.*
3 – *Me gusta mucho la religión porque es fácil.*
4 – *¡Odio el dibujo!*
5 – *No me gustan nada las ciencias – la profesora es muy estricta.*
6 – *Me encanta el alemán – es mi asignatura preferida.*

Answers

	Asignatura	😃	😞	¡Extra!
1	los trabajos manuales	✓		profesor – simpático
2	el inglés		✓	difícil
3	la religión	✓		fácil
4	el dibujo		✓	
5	las ciencias		✓	profesora – estricta
6	el alemán	✓		asignatura preferida

1c Haz preguntas a tu compañero/a.

Speaking. Likes and dislikes with school subjects. In pairs, students take it in turns to ask each other about their school subjects. The *¡Ojo!* feature reminds them that they need to use the definite article when saying whether they like or dislike subjects.

1d Ahora escribe tus opiniones.

Writing. Likes and dislikes with school subjects. Students write a sentence about each of their subjects.

➕ Some could be encouraged to use conjunctions such as *y* and *pero*, and adjectival expressions such as *también* and *sin embargo*, which were featured in Module 1. More able students also could be encouraged to give reasons, drawing on the language used in **1b**. Giving reasons is dealt with more fully in *Repaso 2*.

2a Escucha y escribe la hora (1–9).

Listening. Telling the time (on the hour, half-past, quarter-past and quarter-to.) Students listen and note down the times. The language support grid reminds students of how these times are expressed in Spanish and teachers may wish to use this as a springboard for aural/oral practice, before students tackle the listening task.

■ ▨ ■ ▨ ■ ▨ ■ ▨ ■ ▨ ■ ▨ ■ ▨ ■ ▨ ■ ▨ ■ ▨ ■ ▨ ■ ▨ ■ ▨ ■ ▨ ■ ▨ ■

Tapescript

Ejemplo – Son las nueve.
1 – Es la una.
2 – Son las cuatro y media.
3 – Son las siete y cuarto.
4 – Son las seis y cuarto.
5 – Son las once.
6 – Son las diez menos cuarto.
7 – Son las doce.
8 – Son las ocho y cuarto.
9 – Es la una y media.

Answers

1 1.00	**2** 4.30	**3** 7.15	**4** 6.15	**5** 11.00
6 9.45	**7** 12.00	**8** 8.15	**9** 1.30	

2b Empareja las frases con las imágenes correctas.

Reading. Telling the time (minutes past and to the hour). Students match up each sentence to the correct picture. Teachers may wish to practise times aurally and orally with students, before they tackle the reading.

Answers

1 E	**2** H	**3** B	**4** F	**5** A	**6** D	**7** C	**8** G

2c ¿Qué hora es? Pregunta a tu compañero/a.

Speaking. Pairwork practice on telling the time. Students take it in turns to ask one another the time, using the prompts given. The *Gramática* feature reminds them to use *son las* with all times, except those surrounding one o'clock.

Main topics and objectives

Classroom equipment and language
Reasons for liking or disliking school subjects

Grammar

Adjective endings

Key language

Necesito un(a) …, por favor.
No tengo un(a) …
He olvidado mi …
… bolígrafo/cuaderno/libro/lápiz/regla/goma.
¿Cómo se dice … en español/inglés?
No entiendo.

Más despacio, por favor.
Lo siento, no lo sé.
… es/son (muy/bastante) divertido/a/os/as/
aburrido/a/os/as /difícil(es)/fácil(es)/útil(es)/
interesante(s)
El profesor/La profesora es simpático/a /(muy)
estricto/a.
Nos mandan demasiados deberes.
¿Cuál asignatura te gusta más/menos?

Resources

Cassette A, side 2
CD 1, track 6
Cuaderno pages 8–13
Gramática 3, page 167

1a ¿Qué necesitan estos alumnos? (1–6)
Escribe la letra correcta.

Listening. Classroom equipment. Students match up
each sentence with the correct picture. Students
could brainstorm the names of classroom equipment
before tackling the listening.

Tapescript

1 – *Necesito una regla.*
2 – *He olvidado mi lápiz.*
3 – *Lo siento, no tengo cuaderno.*
4 – *Por favor, señor, necesito una goma.*
5 – *He olvidado mi libro.*
6 – *No tengo un bolígrafo.*

Answers

| 1 A | 2 F | 3 C | 4 E | 5 D | 6 B |

1b Empareja las frases con las
imágenes correctas.

Reading. Classroom language (explaining problems).
Students match up each sentence with the
correct picture.

Answers

| 1 C | 2 A | 3 D | 4 B | 5 E |

1c Túrnate con tu compañero/a.

Speaking. Role-play on classroom language and
equipment. Teachers may wish to give students oral
practice of the key language, before they work on the
role-play.

1d ¿Eres organizado/a? Escribe seis frases.

Writing. Classroom equipment. Students write six
sentences about the classroom equipment they have
or don't have with them. The key language grid,
earlier on the page, supports spelling.

2a Lee las opiniones. ¿Son positivas o negativas?

Reading. Reasons for liking or disliking school
subjects. Students read each sentence and categorise
it as positive or negative, by completing the grid with
smiling and frowning faces. Teachers should make
sure students are familiar with the key adjectives and
other phrases, before they tackle the reading.
Students could be given aural practice of these: the
teacher says each adjective/phrase and students give
a 'thumbs up' sign for positive expressions and a
'thumbs down' sign for negative expressions.

Answers

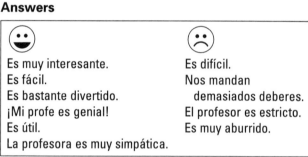

😃	😞
Es muy interesante.	Es difícil.
Es fácil.	Nos mandan
Es bastante divertido.	demasiados deberes.
¡Mi profe es genial!	El profesor es estricto.
Es útil.	Es muy aburrido.
La profesora es muy simpática.	

2b Escucha y toma notas breves (1–5).

Listening. Reasons for liking or disliking school
subjects. Students take notes in Spanish about the
speakers' reasons for liking or disliking certain subjects.

Tapescript

1 – *Prefiero el inglés porque es interesante.*
2 – *Mi asignatura preferida es el español porque es*
divertido.
3 – *Odio el diseño porque es difícil.*
4 – *No me gustan las ciencias porque nos mandan*
demasiados deberes.
5 – *Me encanta la informática – es útil y mi profe es genial.*

Answers

1 inglés – interesante
2 español – divertido
3 diseño – difícil
4 las ciencias – demasiados deberes
5 informática – útil + profe – genial

Gramática

Building on the work on adjective endings and agreement in Module 1, this reminds students that the same rules apply to adjectives used to describe school subjects. Further explanation and practice is given in the grammar section at the back of the Student's Book.

2c Túrnate con tu compañero/a.

Speaking. Pairwork on giving reasons for liking/disliking certain subjects. Students take it in turns to ask each other *¿Cuál asignatura te gusta más/menos?* and to give reasons. Students should be referred to the examples used in the *Gramática* feature for good model answers and also to the language support box on page 18.

2d Completa las frases con tus opiniones.

Writing. Giving opinions and reasons about school subjects. This combines the singular and plural forms of *(No) Me gusta(n), es/son* and adjective endings. Teachers should draw students' attention to the way in which the singular and plural answer prompts on the page have been divided up, ensuring that students understand why, and also how to complete their answers. Once corrected, students could add this piece of writing to their *fichero personal*, as a record for revision and exam preparation.

1 Mi colegio

(Student's Book pages 22–23)

Main topics and objectives

Talking about your school timetable
Describing your school uniform
Describing your school

Grammar

Tener
Tener que + infinitive
Question forms
Time

Skills

Including opinions and reasons
Question words

Key language

¿Qué tienes el lunes? (etc.)
El lunes/martes (etc.) *tengo (matemáticas).*
Tengo recreo/comida a la/las + time.
(No) Tengo que llevar uniforme.
Tengo que llevar …
Llevo …

… un vestido/jersey negro (etc.)
… una corbata/falda/camisa/gorra negra (etc.)
… unos vaqueros/unas zapatillas deportivas negros/as (etc.)
(No) Me gusta (mucho) mi uniforme porque es cómodo/moderno/feo.
¿ Cómo se llama tu colegio? Se llama …
¿ Qué tipo de colegio es? Es un colegio mixto/femenino/masculino.
¿Es grande o pequeño? Es (muy/bastante) grande/pequeño.
¿Cuántos alumnos/profesores hay? Hay (mil) alumnos y (ochenta) profesores.
¿Cómo es el edificio? Es (muy/bastante) moderno/antiguo/feo.
(No) Hay un gimnasio/una biblioteca/una sala/una sala de teatro/una sala de informática/una sala de profesores/(muchos) laboratorios/(ciento) aulas.

Resources

Cassette A, side 2
CD 1, track 7
Cuaderno pages 8–13
Gramática 4.1, page 169 and 11.3, page 179

1a ¿Verdad o mentira?

Reading. School timetable. Students read a Spanish student's school timetable and do a true/false exercise. Teachers could begin by asking questions in Spanish about the timetable, ensuring that students understand the new vocabulary items: *recreo, comida, lengua española, física, química* and *gimnasia.*

➕ More able students could be encouraged to correct the false statements. Teachers could also use the opportunity to discuss differences between the Spanish school timetable and the students' own, including starting and finishing times of the school day and the length of the lunchbreak.

Answers

1 verdad	**2** mentira	**3** mentira
4 verdad	**5** verdad	**6** mentira

1b ¿De qué día hablan? (1–7)

Listening. School timetable. Students listen and note down in Spanish which day each speaker refers to.

Tapescript

1 *Tengo trabajos manuales a las ocho y media.*
2 *Tengo inglés a las tres.*
3 *Tengo geografía a las cuatro.*
4 *Tengo música a las once menos diez.*
5 *Tengo inglés a las doce menos diez.*
6 *Tengo lengua española a las nueve y media.*
7 *Tengo informática a las tres.*

Answers

1 miércoles	**2** lunes	**3** lunes	**4** martes
5 miércoles	**6** miércoles	**7** miércoles	

1c Túrnate con tu compañero/a.

Speaking. Talking about your school timetable. Students work in pairs to ask each other what subjects they have on different days of the week. Before tackling the pairwork task, students need to be confident about saying the days of the week in Spanish, including *jueves* and *viernes*, which are not shown on the timetable in the Student's Book.

2 Mira los dibujos de Alfredo y Alicia. Adivina quién habla.

Reading. School uniform. Students look at the pictures of two Spanish students, one of whom wears a school uniform and the other who does not. They then read a series of statements and decide who says each one. Before students tackle the reading task, teachers should ensure students are familiar with the clothing vocabulary which is given on the page, as well as the expressions *hay/no hay, llevo* and *(no) tengo que llevar.* The last of these is explained in the *Gramática* feature.

Answers

1 Alfredo	**2** Alicia	**3** Alicia	**4** Alfredo
5 Alfredo	**6** Alicia		

As a follow-up to this task, students could be encouraged to speak and write about their own school uniform. The *¡Ojo!* feature on the next page reminds them of the importance of giving opinions and reasons, in order to boost their examination marks. Students could brainstorm adjectives which they could use to give reasons for liking or disliking their school uniform.

3a Lee y completa las frases.

Reading. Describing your school. Students read a description of a Spanish student's school and complete a series of sentences in Spanish. For each gap to be filled, two options are given in Spanish, only one of which is correct. The text introduces a number of new vocabulary items, which are listed on the page in both Spanish and English, for support. The text is quite challenging and teachers may prefer to work through it with students, encouraging them to use their skills (looking for cognates/ near cognates, inferring meaning from context, etc.), rather than leaving them to work on it independently.

Answers

1 Es un colegio *mixto*.
2 Es muy *grande*.
3 Tiene *1.000* alumnos.
4 Empieza a las *8.30*.
5 Termina a las *cuatro*.
6 Tenemos *6* clases por día.
7 Cada clase dura *50* minutos.
8 Durante el recreo *juega al fútbol*.
9 Hay *180* aulas.

3b Escucha y contesta a las preguntas.

Listening. Describing your school. Students listen to a short description of a school and answer five questions in Spanish. The *¡Ojo!* feature reminds students of important question words and encourages them to list these, as well as others they may come across, and learn them. Given the importance of being able to answer and ask questions in the GCSE/Standard Grade examination, teachers may wish to spend some time on this, for example by encouraging pupils to make up as many questions as possible, using the different interrogatives given. Further explanation and practice of question forms is provided in the grammar section at the back of the Student's Book.

Tapescript

Mi colegio es mixto y es bastante grande. Hay quinientos alumnos y treinta profesores. Es un edificio bastante antiguo con veinte aulas y tres laboratorios.

Answers

1 Es un colegio mixto.   2 Es bastante grande.
3 Hay 500 alumnos.   4 Es bastante antiguo.
5 Hay 20 aulas.

3c Contesta a estas preguntas.

Speaking. Describing your school. Students prepare answers to three questions about their school, in Spanish. They should be encouraged to adapt the language used in 3a and 3b, to formulate their own answers.

➕ Depending on the ability of students, teachers could add further questions, such as *¿Cuántos profesores hay? ¿Cómo es el edificio? ¿Cuántas aulas hay? ¿Hay un gimnasio/una biblioteca (etc.)? ¿A qué hora empieza/termina? Hay recreo/hay comida?* (etc.)

As a follow-up, students should be encouraged to write up their answers and, once corrected, add these to their *fichero personal*, for revision and exam preparation.

2 ¿Qué se puede hacer en el colegio?

(Student's Book pages 24–25)

Main topics and objectives

Talking about after-school clubs and activities
Saying what you do at break and lunchtimes

Grammar

Present tense
Preterite tense of regular verbs and *ser*
Expressions of time and frequency

Skills

Adding time indicators to spoken answers *(siempre, a veces/de vez en cuando, nunca)*

Key language

Hay un club de lectura/atletismo/teatro/deportes/ idiomas (etc.) en mi colegio.
¿Eres miembro de algún club?
Soy miembro del club de fútbol/natación/idiomas/ajedrez (etc.)
¿Qué haces durante el recreo/en la hora de comer/ después del colegio?
Siempre/a veces/de vez en cuando/nunca/el martes …
… canto en el coro/toco el piano (en la orquesta)/ practico deporte/como en el comedor /voy al club/ taller de … /estudio en la biblioteca
… juego en el patio/en un equipo de …
Ayer/la semana pasada/el lunes pasado …
… fui al/a la… /canté …/toqué …/jugué …/practiqué …

Resources

Cassette A, side 2
CD 1, track 8
Cuaderno pages 8–13
Gramática 7.2, page 171, 7.6 page 173, 4.1 page 169
and 11.3 page 179

1a Lee estos anuncios escolares. Empareja los alumnos con los "clubs".

Reading. School clubs and activities. Students read three short adverts and match them to sentences in which people express their interests. Students should be encouraged to look for familiar vocabulary and cognates/near-cognates, then to guess the meaning of new expressions such as *cantar en el coro, tocar* and *idiomas.*

Answers

1 B	2 A	3 C	4 B	5 C

As follow-up, teachers may wish to ask students questions in Spanish, including questions relating to the days and times when each of the three clubs take place. This will help prepare students for the written task which follows.

1b Identifica la imagen correcta. Escribe el día (en inglés) y la hora también.

Writing. School clubs and activities. Students read the phrases and match what each person says to the correct picture, also noting the day (in English) and the time of each club or activity. Before tackling this exercise, teachers may wish to ask students questions about the pictures, in order to revise/teach key vocabulary such as *lectura, cartas* and *ajedrez.*

Answers

1 D– Friday, 4pm	2 E– Monday, 6pm	3 C– Tuesday, 1pm
4 A– Tuesday, 4.30pm	5 B– Thursday, 12.30pm	

1c Contesta a las preguntas.

Speaking. What you do at break and lunchtime and which clubs you are a member of. Students prepare answers to three questions about what they do outside lessons. They are supported by a key language grid and should work in pairs to ask and answer the questions. The *¡Ojo!* feature encourages students to use expressions of frequency to enhance their speaking and writing: a valuable way of gaining extra marks in their examination.

2a Escucha y rellena los espacios. Identifica los verbos. ¿Cuáles están en el presente y cuáles en el pasado? ¿Qué significan?

Listening. School clubs and activities. A two-part activity which begins revision of the preterite tense, introduced in the previous stage of the course and which will be covered more fully in Module 3. In the first part of the task, students listen and fill in the gaps in the text, from a 'menu' of words on the page.

Tapescript

– Hola, Gustavo, ¿cómo estás?
– Muy bien. ¿Vas al club de tenis mañana?
– No, porque normalmente voy al club de atletismo los viernes.
– ¡Qué lástima! ¿Fuiste al club de baloncesto ayer?
– Sí, fui al club de baloncesto y después fui a la sala de teatro. Toqué el piano en la orquesta y también canté en el coro.
– ¡Qué bien!

Answers

As tapescript.

In the second part of the task, students are asked to pick out the verbs in the text and decide whether each one is in the present or the past (preterite), then say what each one means. The key language list provides support and students should be encouraged to look for clues in the text, such as words like *ayer*, as well as what they remember about the endings of regular verbs in the preterite tense. They could draw up two lists of verbs from the text, either on the board/OHP or in their exercise books.

Answers

Present tense: estás (you are/are you?)   vas (you go/are going/are you going?)   voy (I go/am going)
Past (preterite tense): fuiste (you went/did you go?)
fui (×2) (I went)   toqué (I played)   canté (I sang)

2b ¿Verdad o mentira?

Reading. School clubs and activities. A true/false exercise, based on a short text.

Answers

1 mentira	**2** verdad	**3** verdad	**4** verdad
5 mentira	**6** mentira	**7** verdad	

2c Escribe un texto parecido. Cambia la carta de Pili.

Writing. School clubs and activities. Students adapt the text in **2b** to write about their own school. Students should be encouraged to include an example of the past tense, where possible, to get them into the habit of demonstrating their ability to use more than one tense, for their GCSE/Standard Grade exam. The key language box gives them some phrases in the preterite for support.

3 Mi rutina diaria

(Student's Book pages 26–27)

Main topics and objectives

Describing your daily routine
Saying how you travel to school and why

Grammar

Present tense of reflexive verbs.
Comparatives

Key language

¿A qué hora te despiertas/levantas/duchas/lavas los dientes/relajas/acuestas?
Me despierto/levanto/ducho/lavo los dientes/relajo/
acuesto a …
Tomo el desayuno/Salgo de casa/Vuelvo a casa/
Ceno/Hago los deberes a …
¿Cómo vas al colegio? Voy en autobús/a pie/en tren/
en coche/en metro/en bicicleta porque …
… es más fácil/rápido/barato/divertido/interesante
(que …)

Resources

Cassette A, side 2
CD 1, track 9
Cuaderno pages 8–13
Gramática 7.12, page 176 and 3.3 page 168

1a Completa las frases con la hora correcta.

Listening. Daily routine. Students listen and note down the time of each activity shown in the pictures. Teachers may wish to remind students briefly of the work they did on telling the time in *Repaso* 1, at the beginning of this module, before they tackle the listening.

Tapescript

1 – Me despierto a las 6:30.
2 – Me levanto a las 6:45.
3 – Me ducho a las 7:00.
4 – Tomo el desayuno a las 7:20.
5 – Me lavo los dientes a las 7:30.
6 – Salgo de casa a las 7:45.
7 – Vuelvo a casa y ceno a las 18:00.
8 – Hago los deberes a las 18:30.
9 – Me relajo a las 19:30.
10 – Me acuesto a las 22:00.

Answers

As tapescript.

1b Túrnate con tu compañero/a. Contesta a las preguntas.

Speaking. Daily routine. Students work in pairs to ask and answer questions about their daily routine. Before asking them to tackle the pairwork task, teachers should encourage students to adapt the phrases in **1a** to describe their own routine.

Gramática

A brief explanation of reflexive verbs in the present tense. Further explanation and practice is provided in the grammar section at the back of the Students' Book.

1c Lee el texto y pon las frases en el orden correcto.

Reading. Daily routine. This moves students from the first and second persons singular to the third person singular of reflexive verbs. Students read the text and put the English sentences into the correct order.

Answers

E, B, F, C, D, A

2a ¿Cómo van al colegio? Escucha y escribe la letra correcta (1–7).

Listening. Travel to school. Students listen and match each speaker with the correct picture. Some of the means of transport were covered in Module 1, but teachers may wish to check students' understanding of *en moto, en metro* and *en coche*, in particular, before they tackle the listening.

➕ More able students could be encouraged to note down the reasons the speakers give for using a particular form of transport.

Tapescript

1 – Voy en moto porque es divertido.
2 – Voy a pie porque vivo a sólo dos kilómetros del colegio.
3 – Voy en bicicleta porque es más rápido que el autobús.
4 – Voy en tren y el viaje dura 10 minutos.
5 – Siempre voy en metro porque es más fácil.
6 – Voy en coche con mis padres.
7 – Normalmente voy al colegio en autobús.

Answers

1 A	2 F	3 E	4 G	5 C	6 D	7 B

2b Túrnate con tu compañero/a.

Speaking. Travel to school. Students work in pairs to ask and answer questions about how they travel to school and why. The key language box provides support and teachers should practise this language orally with students before they tackle the pairwork task.

2c Lee la carta y contesta a las preguntas en inglés.

Reading. Daily routine. A text about the life of a Colombian schoolboy. Students answer questions in English. This is a challenging text, but, as always, students should be encouraged to use their reading skills to make sense of it, and only look up unknown vocabulary sparingly (a small amount of vocabulary help is provided on the page.)

Answers

1 He is from Colombia.
2 He gets up at 5.30.
3 He has a cold shower.
4 Because many of his friends don't have a shower.
5 He wears trousers and a white shirt.
6 He walks to school because it's cheaper.
7 The journey lasts an hour.
8 He works with his father.

2d Escribe una carta a Luis sobre tu rutina diaria, apréndetela de memoria, y luego haz una presentación.

Writing and speaking. Daily routine. Students adapt the text in **2c** to write to Luís about their own daily routine. If possible, they should then learn it by heart and do a spoken presentation.

Topics revised

Talking about your family and your home
Talking about the area where you live
Talking about school and daily routine

Módulo 1 Me presento

Conversación 1 and Conversación 2

Two sets of general conversation questions: one on describing your family and the other on describing the area where you live. Students could work in pairs to ask and answer the questions. They should be encouraged from the start to avoid giving brief answers and volunteer as much detail as possible. The advice about general conversation questions, at the top of page 30, emphasises the importance of demonstrating an ability to use a range of tenses. As students are more likely to be able to apply this advice to the conversations for Module 2, on the next page, teachers may wish to wait before directing students to this advice.

Juego de rol 1

Role-play on talking about your bedroom. Students should first read the general guidance about role-plays, at the top of page 30, which includes advice about taking turns with their partner to play both roles, so that they both have adequate practice of the candidate's role.

Juego de rol 2

Role-play about family and birthdays.

Módulo 2 En el instituto

Conversaciones 1, 2, 3 and 4

Four general conversation areas, covering:

- Describing your school
- School subjects and teachers
- What you do at break and lunchtime
- After-school activities

Before tackling these, students should be referred to the general advice about conversations, at the top of page 30, which emphasises the importance of using a range of tenses. The preterite tense crops up in Module 2 (it is covered more fully in Module 3) and some students should be able to use this, especially in the conversations about school subjects and after-school activities. Although the future with *ir a* is not covered until Module 3, some students may remember it from previous years and could be asked to suggest ways of including a future reference in one or more of the conversations.

The conversations also provide opportunities for students to give opinions and back up their views with reasons. Again, students should be coached, from the beginning, to volunteer opinions whenever possible, rather than waiting to be asked.

Juego de rol

A role-play about school subjects and routine.

Presentación

Students are offered a choice of three oral presentation topics:

- Your home
- Your family and friends
- Your school

Again, students' attention should be drawn to the general advice about preparing presentations, at the top of page 30, before tackling these.

Leer y escribir

(Student's Book pages 148–149)

Leer 1a Lee las cartas y contesta a las preguntas en inglés.

Three short texts about school, followed by questions in English.

Answers

1 Her favourite day is Monday, because she has Spanish, maths and PE.
2 Because the teachers are nice, he doesn't have to wear a uniform and the school has good facilities.
3 Because Pepe's school is mixed.
4 Alicia.
5 José.
6 10.30.
7 Latin. He thinks it's useless.

Leer 1b Lee el texto y rellena los espacios con las palabras de abajo.

A gapped text about schoolday routine.

Answers

Normalmente mi día escolar **empieza** a las ocho. **Salgo** de casa y **voy** en autobús al colegio. El viaje **dura** veinte minutos más o menos. Cuando llego **tomo** té con tostada en la cantina. Luego las **clases** empiezan a las nueve. Tenemos el **recreo** a las **once** y por lo general **juego** al fútbol en el patio con mis amigos. El día **termina** sobre las tres y media y casi todos los días voy al club de informática porque me encanta **escribir** por correo electrónico a mi amigo por correspondencia colombiano.

Escribir 1c Ahora escribe algo sobre tu rutina diaria.

Students adapt the text in 1b to write about their own schoolday routine.

Escribir 2 Mira las notas de María y termina sus frases.

A Spanish girl's school report, followed by a sentence-completion exercise.

Answers (in bold)

Soy fuerte en **inglés** y **teatro**.
Trabajo bien en **lengua española** y **francés**.
No voy bien en **historia** y **tecnología**.
Soy floja en **geografía**.

Escribir 2b Escribe una lista de tus asignaturas y añade una nota al lado de cada una.

Students write their own school report, using the grading system outlined on the page.

Escribir 2c Ahora escribe comentarios positivos y negativos sobre seis de tus asignaturas.

Students then write comments about some of their subjects, following the model in 2a.

módulo 2 · Cuaderno

(Workbook pages 8–13)

page 8

1a

Answers

a V	b M	c V	d M	e V	f M	g M	h V

1b

Pupils choose a day and describe their timetable.

2a

Answers

Name	Subject —	Positive opinion	Subject —	Negative opinion
Tania	English/French	Likes English and French	IT	IT is difficult
Pedro	biology/	Favourite subject is biology	French	French is boring
Sofia	science	Loves science	History	History teacher is strict
Cristina	RE	RE is interesting	Art	Hates art
Paco	history	The history teacher is friendly	Biology	Biology isn't useful
Fernando	technology	Technology is easy	Maths	Doesn't like maths

page 9

2b

Pupils complete the table about their own school subjects.

3a

Answers

1 G	2 B	3 E	4 A	5 F	6 D	7 C

page 10

4a

Answers (in bold)

B Hay un club de **idiomas** los **lunes**.
B Hay un club de **orquestra** los **viernes**.
B Hay un club de **baloncesto** los **lunes**.
B Hay un club de **informática** los **miércoles**.
B Hay un club de **natación** los **viernes**.

4b

Answers (in bold)

nada, actividades, informática, lunes, fútbol, música, coro, simpático.

page 11

5a

Answers

Es bastante grande y moderno.
terminan …
No me gustan nada las matemáticas.
la profesora es estricta
lo bueno en el instituto son …

5b

Answers

1 It is quite big and modern.
2 No, she does not.
3 They finish at four o'clock.
4 Her favourite subject is German because it is interesting.
5 She does not like maths at all because the teacher is strict.
6 On Tuesdays she goes to the art club and on Wednesdays she goes to the photography club.
7 She goes swimming on Mondays.

page 12

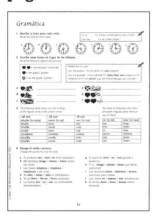

Gramática

1

Answers

A Son las ocho.
B Es la una.
C Son las siete y media.
D Son las seis menos cuarto.
E Es la una y cuarto.
F Son las tres.
G Es la una y media.

2

Answers

A Me gusta el deporte.
B Me gustan la geografía y la informática.
C No me gusta el teatro.
D No me gustan el dibujo y el inglés.
E Me encanta el español.
F Me encantan las matemáticas.

4

Answers (in bold)

a El profesor **es** muy simpático.
b Mi hermana **tiene** teatro los lunes.
c Las clases **empiezan** a las ocho.
d Yo **odio** la informática.
e Yo no **llevo** uniforme.
f Lo bueno **son** las actividades extraescolares.
g El instituto **es** grande y moderno.
h ¿Y tú, **tienes** que llevar uniforme?
i Los alumnos **tienen** una hora para comer.
j Las clases **son** interesantes.
k El recreo **dura** veinte minutos.

módulo 3 · De vacaciones

(Student's Book pages 32–43)

Main topics and objectives	Grammar	Skills
Repaso 1 (pp. 32–33) Saying where you are going on holiday and with whom The weather Saying what you are going to do, depending on the weather	*Al* and *del* *Ir a* + infinitive	
Repaso 2 (pp. 34–35) Expressing opinions about food and drink Ordering a meal in a restaurant or tapas bar	*Gustar/encantar*	
1 En el restaurante (pp. 36–37) Booking a table and ordering a meal Complaining in a restaurant	Numbers/time	
2 ¡Infórmate! (pp. 38–39) Asking for items in a tourist office Discussing holiday plans	*Tú* and *usted*	
3 Mis vacaciones pasadas (pp. 40–41) Discussing past holidays	The preterite	Expressing opinions in the past (e.g. *¡Fue fatal!*)

Key language

¿Adónde vas de vacaciones?	*Hace sol/calor/frío/viento.*
Voy a Alemania/ Cuba/Escocia/España/Francia/Gales/	*Llueve. Hay tormenta.*
Grecia/Inglaterra/Irlanda/La India/Los Estados	*Si (hace sol) voy a comer en un restaurante/ir al cíne/*
Unidos/México …	*a la playa/ hacer windsurf/quedarme en el hotel/*
… con mi madre/mis padres (etc.)	*ver la televisión/jugar al tennis.*

¿Qué vas a tomar? ¿Y para beber?	*… los calamares/champiñones/guisantes/helados/ quesos.*
(No) me gusta(n)/Me encanta(n)/Quisiera/Para mí …	*… las chuletas de cordero/gambas/judías verdes/manzanas/*
… el agua/arroz con leche/bistec/filete de cerdo/	*naranjas/patatas bravas/uvas/verduras/ zanahorias.*
gazpacho/jamón serrano/pan/pescado/pollo/	*Soy vegetarian.*
salchichón/salmón/vino/yogur/zumo de naranja.	
… la carne/ensalada/fruta/limonada/paella/piña/	
sopa de cebolla/sopa de mariscos/tortilla española/	
tortilla francesa.	

Quisiera reservar una mesa.	*… los guisantes con jamón/quesos regionales.*
¿Para qué fecha? Para (el sábado).	*La cuenta, por favor.*
¿Para cuántas personas? Para (cuatro personas).	*¿Te gustó la comida? Sí, me gustó mucho.*
¿A qué hora? A (las diez).	*No tengo vaso/tenedor.*
Lo siento, a (las once), sí.	*El cuchillo está sucio./La cuchara está sucia./La sopa está fría.*
Vale.	*No hay sal ni pimienta en la mesa.*
¿De parte de quién? De parte de …	*Lo siento. Aquí hay un vaso./Le traigo otro/a en seguida.*
¡Camarero!	*Hay un error con la cuenta.*
¿Qué desea usted?	*Sí, hay un error. Le traigo otra cuenta.*
De primer plato/de segundo plato/de postre …	
… el bistec a la pimienta/cóctel de gambas/cordero	
asado/flan/pollo al ajillo/sorbete.	
… la ensalada especial de la casa/ensaladilla rusa/fruta	
del tiempo/merluza a la vasca/tarta helada/trucha	
con almendras.	

¿Qué quiere usted?	*¿Cuánto tiempo vas a estar allí?*
Quisiera/Necesito …	*Voy a estar allí 15 días/tres semanas/un mes (etc.)*
… un mapa de la región/plano de la ciudad/folleto de	*¿Cómo vas a ir allí? Voy a ir en avión (etc.)*
excursiones/horario de trenes.	*¿Con quién vas a ir? Voy a ir con mi familia (etc.)*
… una lista de hoteles/hostales/campings/albergues.	*¿Dónde vas a quedarte? Voy a quedarme en …*
… información sobre (Barcelona/los hostales aquí).	*… un hotel/un albergue juvenil/una caravana/la casa de mi*
¿Tiene usted (un folleto de excursiones)?	*abuela (etc.)*
Por supuesto. Aquí tiene usted.	*¿Qué vas a hacer allí? Voy a …*
¿Algo más?	*… ir a la playa/al teatro/a un concierto.*
¿Adónde vas a ir de vacaciones? Voy a ir a Las Islas	*… visitar museos/monumentos/muchas ciudades/*
Canarias/a Canadá (etc.)	*a amigos (etc.)*
¿Cuándo vas a ir? Voy a ir en agosto (etc.)	

¿Adonde fuiste?	*Hice windsurf/vela.*
Fui a España/la costa/la montaña (etc.)	*Jugué al voleibol/fútbol.*
¿Cuándo fuiste?	*Visité castillos/museos.*
El año/agosto pasado (etc.)	*¿Qué tiempo hizo? Hizo sol/Llovió.*
¿Con quién fuiste? Fui con mis amigos (etc.)	*Hizo buen/mal tiempo.*
¿Cómo fuiste? Fui en coche (etc.)	*El viaje fue muy lento.*
¿Cuánto tiempo pasaste allí? Pasé diez días (etc.) allí.	*El hotel fue estupendo.*
¿Dónde te alojaste? Me alojé en un hotel/un camping.	*El tiempo fue muy bueno.*
¿Qué hiciste? Fui a la playa./Tomé el sol./Nadé en la	*La comida fue rica.*
piscina./Saqué fotos./Bailé en una discoteca./Comí	*Me gustó mucho el postre.*
platos típicos.	*Lo pasé bomba (en la piscina).*

módulo 3 · Repaso 1

(Student's Book pages 32–33)

Main topics and objectives

Saying where you are going on holiday and with whom
The weather
Saying what you are going to do, depending on the weather

Grammar

Al and *del*
Ir a + infinitive

Key language

¿Adónde vas de vacaciones?
Voy a Alemania/Cuba/Escocia/España/Francia/Gales/
Grecia/Inglaterra/ Irlanda/La India/Los Estados Unidos/México/Italia/Portugal …
… con mi madre/mis padres (etc.)
Hace sol/calor/frío/viento.
Llueve. Hay tormenta.
Si (hace sol) voy a comer en un restaurante/ir al cine/ a la playa/hacer windsurf/quedarme en el hotel/ ver la televisión/jugar al tenis.

Resources

Cassette B, side 1
CD 2, track 2
Cuaderno pages 14–20
Gramática 7.8, page 174

1a ¿Adónde van de vacaciones? Escribe la letra correcta e identifica el miembro de la familia. (1–5)

Listening. Holiday destinations. Students match up the holiday destinations mentioned with the flags on the shirts in the Student's Book. In addition, students note down whom each speaker is going on holiday with. The grid below in 1b lists a number of key countries in Spanish. Teachers may wish to use this for revision of the names of countries, before tackling the listening, drawing students' attention to the names which are cognates or near cognates of English and those which are non-cognates.

Tapescript

1 – *¿Adónde vas de vacaciones?*
 – *Voy a Italia con mis padres.*
2 – *¿Adónde vas de vacaciones?*
 – *Voy a Portugal con mis abuelos.*
3 – *¿Adónde vas de vacaciones?*
 – *Voy a los Estados Unidos con mi madre.*
4 – *¿Adónde vas de vacaciones?*
 – *Voy a Francia con mi padrastro.*
5 – *¿Adónde vas de vacaciones?*
 – *Voy a Alemania con mi hermano.*

Answers

1 c – padres	**2** e – abuelos	**3** b – madre
4 d – padrastro	**5** a – hermano	

1b Túrnate con tu compañero/a. Inventa seis ejemplos. Toma notas en inglés.

Speaking. Saying where you are going on holiday and with whom. Pairwork activity. Students use the support grid provided to ask and answer questions about holiday plans, each taking notes in English to demonstrate comprehension of what their partner says.

More able students could be encouraged to do the activity without referring to the support grid, or could look up the names of other countries in a dictionary and use those in their conversation.

2a Lee la postal. Empareja las actividades con el tiempo.

Reading. Weather and holiday activities. Students read the postcard and pair up the weather with the activities the writer says she will do. Teachers may wish to revise weather phrases before tackling this activity.

Answers

1 C	**2** D	**3** A	**4** B

2b ¿Puedes identificar estas frases sobre el tiempo?

Writing. Weather. Students unmuddle the weather phrases and write them out correctly.

Answers

1 hace frío	**2** hace calor	**3** llueve
4 hay tormenta	**5** hace viento	

Gramática

Al and *del*

Gramática

Ir a + infinitive: This key way of expressing the future is covered in more depth in the grammar section, at the back of the Student's Book, with practice exercises.

2c Completa las frases. ¿Qué vas a hacer?

Writing. Weather and activities. Students create sentences, using *si* followed by a weather phrase and *voy a* + infinitive. Support is given in the form of eight activity phrases.

2d Túrnate con tu compañero/a.

Speaking. Pairwork activity on weather and activities. Students ask and say what they are going to do, depending on the weather.

Repaso 2

(Student's Book pages 34–35)

Main topics and objectives

Expressing opinions about food and drink
Ordering a meal in a restaurant or tapas bar

Grammar

Gustar/encantar

Key language

¿Qué vas a tomar? ¿Y para beber?
(No) me gusta(n)/Me encanta(n)Quisiera/Para mí …
… el agua/arroz con leche/bistec/filete de cerdo/
gazpacho/jamón serrano/pan/pescado/pollo/
salchichón/salmón/vino/yogur/zumo de naranja.

… la carne/ensalada/fruta/limonada/paella/piña/
sopa de cebolla/sopa de mariscos/tortilla española/
tortilla francesa.
… los calamares/champiñones/guisantes/helados/
quesos.
… las chuletas de cordero/gambas/judías verdes/
manzanas/naranjas/patatas bravas/uvas/verduras/
zanahorias.
Soy vegetarian.

Resources

Cassette B, side 1
CD 2, track 2
Cuaderno pages 14–20

1a Clasifica las imágenes de abajo en las categorías correctas.

Reading. Food and drink. Students categorise the food and drink listed under five headings in Spanish. Listing and learning vocabulary in categories like this can be helpful to students, as it breaks down long lists into smaller chunks. Teachers may wish to encourage students to treat other areas of vocabulary (e.g. places in a town, or clothes) in a similar way.

1c Escribe tu opinión sobre algo de cada categoría en **1a**.

Writing. Opinions about food and drink. Students write an opinion about one item from each category in **1a**. Some students may need reminding about how *me gusta/me encanta* change in the plural.

Answers

Carne	Pescado	Verduras	Fruta	Bebidas
El pollo	La sopa de mariscos	La sopa de cebolla	Las naranjas	El vino
El bistec	El salmón	Los guisantes	Las manzanas	El agua
		Las judías verdes	Las uvas	El zumo de naranja
		Los champiñones		La limonada
		Las zanahorias		

1b Escucha las palabras y comprueba tu pronunciación.

Listening. Pronunciation exercise on food and drink. This activity could be tackled in a number of ways, depending on preferred teaching and learning styles. One approach would be to invite a student to read out the items they have listed under each category in **1a** (either as individual items or as a complete category), then play the recorded version and ask either the same student or his/her classmates to compare the student's pronunciation with that of the native speaker. The recorded version could also be used for whole class repetition or drilling, if desired.

Tapescript

– Carne: *El pollo, el bistec.*
– Pescado: *La sopa de mariscos, el salmón.*
– Verduras: *La sopa de cebolla, los guisantes, las judías verdes, los champiñones, las zanahorias.*
– Frutas: *Las naranjas, las mananzas, las uvas.*
– Bebidas: *El vino, el agua, el zumo de naranja, la limonada.*

1d Escucha la conversación. ¿Verdad (✓) o mentira (✗)?

Listening. Ordering food and drink. True/false activity based on a conversation in a restaurant.

✚ Able students could correct the false statements.

Tapescript

– Ernesto:	*¡Camarero!*
– Camarero:	*Buenos días, ¿Qué van a tomar?*
– Sandra:	*Para mí, un bistec con judías verdes, ¿y tú, Ernesto?*
– Ernesto:	*Quisiera el salmón con guisantes.*
– Camarero:	*¿Y para beber?*
– Ernesto:	*Dos copas de vino y una botella de agua sin gas.*
– Camarero:	*Muchas gracias.*

Answers

1 mentira (✗)   **2** mentira (✗)   **3** verdad (✓)   **4** verdad (✓)
5 mentira (✗)

1e Túrnate con tu compañero/a.

Speaking. Ordering a meal in a restaurant. Pairwork. Students work in pairs to create a dialogue, using the written prompts and artwork on the page.

2a ¿Qué van a tomar? Escucha y escribe notas breves en español. (1–6)

Listening. Ordering food in a tapas bar. Note-taking activity in Spanish. Before tackling this activity, teachers may wish to find out what students know about tapas bars and the kind of food they offer, as well as ensuring students understand what the labelled illustrations of typical tapas consist of.

Tapescript

1 – Quisiera una tortilla española y calamares.
2 – Para mí, las patatas bravas.
3 – Me gustan mucho los mariscos – voy a tomar los calamares.
4 – Voy a pedir jamón serrano.
5 – Quisiera una ración de salchichón y de queso.
6 – Para mí, gambas y jamón serrano.

Answers

As tapescript.

2b Lee los menús del día. Busca las palabras nuevas en el diccionario.

Reading. Menus. Dictionary exercise based on two restaurant menus. Students should be encouraged to use their reading skills and strategies (identifying cognates or near-cognates, predicting from context, etc.) to minimise the number of words they need to look up in the dictionary. Sharing their hypotheses and reasoning about unknown vocabulary with the rest of the class can be a valuable exercise for developing the whole class's reading skills.

2c Decide qué menú corresponde a estas personas.

Reading. Food and drink preferences. Students decide which menu in **2b** would best suit each person. As a follow-up, students could choose one of the two menus and say what they would order, perhaps leading to pairwork in which one of them plays the waiter (using the phrases from **1e**, opposite) and the other orders a meal.

Answers

1 Menu B   **2** Menu A   **3** Menu B   **4** Menu A   **5** Menu A

2d Inventa un menú del día para un restaurante español. Utiliza el ordenador para diseñar el menú.

Writing. Creative task to design a menu, using ICT if possible. Categories and headings for the menu are given as support. If they use ICT, students could incorporate clipart or scanned-in photographs.

1 En el restaurante

(Student's Book pages 36–37)

Main topics and objectives

Booking a table and ordering a meal
Complaining in a restaurant

Grammar

Numbers/time

Key language

Quisiera reservar una mesa.
¿Para qué fecha? Para (el sábado).
¿Para cuántas personas? Para (cuatro personas).
¿A qué hora? A (las diez).
Lo siento, a (las once), sí.
Vale.
¿De parte de quién? De parte de ...
¡Camarero!
¿Qué desea usted?
De primer plato/de segundo plato/de postre ...
... el bistec a la pimienta/cóctel de gambas/cordero asado/flan/pollo al ajillo/sorbete.
... la ensalada especial de la casa/ensaladilla rusa/fruta del tiempo/merluza a la vasca/tarta helada/trucha con almendras.
... los guisantes con jamón/quesos regionales.
La cuenta, por favor.
¿Te gustó la comida? Sí, me gustó mucho.
No tengo vaso/tenedor.
El cuchillo está sucio./La cuchara está sucia./La sopa está fría.
No hay sal ni pimienta en la mesa.
Lo siento. Aquí hay un vaso./Le traigo otro/a en seguida.
Hay un error con la cuenta.
Sí, hay un error. Le traigo otra cuenta.

Resources

Cassette B, side 1
CD 2, track 3
Cuaderno pages 14–20

Note: the three menus at the top of page 36 are presented mainly for decorative purposes. However, teachers may wish students to read the menus and summarise what they understand.

➕ In particular, teachers may wish to use these menus as extension work for able students.

1a Escucha la conversación y rellena los espacios.

Listening. Booking a restaurant table. Gap-filling exercise.

🅁 The missing words are all ones which students have met before. However, teachers may wish to provide some students with a list of the missing words, to help them with spelling.

Tapescript

– *Restaurante Los Pescadores, dígame.*
– ***Quisiera*** *reservar una mesa.*
– *¿Para qué fecha?*
– *Para el sábado.*
– *¿Para cuántas* ***personas***?
– *Para* ***cuatro*** *personas.*
– *¿A qué hora?*
– *A las* ***diez***.
– *Lo siento, a las* ***once***, *sí.*
– *Vale.*
– *¿De parte de quién?*
– *De parte de Marisa Velázquez.*
– *Muy bien.*
– ***Adiós***.

Answers

See words in bold in tapescript.

1b Túrnate con tu compañero/a. Practica la conversación con la información de abajo.

Speaking. Booking a restaurant table. Pairwork activity. Students should first practise the completed dialogue in **1a**, then use the prompts in **1b** to change details in the dialogue.

🅁 Teachers may wish to support some students, by putting the dialogue from **1a** on to an OHT or the board and gapping or highlighting the sections which are to be changed.

➕ More able students could cover up the dialogue in **1a** and try creating the new version from memory.

1c Lee el menú y escoge un plato apropiado para cada cliente.

Reading. Restaurant menu. Students choose items from the menu to match a set of criteria in English. The menu contains a number of new items of vocabulary and students could first work in pairs, with a dictionary, to ensure they understand everything on the menu. As always, they should be encouraged to employ their reading skills and strategies and only use the dictionary as a last resort.

Answers

1 sopa de cebolla **2** cóctel de gambas **3** cordero asado
4 merluza a la vasca/salmón del Pacífico **5** fruta (del tiempo)

1d Escribe la conversación en el orden correcto.

Writing. Ordering a meal and asking for the bill. Students write out the dialogue in the correct order.

Answers

- ¡Camarero!
- Sí, ¿qué van a tomar?
- De primer plato, la ensaladilla rusa.
- ¿Y de segundo plato?
- El bistec a la pimienta, por favor.
- ¿Y de postre?
- El flan.
- ¿Le gustó la comida?
- Sí, me gustó mucho. La cuenta, por favor.
- Son 20 euros.

2a Los problemas. Empareja la frase con las imágenes correctas.

Reading. Complaining in a restaurant. Matching sentences to pictures.

Answers

| **1** B | **2** A | **3** F | **4** C | **5** E | **6** G | **7** D |

2b ¿Cuál es el problema? Mira los dibujos en **2a** y escribe la letra correcta. (1–5)

Listening. Complaining in a restaurant. Students note down the letter of the picture which goes with each complaint.

✚ Some students could note down any extra information they hear, such as what the person in number 4 is eating, or how much is on the bill in number 5 and how the mistake has occurred.

Tapescript

1 – ¡Camarero! Tráigame sal y pimienta por favor.
2 – No puedo comer la sopa – está fría. Quiero ver el menú otra vez.
3 – ¡Camarero! Necesito otro cuchillo. Está muy sucio.
  – En seguida, señorita.
4 – ¡Camarera! No puedo comer el helado con esta cuchara. Está sucia. Tráigame otra, por favor.
  – Muy bien, señor.
5 – ¡Camarera! Mire. El total no puede ser 25 euros porque no comimos postre.
  – ¡Ay! Lo siento, señor. Aquí está la cuenta para esta mesa.

Answers

| **1** G | **2** D | **3** F | **4** C | **5** A |

2c Túrnate con tu compañero/a.

Speaking. Complaining in a restaurant. Role-play. This provides valuable preparation for the speaking test section of examinations.

✚ Once they have perfected the role-play, some students could be encouraged to change the details, to create a different conversation.

Main topics and objectives

Asking for items in a tourist office
Discussing holiday plans

Grammar

Tú and *usted*

Key language

¿Qué quiere usted?
Quisiera/Necesito ...
... un mapa de la región/plano de la ciudad/folleto de excursiones/horario de trenes.
... una lista de hoteles/hostales/campings/albergues.
... información sobre (Barcelona/los hostales aquí).
¿Tiene usted (un folleto de excursiones)?
Por supuesto. Aquí tiene usted.
¿Algo más?
¿Adónde vas a ir de vacaciones? Voy a ir a Las Islas

Canarias/a Canadá (etc.)
¿Cuándo vas a ir? Voy a ir en agosto (etc.)
¿Cuánto tiempo vas a estar allí?
Voy a estar allí 15 días/tres semanas/un mes (etc.)
¿Cómo vas a ir allí? Voy a ir en avión (etc.)
¿Con quién vas a ir? Voy a ir con mi familia (etc.)
¿Dónde vas a quedarte? Voy a quedarme en ...
... un hotel/un albergue juvenil/una caravana/la casa de mi abuela (etc.)
¿Qué vas a hacer allí? Voy a ...
... ir a la playa/al teatro/a un concierto.
... visitar museos/monumentos/muchas ciudades/a amigos (etc.)

Resources

Cassette B, side 1
CD 2, track 4
Cuaderno pages 14–20
Gramática 6.1, page 170

1a Empareja los folletos con la lista.

Reading. Tourist office items. Students match the Spanish to the English.

Answers

1 c	2 f	3 d	4 a	5 b	6 e

1b Escucha y apunta la información que reciben. Escribe las letras correctas. (1–4)

Listening. Asking for information in a tourist office. Students note down the letters of the things from **1a** each speaker asks for. NB In dialogue 3, students should be encouraged to spot the difference between what the speaker asks for and what is received. Once they have completed the exercise, students should also be encouraged to listen again and spot, for example, the different ways in which the tourists ask for things (*Quisiera ..., Necesito ... ¿Tiene usted ...?*), how the employee asks whether they need anything else, how the speakers show they are polite to one another, etc.

Tapescript

1 – *Perdone, señor*
  – *¿Qué desea usted?*
  – *Quisiera un horario de trenes.*
  – *¿Algo más?*
  – *Sí, una lista de hoteles.*
  – *Aquí tiene usted.*
  – *Gracias.*
  – *De nada.*
2 – *Buenos días.*
  – *¿Qué desea usted?*
  – *Necesito información sobre Barcelona.*
  – *Aquí tiene un plano de la ciudad.*
  – *¿Tiene usted una lista de campings y albergues?*

  – *Sí, por supuesto.*
3 – *Buenas tardes. Quisiera información sobre los hostales aquí en Almería.*
  – *Tome esta lista.*
  – *¿Tiene usted un folleto de excursiones?*
  – *No, lo siento no tenemos pero hay un plano de la ciudad.*
  – *Muchas gracias.*
4 – *Buenas tardes.*
  – *Muy buenas. ¿Qué quiere usted?*
  – *Quisiera un plano de Zaragoza.*
  – *Aquí tiene. ¿Algo más?*
  – *Necesito información sobre los campings en la región.*
  – *Tome la lista.*
  – *Muchísimas gracias.*

Answers

1 a, b	2 f, e	3 b, d, f	4 f, e

Gramática

Tú and *usted*. The dialogues in **1b** provide a number of examples of the use of *usted*. The grammar section at the back of the Students' Book provides further explanation and a practice exercise.

1c Haz el diálogo con tu compañero/a.

Speaking. Asking for items in a tourist office. Role-play. Students should be encouraged to repeat the role-play as many times as possible, varying the details each time, by using the options given in the prompts.

2a Empareja las preguntas con las respuestas.

Writing. Discussing holiday plans. Students match questions to answers. All the questions and answers use *ir a* + infinitive (covered in *Repaso 1*, page 33).

These questions often crop up in the general conversation section of the examination speaking test. The variety of key question words used (¿*Dónde?* ¿*Adónde?* ¿*Cuándo?* ¿*Cuánto?* ¿*Cómo?* ¿*Qué?*) provides an opportunity to develop students' skills in distinguishing between the different types of information elicited by each question. Their understanding of question forms can be a key factor in students' examination success.

Answers

1 d	**2** g	**3** e	**4** b	**5** c	**6** a	**7** f

2b Escucha las conversaciones en una agencia de viajes. Copia y completa la ficha con la información correcta.

Listening. Holiday plans. Students complete the grid, using the list of words and phrases given. This is quite a demanding activity, with four pieces of information to listen for in each dialogue, so teachers may wish to break it down for students, for example, by pausing the tape and by playing each dialogue several times.

R Some students might find it easier and quicker to note down their answers in English. Alternatively, teachers could write the list of words and expressions onto an OHT, giving each one a letter, so that students can simply note down the letters, instead.

Tapescript

1 – Buenos días.
– Buenos días. ¿Adónde quiere ir?
– Quisiera visitar Inglaterra.
– ¿Cuánto tiempo quiere pasar allí?
– Quince días.
– ¿Dónde quiere quedarse?
– En un albergue juvenil.
– ¿Qué le interesa hacer?
– Bueno, visitar monumentos y museos.

2 – Buenas tardes.
– Sí, señora. ¿Qué desea?
– Quisiera ir de vacaciones a los Estados Unidos.
– ¿Adónde exactamente?
– Quiero ir de Los Angeles a Nueva York.
– ¿Cúanto tiempo quiere pasar allí?
– Un mes.
– ¿Cómo va a viajar?
– Vamos a alquilar una caravana y visitar muchas ciudades en el camino.
– ¡Ay! Qué bien!

3 – Perdone, señor.
– ¿Sí?
– Quisiera ir a Francia, a París, para pasar un fin de semana.
– Muy bien. ¿Usted quiere un hotel en el centro de París
– Sí, por favor. Vamos a ir al teatro y a un concierto.
– Bueno …

4 – Buenos días, ¿qué desea?
– Quiero ir a Canadá a ver a mi abuela que vive allí.

– ¿Cuánto tiempo quiere pasar en Canadá?
– Tres semanas.
– Usted va a quedarse en casa de su abuela. ¿Verdad?
– Sí. Vamos a visitar a unos amigos.
– Muy bien.

Answers

	País	**Estancia**	**Alojamiento**	**Actividades**
1	Inglaterra	15 días	Albergue juvenil	Visitar monumentos y museos
2	Estados Unidos	1 mes	Caravana	Visitar muchas ciudades
3	Francia	1 fin de semana	Hotel	Ir al teatro y a un concierto
4	Canadá	3 semanas	Casa de su abuela	Visitar a amigos

2c Imagina que vas de vacaciones. Contesta a las preguntas en **2a**. Escribe las respuestas.

Speaking. Students work in pairs to ask and answer the questions about holiday plans in **2a**. This is useful preparation for the speaking test in their examination. After oral practice, students write down their answers. Once these have been corrected, students could add them to their *fichero personal*.

2d Lee el mensaje electrónico. ¿Verdad o mentira?

Reading. Holiday plans. True/false exercise.

+ More able students could correct the false statements. As a follow-up, teachers may wish students to write a reply to Lauren's e-mail, answering her question about their holiday plans.

Answers

1 mentira	**2** verdad	**3** mentira	**4** mentira
5 verdad	**6** verdad		

3 Mis vacaciones pasadas

(Student's Book pages 40–41)

Main topics and objectives

Discussing past holidays

Grammar

The preterite

Skills

Expressing opinions in the past (e.g. *¡Fue fatal!*)

Key language

¿Adónde fuiste?
El año/agosto pasado, fui a España/la costa/la montaña (etc.)
¿Cuándo fuiste?
El año/agosto pasado (etc.)
¿Con quién fuiste? Fui con mis amigos (etc.)
¿Cómo fuiste? Fui en coche (etc.)
¿Cuánto tiempo pasaste allí? Pasé diez días (etc.) allí.
¿Dónde te alojaste? Me alojé en un hotel/un camping.

¿Qué hiciste?
Fui a la playa/Tomé el sol/Nadé en la piscina/Saqué fotos/Bailé en una discoteca/Comí platos típicos.
Hice windsurf/vela.
Jugué al voleibol/fútbol.
Visité castillos/museos.
¿Qué tiempo hizo? Hizo sol/Llovió.
Hizo buen/mal tiempo.
El viaje fue muy lento.
El hotel fue estupendo.
El tiempo fue muy bueno.
La comida fue rica.
Me gustó mucho el postre.
Lo pasé bomba (en la piscina).

Resources

Cassette B, side 1
CD 2, track 5
Cuaderno pages 14–20
Gramática 7.6, page 173

1a Mira las frases de abajo y busca las palabras que no conoces.

Reading. Questions and answers about past holidays. The spider diagram introduces key questions and example answers for discussing past holidays. The majority of the questions are past tense versions of the questions used to describe future holiday plans in the previous unit (see page 39). Teachers could use this opportunity to draw students' attention to the differences between the future and past tense versions of the same question and the importance of listening to or looking carefully at which tense the question is in, in order to answer correctly, especially in their examination.

1b Escucha las descripciones y rellena la ficha. (1–4)

Listening. Accounts of past holidays. Students should be encouraged to complete the grid in note form, in Spanish, as in the example.

R As with activity **2b** on page 39, there is quite a lot of information to listen for in each account. Some students will need further support with this (see suggestions under **2b**, above, on page 41).

➕ More able students should be encouraged to listen for any extra information (such as means of transport, accommodation, weather, speaker's opinion of the holiday, etc.)

Tapescript

– El año pasado fui a Madrid con mi familia. Pasamos tres semanas allí y ¡fue fenomenal! Nadé en la piscina mucho, hice windsurf y comí platos típicos como la paella y las patatas bravas.

– El junio pasado fui a Portugal con mis amigos. Fuimos en coche y pasamos quince días allí. Me gustó mucho. Saqué fotos de Lisboa y visité muchos museos.

– Fui a Mallorca el julio pasado para las vacaciones. Pasé diez días en un camping. ¡Fue fantástico! Bailé salsa en una discoteca y jugué al voleibol en la playa.

– En enero, fui de vacaciones a Cuba con mi hermano. Hizo buen tiempo en Cuba y por eso nadé en la piscina, tomé el sol y fui a la playa. Pasé una semana allí.

Answers

¿Cuándo?	¿Adónde?	¿Con quién?	¿Cuánto tiempo?	¿Actividades?
el año pasado	Madrid	familia	3 semanas	nadé, windsurf, platos típicos
junio pasado	Portugal	amigos	15 días	saqué fotos, visité museos
julio pasado	Mallorca	(no se sabe)	10 días	bailé en una discoteca, jugué al voleibol
enero	Cuba	hermano	1 semana	nadé en la piscina, tomé el sol, fui a la playa

1c Lee la carta. ¿Verdad (✓) o mentira (✗)?

Reading. Account of a past holiday. True/false exercise.

➕ More able students could correct the false statements. Before tackling this activity, teachers should draw students' attention to the *¡Ojo!* feature on the next page, which suggests strategies for dealing with longer texts in Spanish.

Answers

1 mentira	**2** mentira	**3** verdad	**4** verdad	**5** mentira
6 mentira	**7** mentira	**8** mentira		

¡Ojo!

A checklist of reading strategies for students to use when tackling longer texts in Spanish.

2a Prepara una presentación oral sobre tus vacaciones pasadas.

Speaking. Students prepare a presentation about a past holiday. They could record their presentation, perfecting and re-recording it until they (and you!) are happy with the standard. A tape-recorded version of important spoken pieces of work could sit alongside students' written *fichero personal*, as a valuable record of learning and revision aid.

2b Ahora escribe tu presentación.

Writing. Students' written version of their presentation could form part of their *fichero personal*.

Gramática

The preterite.

This major tense is covered in more detail in the grammar section at the back of the Student's Book, with practice exercises.

2c Empareja las opiniones con las imágenes correctas.

Reading. Opinions about past holidays. Matching phrases to pictures. Given the importance of opinion-giving in the examination, teachers may wish to encourage students to use some of these opinions in their spoken and written presentations, in **2a** and **2b**, above.

➕ More able students could adapt the phrases used in 2c, to create different opinions.

Answers

1 B	**2** A	**3** C	**4** D

2d Describe unas vacaciones interesantes. Usa tu imaginación. Incluye tu opinión.

Writing. Past holidays. Students write about a past holiday, incorporating their opinión. The *¡Ojo!* feature shows them a simple way of giving opinions about past events, using *fue* followed by an adjective. Once corrected, this piece of work could be added to students' *fichero personal*.

¡Ojo!

Giving opinions about past events, using *fue* followed by an adjective.

Trabajo de curso

(Student's Book pages 136–137)

Mis vacaciones: a coursework-style task to write about your holidays. Students are presented with a model text, comprehension exercises and preparation activities. The *Ayuda* section gives guidance to students on enhancing their coursework assignment, including a reminder of how to use past, present and future tenses; the conditional is also touched upon, as a lexical item only at this stage (introduced fully in Module 10). Students are further reminded to give opinions and are encouraged to use time markers.

1 Empareja las expresiones del texto en verde con estas expresiones inglesas.

Answers

last year I went to	el año pasado fui a
normally I go on holiday to	normalmente voy de vacaciones a
I went to the beach	fui a la playa
I ate (in various restaurants)	comí (en varios restaurantes)
I went (by plane)	fui (en avión)
I bought (a Catalan dictionary)	compré (un diccionario de catalán)
if I win the lottery	si me tocara la lotería
it was sunny and hot	hizo mucho sol y calor
I stayed in (a hotel)	me alojé en (un hotel)
I spent (a week there)	pasé (una semana allí)
I would like to go to	me gustaría ir a
It was (delicious)	era (deliciosa)
next year I am going to visit	el año próximo voy a visitar
I took (many photos)	saqué (muchas fotos)
they speak (two languages)	hablan (dos lenguas)

2 Imagina que eres Carlos y escribe tus respuestas a las siguientes preguntas.

Answers

¿Adónde vas de vacaciones normalmente?	Normalmente voy a las Islas Canarias.
¿Adónde fuiste el año pasado?	Fui a Barcelona.
¿Con quién fuiste?	Fui con mi mejor amigo y su madre.
¿Cómo fuiste?	Fui en avión.
¿Cuántos días pasaste allí?	Pasé una semana allí.
¿Dónde te alojaste?	Me alojé en un hotel.
¿Qué hiciste?	Visité muchos monumentos/Fui al estadio Camp Nou para ver un partido de fútbol/Saqué muchas fotos/Fui a la playa.
¿Dónde comiste?	Comí en varios restaurantes.
¿Te gusta Barcelona?	Me gusta mucho.
¿Adónde vas a ir de vacaciones el año próximo?	Voy a visitar Madrid.
Si te tocara la lotería, ¿adónde te gustaría ir de vacaciones?	Me gustaría ir a Miami en los Estados Unidos.

Leer **1a** Lee la postal de Mónica y rellena los espacios.

A gapped postcard, with picture prompts in each gap. Students copy and complete the text, replacing the pictures with words.

Answers (in bold)

Alicante, 3 de julio

Hola Nestor,
Aquí estoy de vacaciones en **España**. Estoy con mi **familia**. Me quedo en un hotel grande de lujo. ¡Nos lo pasamos bomba! Hace muy buen tiempo, hace **sol** y hace **calor**. Durante el día **nado** en el mar o en la **piscina**. También tomo mucho **sol** en la playa. Ayer fui a la oficina de turismo para coger **un mapa** de la región. Manaña vamos de excursión a las **montañas** o quizás a visitar los **museos**.

Un abrazo,

Mónica

Escribir **1b** Escribe una postal a un/a amigo sobre tus vacaciones. Usa la postal de Mónica como modelo.

Students adapt the postcard in **1a** to create their own version.

Leer **2a** Pon los cuadros en el orden correcto.

A recipe for Spanish omelettes. Students read the instructions and number the pictures in the correct order.

Answers

1 C	**2** F	**3** H	**4** B	**5** G	**6** A	**7** E	**8** D

Escribir **2b** Escribe los ingredientes y las instrucciones en español para el gazpacho (una sopa fría). Usa el diccionario si es necesario.

Students use the list of ingredients and instructions in English to write a recipe in Spanish for gazpacho. They will need to refer to a dictionary for some of the vocabulary, but the instructions can be adapted from the recipe in Leer **2**.

Answers

¼ kilo de tomates
2 pimientos
1 diente de ajo
5 cucharadas de vinagre
150 gramos de pan rallado

Pela los tomates. Pica los pimientos. Fríe el ajo. Añade el vinagre. Mete el pan rallado con los pimientos.

Leer **3** Lee el folleto y contesta a las preguntas en inglés.

A brochure for a holiday village. Students answer questions in English.

Answers

1 35 kilometres from Cartagena.
2 Campsite or apartments/flats.
3 Restaurants, cafés, supermarkets.
4 Water sports: swimming, scuba-diving/sub-aqua, windsurfing, sailing, water skiing. Non-water sports: golf, tennis, horse riding.
5 (Individual answers)
6 Yes.
7 rice dishes, fish, meat.

page 14

1a

Answers

Name	Country	With whom	Accomodation	How long for
Paco	USA	his parents	hotel	3 weeks
Isabel	France	her sister	her aunt's house	1 month
Ana	Germany	her friend	youth hostel	1 week
Miguel	Greece	his family	campsite	15 days
Sofia	Ireland	alone	her penfriend's house	2 weeks

1b

Answers

a Llueve y hace 15 °C.
b Hace calor y hace 30 °C.
c Hace sol y hace 20 °C.
d Hace viento y hace frío (4° C).
e Hay niebla y hace 12 °C.

page 15

2a

Answers

bañarse en el mar	to go swimming in the sea
hacer ciclismo	to go cycling
ir a la pista de hielo	to go to the ice rink
jugar al ajedrez	to play chess
ir de compras	to go shopping
ir de excursión	to go on a trip
montar a caballo	to go riding
nadar	to swim
tomar el sol	to sunbathe

2c

Answers

1 b	**2** c	**3** b	**4** c	**5** b

page 16

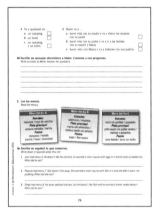

3a

Answers

Juan had salad, Spanish omelette and strawberry ice cream.
Paquita had prawn cocktail, hake with peas, and rice pudding.
Diego had squid, roast lamb with potatoes, and créme caramel.

page 17

4a

Answers

1 tenedor	**2** cuchillo	**3** vino	**4** cuenta	**5** cuchera
6 sal	**7** café	**8** vaso		

4b

Answers

1 un folleto de excursiones
2 un horario de trenes
3 una lista de albergues
4 un plano de la ciudad
5 un mapa de la región

5a

Answers

1 V	**2** M	**3** M	**4** M	**5** M	**6** V

page 18

5d

Answers

1 By train
2 Barcelona
3 He stayed at his uncle's house.
4 It was quite long.
5 Visited 3 parks
6 He went to the beach, swam, played football and sunbathed.
7 He got a brochure of excursions.
   It was windy.
   A cold tomato soup and ice-cream tart.
   He went to dance in a club.
   He will send some pictures of his holidays.

page 19

Gramática

1

Answers

Present tense
Viajo en tren.
Como mariscos en un restaurante.
Sacamos muchas fotos durante las vacaciones.
¿Tomas el sol?
Visito el castillo.
¿Vas a España?
Nadamos en la piscina.
Immediate future (going to)
Voy a viajar en tren.
Voy a comer mariscos en un restaurante.
Vamos a sacar muchas fotos durante las vacaciones.
¿Vas a tomar el sol?
Voy a visitar el castillo.
¿Vas a ir a España?
Vamos a nadar en la piscina.

2

Answers

1 PRESENTE	**2** PRETÉRITO	**3** PRETÉRITO
4 PRETÉRITO	**5** PRESENTE	**6** PRETÉRITO
7 PRETÉRITO	**8** PRESENTE	**9** PRESENTE
10 PRETÉRITO		

3

Answers

1 Fui a Barcelona.
2 Viajé en tren.
3 Comí una tortilla en un restaurante.
4 Saqué fotos en la playa.
5 Hizo sol.
6 Visité la catedral.

En ruta

(Student's Book pages 44–57)

Main topics and objectives	Grammar	Skills
Repaso (pp. 44–45) Directions and places in a town	Imperative Prepositions	
1 En camino (pp. 46–47) Asking about distances and the best means of transport to reach your destination Discussing transport preferences	*Hay* and *hay que* + infinitive	
2 En la estación (pp. 48–49) Railway station facilities Buying a train ticket and obtaining travel information	Time (24-hour clock)	
3 En la carretera (pp. 50–51) Dealing with car breakdowns	Numbers	
4 ¿Qué pasó? (pp. 52–53) Reporting accidents	The imperfect tense The preterite	Importance of using different tenses in your written work

Key language

Perdón, señor/señora.	*Siga todo recto.*
¿(Me puede decir) dónde está(n) …	*Tuerza a la izquierda/derecha (en los semáforos).*
… el centro comercial/teatro/cine/colegio?	*Tome la primera/segunda/tercera calle a la derecha/*
… la oficina de turismo/comisaría?	* izquierda.*
… los Correos?	*Cruce la plaza.*
¿Por dónde se va …	*Pase el puente/por los semáforos.*
… al mercado/hospital/camping?	*Está cerca/enfrente (de la estación)/entre el camping y la*
… a la estación de autobuses/estación de autocares/	* piscina/al lado del cine.*
* estación de trenes/piscina?*	*Está a mano derecha/izquierda.*

¿Por dónde se va al aeropuerto/a la estación de autocares?	*No me gusta viajar en autobús porque es (demasiado)*
Está lejos de aquí/a unos cinco kilómetros.	* lento/sucio/caro/malo para el medio ambiente.*
¿Hay un autobús/tren?	*En mi opinión, los trenes son muy rápidos/fáciles (etc.)*
No, hay que coger el metro/un taxi.	*El problema con los autobuses es que son muy lentos (etc.)*
¿Cuánto tiempo hace falta?	*Creo que hay demasiada polución a causa de los coches.*
Treinta minutos (más o menos).	
Prefiero viajar en tren/coche/porque es …	
Voy a pie o en bicicleta porque es …	
* más barato/cómodo/ecológico/fácil/limpio/rápido/*	
* sano (que el autobús).*	

Cantina/Cambio/Consigna automática/Entrada/	*Fumador/no fumador.*
* Información/Objetos perdidos/Paso subterráneo/*	*¿Cuánto es? Son (20 euros).*
* Quiosco/Sala de espera/Salida de emergencia/Señoras/*	*¿De qué andén sale? Del andén número (cuatro).*
* Caballeros/Taquilla.*	*¡Atención! El AVE/Tren TALGO/INTERCITY …*
Quisiera un billete de ida/ida y vuelta a (Madrid).	*… procedente de (Bilbao)/con destino a (Sevilla) …*
¿A qué hora? A las (diez y veinte).	*… efectuará su llegada a las (13.50)/por vía 3.*
¿Primera o segunda clase?	*… está en la vía (5).*
Primera/segunda clase.	*Faltan (dos minutos) para que efectúe su salida.*
¿Fumador o no fumador?	

Mi coche tiene una avería.	*En la autopista (A7)/la carretera (C246) …*
Tengo un problema con el coche.	*… a (5) kilómetros de (Lérida) dirección (Tarragona).*
Necesito a un mecánico.	*… cerca de la salida de (Tarragona).*
¿Puede usted mandar a un mecánico?	*… entre (Vendrell) y (Valls).*
¿Qué le pasa?	*¿De qué marca es el coche?*
Tengo un pinchazo.	*Es un (SEAT Ibiza.)*
Hay/Tengo un problema con el motor/la batería.	*¿De qué color? (Blanco/azul, etc.)*
No tengo una rueda de emergencia.	*¿Qué es la matrícula?*
Los frenos/Los faros no funcionan.	*Vengo en seguida.*
Se ha roto el parabrisas.	*Llegaré dentro de una hora.*
¿Dónde está usted?	

Tuve/Hubo un accidente.	*El coche era (blanco).*
Hacía sol/Estaba lloviendo.	*El peatón/perro/conductor (del coche/camión) …*
Había mucha gente.	* (no) fue herido/tuvo que ir al hospital.*
Un coche/camión/una moto chocó con …	
… un peatón/ perro/otro coche.	

Main topics and objectives

Directions and places in a town

Grammar

Imperative
Prepositions

Key language

Perdón, señor/señora.
¿(Me puede decir) dónde está(n) …
… el centro comercial/cine/colegio/teatro?
… la oficina de turismo/comisaría?
… los Correos?
¿Por dónde se va …
… al mercado/hospital/camping?
… a la estación de autobuses/la estación de
autocares/la estación de trenes/piscina?
Siga todo recto.
Tuerza a la izquierda/derecha (en los semáforos).
Tome la primera/segunda/tercera calle a la
derecha/izquierda.
Cruce la plaza.
Pase el puente/por los semáforos.
Está cerca/enfrente (de la estación)/entre el camping
y la piscina/al lado del cine.
Está a mano derecha/izquierda.

Resources

Cassette B, side 1
CD 2, track 6
Cuaderno pages 21–27
Gramática 7.11, page 176

1a Empareja los símbolos con las direcciones.

Reading. Directions. Matching phrases to pictures.

Answers

1 D	2 A	3 G	4 C	5 E	6 H	7 F	8 B

1b Mira el plano. ¿Las direcciones (1–6) son correctas o falsas?

Listening. Asking the way and directions. True/false exercise based on a simple map.

➕ Able students could correct the false directions they hear.

Tapescript

1 – *Perdone, señor. ¿Por dónde se va a la estación de autobuses?*
– *La estación de autobuses, vamos a ver, la tercera a la derecha. Sí.*
– *Gracias.*
2 – *Señorita. ¿Dónde está el hospital?*
– *Bueno, tome la tercera calle a la izquierda.*
3 – *¿Me puede decir dónde está el mercado?*
– *Sí, tome la segunda a la izquierda.*
– *Gracias.*
– *De nada, adiós.*
4 – *¿El centro comercial, por favor?*
– *Tuerza a la derecha y siga todo recto. Está muy cerca.*
5 – *Perdone, señora.*
– *¿Sí?*
– *¿Por dónde se va al camping?*
– *Tome la tercera calle a la izquierda, todo recto en los semáforos y ya está.*
6 – *Perdón, señor. ¿Dónde está la comisaría?*
– *Bueno, la comisaría. Tome la primera a la izquierda y todo recto. Está a unos trescientos metros.*
– *Gracias. Adiós.*

Answers

1 ✓	2 ✗	3 ✗	4 ✓	5 ✗	6 ✓

Gramática

The imperative (polite form).

1c Mira el plano y haz preguntas a tu compañero/a. ¿Su respuesta es correcta o no? Pues, escribe direcciones para cada lugar en el plano.

Speaking and writing. Asking the way and giving directions. Pairwork. Before tackling this activity, teachers may wish to give students oral practice of asking the way to various places and giving directions. Teachers may also wish to precede the activity by drawing attention to the two *¡Ojo!* features on this page. The first of these reminds students about the *a + el = al* rule (explained in more detail in the previous chapter – see Student's Book page 33.) The second points out that there are a number of different ways of asking for directions. (The listening activity **1b**, above, provides examples of all three ways mentioned.) As a follow-up, students write directions to the places shown on the map.

¡Ojo!

A + el = al.

¡Ojo!

Three different ways of asking for directions.

2a Mira el plano. Estás aquí (X). ¿Cuál es el destino en cada caso?

Reading. Places in a town and directions. Students read a series of directions and work out from the map and the key where each one leads. The small key language support box offers support with prepositions in particular, and teachers may wish to ensure that students are familiar with this key language, before tackling the activity. Students should also be familiar with all the places listed in the map key, before beginning the activity.

Answers

1 Correos	**2** comisaría	**3** cine	**4** centro comercial
5 hospital				

2b Escucha los diálogos (1–5). ¿Adónde van?

Listening. Directions and places in a town. Students listen and refer again to the map, to work out where each speaker is directing someone to.

R This activity may prove demanding for some students, as each item on the CD/tape involves a number of different directions. Teachers may wish to pause the CD/tape after each direction or after every other direction and check that students are making sense of what they hear and are able to follow correctly on the map.

Tapescript

1 – Tuerza a la derecha. Siga todo recto y está a mano izquierda, enfrente del puente.

2 – Tuerza a la izquierda y tome la segunda a la derecha. Tome la primera a la izquierda y está a mano izquierda enfrente de la oficina de turismo. No está lejos.

3 – Tuerza a la derecha. Pase por los semáforos y por el puente. Tuerza a la izquierda en el cruce y está todo recto. Está cerca.

4 – Siga todo recto. Tuerza a la izquierda en los semáforos y siga todo recto. Está a mano derecha enfrente de Correos.

5 – Tuerza a la derecha. Tuerza a la izquierda en los semáforos, pase por delante del hospital y está al lado del camping. La piscina también está cerca.

Answers

1 comisaría	**2** Colegio San Fernando	**3** mercado
4 teatro	**5** cine	

2c Mira el plano. Haz preguntas a tu compañero/a.

Speaking. Asking the way and giving directions. Students work in pairs to ask for and give directions to the places shown by symbols.

R For students who need more structure/support, teachers may wish to put a model dialogue onto an OHT or the board and practise this first.

1 En camino

(Student's Book pages 46–47)

Main topics and objectives

Asking about distances and the best means of transport to reach your destination
Discussing transport preferences

Grammar

Hay and *hay que* + infinitive

Key language

¿Por dónde se va al aeropuerto/a la estación de autocares?
Está lejos de aquí/a unos cinco kilómetros.
¿Hay un autobús/tren?
No, hay que coger el metro/un taxi.
¿Cuánto tiempo hace falta?
Treinta minutos (más o menos.)

Prefiero viajar en tren/coche/porque es ...
Voy a pie o en bicicleta porque es ...
... más barato/cómodo/ecológico/fácil/limpio/rápido/ sano (que el autobús).
No me gusta viajar en autobús porque es (demasiado) lento/sucio/caro/malo para el medio ambiente.
En mi opinión, los trenes son muy rápidos/fáciles (etc.)
El problema con los autobuses es que son muy lentos (etc.)
Creo que hay demasiada polución a causa de los coches.

Resources

Cassette B, side 1
CD 2, track 7
Cuaderno pages 21–27

1a Escucha el diálogo y pon las frases en el orden correcto.

Listening. Asking about means of transport and distances. Students put the dialogue into the correct order.

Tapescript

Turista:	Perdón, señora. ¿Por dónde se va a la estación de autocares, por favor?
Peatón:	Está lejos de aquí a unos cinco kilómetros.
Turista:	¿Hay un autobús?
Peatón:	No, hay que coger el metro.
Turista:	¿Cuánto tiempo hace falta?
Peatón:	Treinta minutos.
Turista:	Gracias, adiós.

Answers

As tapescript.

Gramática

Hay and *hay que.*

1b Escucha los diálogos y copia y completa la tabla (1–3).

Listening. Places in a town. means of transport and travel time. Students complete the grid.

R Students who might find this activity too hard could be provided with a partially completed grid, so that they only have to listen for one (or two) pieces of information per dialogue. They could also fill in the grid in English, rather than Spanish.

+ More able students could be encouraged to listen for extra details, such as whether the train in dialogue 2 is direct and what number bus is needed in dialogue 3.

Tapescript

Ejemplo

– Turista:	Perdón, señor. ¿Por dónde se va a la estación de autocares?
– Peatón:	Está lejos de aquí.
– Turista:	¿Hay un autobús?
– Peatón:	No, hay que coger el metro.
– Turista:	¿Cuánto tiempo hace falta?
– Peatón:	30 minutos.
– Turista:	Gracias, adiós.

1	– Turista:	Perdón, señor. ¿Por dónde se va a la estación de trenes, por favor?
	Peatón:	Está bastante cerca de aquí.
	Turista:	¿Hay un autobús?
	Peatón:	No, hay que coger un taxi.
	Turista:	¿Cuánto tiempo hace falta?
	Peatón:	Diez minutos en taxi.
	Turista:	Gracias, adiós.
2	– Turista:	Perdón, señor. ¿Por dónde se va al polideportivo, por favor?
	Peatón:	Está muy lejos de aquí.
	Turista:	¿Hay un autobús?
	Peatón:	No, hay que coger el tren.
	Turista:	¿Cuánto tiempo hace falta?
	Peatón:	15 minutos. Es directo.
	Turista:	Gracias, adiós.
3	– Turista:	Perdón, señor. ¿Por dónde se va al hospital, por favor?
	Peatón:	Está muy cerca de aquí.
	Turista:	¿Hay una parada de taxis cerca de aquí?
	Peatón:	No, hay que coger el autobús número 5.
	Turista:	¿Cuánto tiempo hace falta?
	Peatón:	25 minutos más o menos.
	Turista:	Gracias, adiós.

Answers

¿Dónde?	¿Transporte?	¿Minutos?
La estación de trenes	Taxi	10 minutos
El polideportivo	Tren	15 minutos
El hospital	Autobús	25 minutos

1c Túrnate con tu compañero/a.

Speaking. Asking the way, means of transport, distances and time. Students work in pairs to create dialogues, using the pictures as prompts. Students should first practise the model dialogue, in which the details to be changed are highlighted in bold.

2a Empareja los dibujos con las palabras.

Reading. Opinions about transport. Students match simple opinions to pictures. Students should recognise most of the adjectives used and others can be guessed, especially if presented in pairs (*barato/caro, limpio/sucio*, etc.)

Answers

| 1 H | 2 F | 3 J | 4 D | 5 I | 6 B | 7 G | 8 A | 9 E | 10 C |

2b Lee las opiniones sobre el transporte. ¿Son positivas o negativas?

Reading. Opinions about transport. This activity presents more complex opinions about transport preferences. However, students should be encouraged to look for the adjectives which they met in the previous exercise, and read each phrase for gist in order to decide whether it is a positive or a negative statement, rather than trying to understand every word.

✚ Able students should be able to manipulate these phrases, to create new opinions about transport and use these in their speaking and writing.

Answers

Positivas: 1, 3, 5, 6.   **Negativas:** 2, 4, 7, 8.

2c Escucha las opiniones. Identifica su medio de transporte preferido y por qué lo prefieren.

Listening. Transport preferences. Students listen to each speaker and note down the means of transport they prefer and why. The example shows them how to do this in very simple Spanish, using only two words.

R Some students might find it easier to take notes in English, or teachers might wish to provide them with lists of the means of transport and reasons given, so that students can demonstrate comprension by simply drawing a line, to join the two.

✚ Able students could note down any extra information they hear.

Tapescript

– Me encanta mi coche porque es muy cómodo. Voy siempre en coche. Es que no me gusta el transporte público.
– Vivo cerca de mi colegio y las tiendas están cerca. Prefiero ir en bicicleta. Hay mucha polución en el mundo; por eso ir en bici es más ecológico.
– Prefiero el tren porque es muy fácil y puedo hablar por teléfono y tomar un café.
– Voy en taxi si puedo porque es muy rápido.

Answers

| 1 coche/cómodo | 2 bicicleta/ecológico | 3 tren/fácil |
| 4 taxi/rápido | | |

2d Con tu compañero/a, dí qué tipo de transporte prefieres y por qué.

Speaking. Transport preferences. Students work in pairs, using the support grid provided, to say which means of transport they prefer and why.

✚ Able students could be encouraged to use *and* or/manipulate and use some of the more complex phrases from **2b**, above, in their speaking.

2e Lee el mensaje. ¿Verdad (✓) o mentira (✗)?

Reading. Transport issues. Students read the e-mail about transport problems in Lima and do the true/false exercise. As a follow-up, students could write a reply to Pablo's questions about transport problems in their area, if teachers wish.

Answers

| 1 verdad | 2 mentira | 3 verdad | 4 mentira | 5 verdad |

2 En la estación

(Student's Book pages 48–49)

Main topics and objectives

Railway station facilities
Buying a train ticket and obtaining travel information

Grammar

Time (24-hour clock)

Key language

*Cantina/Cambio/Consigna automática/
Entrada/Información/Objetos perdidos/
Paso subterráneo/Quiosco/Sala de espera/
Salida de emergencia/Señoras/Caballeros/Taquilla.
Quisiera un billete de ida/ida y vuelta a (Madrid).
¿A qué hora? A las (diez y veinte).*

*¿Primera o segunda clase? Primera/segunda clase.
¿Fumador o no fumador? Fumador/no fumador.
¿Cuánto es? Son (20 euros).
¿De qué andén sale? Del andén número (cuatro).
¡Atención! El AVE/Tren TALGO/INTERCITY ...
... procedente de (Bilbao)/con destino a (Sevilla) ...
... efectuará su llegada a las (13.50)/por vía 3.
... está en la vía (5).
Faltan (dos minutos) para que efectúe su salida.
Salida/Llegada/Prestaciones/Preferente/Prensa*

Resources

Cassette B, side 1
CD 2, track 8
Cuaderno pages 21–27

1a Empareja los símbolos con las palabras.

Reading. Railway station facilities. Students match the words with the symbols. Students could work in pairs, using their reading skills and strategies to work out or guess as much of the new vocabulary as possible, then look up any remaining words in a dictionary.

Answers

1 F	2 D	3 K	4 B	5 J	6 C	7 E	8 L	9 A
10 H	11 I	12 G						

1b Escucha a las personas. Escribe la letra correcta. (1–6)

Listening. Railway station facilities. Students listen to the speakers saying what they need to do and write down the letter of the corresponding symbol in **1a**.

Tapescript

1 – *Tengo hambre. ¿Quieres un bocadillo o patatas fritas?*
2 – *Necesito leer algo en el tren. Voy a comprarme un periódico.*
3 – *No tengo un billete. Necesito comprarlo.*
4 – *Quisiera información sobre el tren para Madrid.*
5 – *¿Dónde está mi bolso? Lo he perdido.*
6 – *No tengo más euros. Tengo que cambiar un cheque de viaje.*

Answers

1 E	2 I	3 H	4 G	5 D	6 F

1c Lee la conversación de la taquilla y rellena los espacios.

Reading. Buying train tickets. Students complete the gapped dialogue from a list of missing words given. They can then check their answers by listening to the tape/CD (see **1d**, below.) If preferred, students could listen to the tape/CD before filling in the gaps.

Answers

1 Málaga	2 diez y veinte	3 Segunda	4 No fumador
5 20 euros	6 cuatro		

1d Escucha la conversación. ¿Es correcta?

Listening. Buying train tickets. Students check their answers against the recorded version.

Tapescript

Empleado:	Buenos días. ¿Qué desea?
Viajero:	Quisiera un billete de ida y vuelta a Málaga.
Empleado:	¿A qué hora?
Viajero:	A las diez y veinte.
Empleado:	¿Primera o segunda clase?
Viajero:	Segunda.
Empleado:	¿Fumador o no fumador?
Viajero:	No fumador. ¿Cuánto es?
Empleado:	20 euros.
Viajero:	Vale. ¿De qué andén sale?
Empleado:	Del andén número cuatro.
Viajero:	Gracias, adiós.

1e Túrnate con tu compañero/a.

Speaking. Buying train tickets. Before tackling the role-play, students should practise the completed dialogue from **1c**, above. The role-play offers several variations, so that it can be practised more than once, if teachers wish.

2a Mira el horario. ¿Verdad o mentira?

Reading. Train timetable. True/false exercise. Before students undertake the activity, teachers should ensure that students understand the train timetable, the symbols for various on-board facilities and the different types of trains mentioned. The following information might be helpful:

In Spain, passengers pay different rates depending on the speed and standard of the trains. TALGOs are a type of long-distance train for which you would expect to pay more. INTERCITY is a standard train. The AVE (Alta Velocidad Española), which means high-speed Spanish train, is quicker than the TALGO and is mainly used between Madrid and Sevilla. *Preferente* means first class and *turista* means second/standard class (abbreviated to P and T in the price columns in the train information on page 49).

✚ Able students could correct the false statements.

Answers

1 verdad	2 mentira	3 verdad	4 mentira

Answers

1 Tiene diez líneas. 2 Es rápido y barato. 3 Cuesta 1 euro.
4 Cuesta 5 euros. 5 El primer tren sale a las seis y cinco.
6 Cierra a la una y media.

2b Escucha los anuncios de la estación. Completa la tabla con la información que falta.

Listening. Rail travel announcements. Students complete the grid. They need to be made familiar with the new expressions *procedente de*, *con destino a*, *efectuará su llegada* and *vía* before tackling this exercise. Teachers may also wish to check students' understanding of the 24-hour clock, which is used in this activity.

R Students requiring extra support could be given a list of the missing information, from which to select their answers.

Tapescript

– ¡Atención! Tren TALGO procedente de Bilbao que tiene su llegada a las 13.50 efectuará su llegada por vía 3.
– ¡Atención tren INTERCITY con destino a Madrid efectuará su llegada a las 14.30 por vía 3.
– ¡Atención! El AVE con destino a Sevilla está en la vía 1. Faltan diez minutos para que efectúe su salida.
– ¡Atención! Tren Expreso Costa Verde con destino a Santiago está en la vía 8. Faltan dos minutos para que efectúe su salida.

Answers (in bold)

Procedente/Destino	Ciudad	Vía	Hora/Minutos
Procedente	Bilbao	a) **3**	b) **13.50**
Destino	c) **Madrid**	3	d) **14.30**
e) **Destino**	Sevilla	1	f) **En 10 minutos**
g) **Destino**	Santiago	h) **8**	i) **En 2 minutos**

2c Lee el texto sobre el metro de Madrid y contesta a las preguntas.

Reading. Underground travel information. A short text, with questions in Spanish. Students may need help with some new vocabulary (e.g. *un viaje sencillo*, *se cierra*), or to have access to a dictionary.

3 En la carretera

(Student's Book pages 50–51)

Main topics and objectives

Dealing with car breakdowns

Grammar

Numbers

Key language

Mi coche tiene una avería.
Tengo un problema con el coche.
Necesito a un mecánico.
¿Puede usted mandar a un mecánico?
¿Qué le pasa?
Tengo un pinchazo.
Hay/Tengo un problema con el motor/la batería.
No tengo una rueda de emergencia.
Los frenos/Los faros no funcionan.

Se ha roto el parabrisas.
¿Dónde está usted?
En la autopista (A7)/la carretera (C246) ...
... a (5) kilómetros de (Lérida) dirección (Tarragona).
... cerca de la salida de (Tarragona).
... entre (Vendrell) y (Valls).
¿De qué marca es el coche? Es un (SEAT Ibiza).
¿De qué color? (Blanco/azul, etc.)
¿ Qué es la matrícula?
Vengo en seguida.
Llegaré dentro de una hora.

Resources

Cassette B, side 1
CD 2, track 8
Cuaderno pages 21–27

1a Identifica las partes del coche.

Reading. Car parts vocabulary. Matching words to the picture. Students could work in pairs or groups, firstly using reading strategies (such as looking for cognates/ near cognates) to work out as many as they can, then using a dictionary to look up any unknown words.

Answers

1 el motor	**2** el parachoques	**3** la matrícula
4 el faro/los faros	**5** la rueda	**6** la batería	**7** el neumático
8 la ventanilla	**9** el tubo de escape	**10** el parabrisas

1b ¿Cuál es el problema? Escribe la letra correcta. (1–7)

Listening. Car breakdowns. Students match what they hear to the pictures.

Tapescript

1 – ¿Aló? Necesito a un mecánico. Mi coche tiene una avería.
2 – Hay un problema con el motor.
3 – Los frenos no funcionan.
4 – Tengo un pinchazo.
5 – No tengo una rueda de emergencia.
6 – Los faros no funcionan.
7 – Tengo un problema con la batería.

Answers

1 G	**2** C	**3** D	**4** B	**5** F	**6** E	**7** A

1c Mira el dibujo del coche y túrnate con tu compañero/a.

Speaking. Car parts vocabulary. Students work in pairs to practise the vocabulary. Teachers may wish to precede this with whole-class 'drilling' of the vocabulary, to ensure correct pronunciation.

2a Empareja las preguntas con las respuestas.

Reading. Reporting a breakdown. Students match up the questions a garage or breakdown service is likely to ask with example answers, including the location, make and colour of the car. After completing the activity, students should practise the questions and answers orally, as a complete dialogue.

➕ Able students could adapt the dialogue, by changing details in the answers.

Answers

1 d	**2** a	**3** b	**4** c

2b Escucha las conversaciones. Toma breves notas en inglés. (1–4)

Listening. Reporting car breakdowns. Students listen and note down in English what the problem is, where the car has broken down, its make and colour.

🅡 As there is quite a lot of information to listen for, teachers may wish to pause the CD/tape after each detail for some students and give them support with the names of the towns mentioned (e.g. by writing them on the board.) Alternatively, students could be asked to simply note down one detail about the location of the car (which is arguably the most difficult part of the information to understand fully.)

Tapescript

1 – ¡Oiga! Tengo un problema con el coche.
  – ¿Qué le pasa?
  – Tengo un problema con los frenos. No funcionan.
  – ¿Dónde está usted?
  – Estamos en la carretera N240 a 5 kilómetros de Lérida dirección Tarragona.
  – ¿De qué marca es el coche?
  – Un SEAT Ibiza, matrícula M306795
  – ¿De qué color?

– *Blanco.*
– *Muy bien.*
2 – *Talleres San Isidro.*
   – *¡Oiga!, tengo un problema con el coche.*
   – *¿Qué le pasa?*
   – *¿Puede usted mandar a un mecánico? El coche tiene una avería.*
   – *¿Qué le pasa exactamente?*
   – *No sé. Es un problema con el motor.*
   – *¿Dónde está usted?*
   – *Estoy en la carretera N11 a 20 kilómetros de Igualada cerca de la A2.*
   – *¿Y su coche?*
   – *Un Volkswagen Passat rojo.*
   – *Vale. Vengo en seguida.*
3 – *¡Oiga!*
   – *¿Sí? Se ha roto el parabrisas.*
   – *¿Dónde está usted?*
   – *En la carretera C246 entre Vendrell y Valls.*
   – *¿Y el coche?*
   – *Un Opel Corsa, negro.*
   – *¿La matrícula?*
   – *B493923.*
   – *Vale. Llegaré dentro de una hora.*
   – *Gracias, adiós.*
4 – *Tengo un problema con el coche.*
   – *¿Sí? ¿Qué le pasa?*
   – *Los faros no funcionan.*
   – *¿Dónde está usted?*
   – *En la autopista A7 cerca de la salida de Tarragona.*
   – *¿Y su coche?*
   – *Un Audi Quattro verde.*
   – *Vale. Voy en seguida.*

Answers

1 Brakes. N240, 5 km from Lérida (Tarragona direction). SEAT Ibiza. White.
2 Engine. N11, 20 km from Igualada, near the A2. Volkswagen Passat. Red.
3 Windscreen. C246, between Vendrell and Valls. Opel Corsa. Black.
4 Headlights. A7, near Tarragona exit. Audi Quattro. Green.

2c Escucha e identifica la matrícula correcta. (1–5)

Listening. Car registration numbers. Students match up what they hear to the registration plates shown. As well as revision of letters of the alphabet (see Module 1, *Repaso 1*, page 7), this activity provides valuable practice of numbers – often a source of lost marks in examinations if misunderstood/wrongly given – and teachers may wish to precede or follow the activity by playing various number games in Spanish.

1 – *La matrícula es CA254472*
2 – *La matrícula es MA369160*
3 – *La matrícula es B346221*
4 – *La matrícula es B264920*
5 – *La matrícula es M369270*

Answers

1 C	2 B	3 E	4 D	5 A

2d Haz diálogos por teléfono con tu compañero/a.

Speaking. Reporting car breakdowns. Students work in pairs, using the prompts on the page to build dialogues. The model dialogue on the page provides support and the sections of the dialogue to be changed are highlighted in bold.

2e Escoge uno de los personajes de abajo y escribe una conversación con el garaje donde piden ayuda.

Writing. An imaginative task in which students create a conversation between a celebrity whose car has broken down and the garage they call for help. The artwork provides a stimulus, or students can use their own ideas.

4 ¿Qué pasó?

(Student's Book pages 52–53)

Main topics and objectives

Reporting accidents

Grammar

The imperfect tense
The preterite

Skills

Importance of using different tenses in your written work

Key language

Tuve/Hubo un accidente.

Hacía sol/Estaba lloviendo.
Había mucha gente.
Un coche/camión/una moto chocó con …
un peatón/perro/otro coche.
El coche era (blanco).
El conductor (del coche/camión)/peatón/perro …
… (no) fue herido/tuvo que ir al hospital.

Resources

Cassette B, side 1
CD 2, track 9
Cuaderno pages 21–27
Gramática 7.7, page 174 and 7.6 page 173

1a Lee las frases y asegúrate de que las entiendes.

Reading. Reporting an accident. The new language for reporting an accident is presented via a flowchart, with picture clues to help convey meaning. Teachers may wish to check first that students understand the language in each box, then begin constructing sentences (orally or in writing) and ask students to explain the details of each sentence, in English. The flowchart could also be used to give students oral practice of the new key language. Teachers could write prompts in English on the board or OHT and ask students to construct sentences, reporting what happened.

➕ Teachers could extend more able students, by asking them to create new phrases, using known (or unknown) vocabulary, e.g. 'It was cold. A bicycle crashed into a child. The child wasn't hurt.' (etc.)

1b Describe los dibujos.

Writing. Reporting an accident. Students write an account of an accident, using the picture prompts.

➕ More able students could write their own account, using different details from those shown in the pictures.

Answers

A Hubo/tuve un accidente.   **B** Hacía sol.
C Una moto chocó con un perro.
D El conductor fue herido. El perro no fue herido.

Gramática

The preterite and imperfect tenses. A brief explanation of the imperfect, in the third person singular only. This new tense is covered more fully in later chapters and in the grammar section at the back of the Student's Book.

1c Escucha la descripción del accidente. ¿Verdad o mentira?

Listening. Reporting an accident. True/false exercise. This extends the language of the flowchart a little, bringing in *era* (for describing the colour of the vehicles involved) and *tuvo que* (*ir al hospital*). Students should be encouraged to use previous knowledge and the context to guess the meaning of these new elements.

➕ Able students could correct the false statements.

Tapescript

Ayer hubo un accidente terrible cerca de mi casa. Estaba lloviendo y hacía mal tiempo. Un coche chocó con un camión. Era un coche rojo y el camión era blanco. Afortunadamente, el conductor del camión no fue herido pero el conductor del coche tuvo que ir al hospital en ambulancia.

Answers

1 mentira	**2** verdad	**3** mentira	**4** mentira	**5** verdad

1d Lee el mensaje y escoge la respuesta correcta.

Reading. Report of a difficult journey. A multiple-choice activity, based on a short letter. The text uses a number of different tenses and the *¡Ojo!* feature below asks students to find and identify what they are. In particular, teachers may wish to build on the *Gramática* feature above, by asking students to say why the preterite or the imperfect has been used in each case.

Answers

1 b	**2** c	**3** a	**4** b	**5** a

¡Ojo!

Using a range of tenses.

Topics revised

- Future and past holidays
- Meeting people
- Ordering a snack in a café
- Transport
- Getting information about train travel
- Asking the way
- Buying coach tickets

Módulo 3 De vacaciones

Conversación 1 and Conversación 2

Two general conversations about holidays: the first requires use of the present and future tenses, the second requires use of the preterite. The general advice at the top of page 56 encourages students to make use of 'time-filler' expressions in Spanish and to listen carefully for past and future tense questions.

Juegos de rol 1 and 2

Two role plays: one on meeting a young Spanish person, the other on ordering a snack in a café. The first requires the use of tú and the second one usted. The general advice at the top of page 56 gives students guidance about the two modes of address. It also suggests students get into the habit of perfecting role-plays and then tape-recording them.

Módulo 4 En ruta

Conversación 1 and Conversación 2

General conversations covering travel to school and preferred means of transport. There are opportunities in both topics for students to give opinions and reasons. Some students could also be encouraged to take the initiative, by including reference to the past or the future (e.g. yesterday my journey to school took … Tomorrow, I'm going to go to the shopping centre by bus, etc.)

Juegos de rol 1, 2 and 3

Role plays on:

- Asking for information about train travel
- Asking for directions
- Buying a coach ticket

Presentación

Students are asked to prepare a presentation about a holiday, using the headings given. They should look carefully at the general advice at the top of page 56, which suggests using *creo que … porque* to express opinions, as well as making sure they use all three tenses and, again, suggests tape-recording their presentation once they have perfected it.

Leer y escribir

(Student's Book pages 152–153)

Leer 1a Rellena los espacios con las palabras.

A series of gapped sentences about directions. Students copy out and complete the sentences, using words from the list to replace the pictures.

Answers (in bold)

> 1 A las **nueve** coja el **autobús**. La **parada de autobuses** está enfrente de nuestro piso.
> 2 Baje en el **hospital** y tome la primera calle a la derecha.
> 3 El **mercado** está al lado del teatro.
> 4 Luego para ir al centro comercial que está muy cerca, cruce la **plaza** y allí está.
> 5 Para ir a Correos, cruce el **puente**, siga todo recto y está a la izquierda de la **peluquería**.
> 6 La oficina de turismo está bastante lejos. Coja el **metro** que está delante de la **piscina**.

Leer 1b ¿Verdad o mentira?

A true/false exercise, based on the sentences in Leer 1.

Answers

> **1** mentira   **2** mentira   **3** verdad   **4** mentira   **5** verdad
> **6** mentira   **7** mentira   **8** mentira

Escribir 1c Ronaldo tiene fiesta en casa. Escribe una nota con direcciones para Raúl.

Students write directions to a party, using their imagination.

Leer 2a Lee y escoge las cuatro frases correctas.

An account of a disastrous journey. Students then read a series of statements and identify the four correct sentences.

Answers

> The four correct statements are: 1, 4, 6 and 8.

Escribir 2b Contesta en inglés.

A series of questions in English based on the text in Leer 4.

Answers

> **1** He got up late.   **2** The car was in the garage.   **3** It was pouring with rain.   **4** He left his book of tickets at home. He realised at the bus stop.   **5** At the main crossroads/junction.   **6** A lorry hit the traffic lights. The driver was taken to hospital.   **7** He went by bicycle. It's cheaper, quicker and healthier.

Escribir 3 Escribe sobre un día horroroso. Usa el pretérito y el imperfecto.

Students write a similar text to the one in Leer 2a, about a disastrous day, using the picture prompts.

módulo 4 *Cuaderno*

(Workbook pages 21–27)

page 21

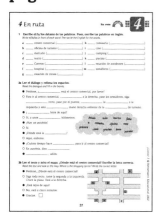

page 22

1

Answers

a el centro comercial **b** la oficina de turismo
c el mercado **d** el teatro **e** los correos **f** el hospital
g la estación de trenes **h** la comisaría **i** el cine
j el camping **k** la piscina **l** la estación de autocares
m los semáforos

2a

Answers (in bold)

A: Perdone ¿**dónde** está el centro comercial, por favor?
B: Para ir al centro comercial, **tuerza** a la derecha, pase los semáforos, siga **todo** recto, pase por el puente, **tome** la **primera** a la izquierda y está **a** mano derecha enfrente de la **oficina** de turismo.
A: ¿**Está** lejos de aquí?
B: Sí, a unos **cinco** kilómetros.
A: ¿Hay un autobús?
B: Sí.
A: ¿Dónde está la **parada**?
B: Aquí enfrente.
A: ¿Cuánto tiempo hace **falta** para ir al centro comercial?
B: En autobús, diez **minutos**.
A: **Gracias**, adiós.

2b

Answers

c

3a

Answers

1 caballeros **2** consigna automática **3** andén
4 objetos perdidos **5** cantina **6** paso subterráneo
7 cambio **8** salida **9** quiosco **10** taquillas **11** entrada

3b

Answers

1 B **2** C **3** I **4** K **5** G **6** H **7** J **8** A **9** E **10** D **11** F

page 23

3c

Answers

a mentira **b** mentira **c** verdad **d** no se sabe
e no se sabe **f** mentira **g** mentira

Cuaderno

(Workbook pages 21–27)

page 24

4

Answers

1 60 euros	**2** 14.00	**3** 11	**4** no	**5** sí

5a

Answers

1 e	**2** b	**3** f	**4** a	**5** g	**6** c	**7** h	**8** d

page 25

6a

Answers

a V	**b** M	**c** M	**d** V	**e** M	**f** M

page 26

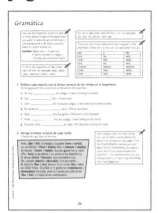

Gramática

1

Answers (in bold)

> **1** Yo **viajaba** al colegio. (I was travelling to school)
> **2** **Hacía** frío. (It was cold)
> **3** **Llevaba** mi chaqueta negra. (I was wearing my black jacket)
> **4** El coche **era** azul. (The car was blue)
> **5** **Había** mucha gente. (There were a lot of people)
> **6** **Hablaba** con mi amiga. (I was talking to my friend)
> **7** El perro **cruzaba** la calle. (The dog was crossing the road)

2

Answers (in bold)

> Ayer, **iba** al colegio cuando **tuve** un accidente. **Hacía** frío y **estaba** lloviendo. **Había** mucha gente en la calle. **Vi** a un chico y su perro en los semáforos. El chico **llevaba** una sudadera roja. Un camión **chocó** con un coche. El camión **era** blanco y el coche **era** un SEAT Ibiza. El chico y el perro no **resultaron** heridos, pero el conductor del coche **fue** al hospital en ambulancia.

¿Qué te ha pasado?

(Student's Book pages 58–69)

Main topics and objectives	Grammar	Skills
Repaso (pp. 58–59) Reporting illness	*Doler* and *tener dolor de*	
1 Me siento mal (pp. 60–61) Describing symptoms and seeking medical advice	Expressions with *tener* *Desde hace* Imperative	
2 Al médico (pp. 62–63) Reporting injuries	Perfect tense (first and third person singular)	
3 Reservas y llegadas (pp. 64–65) Booking hotel rooms and arriving at a campsite		
4 Al llegar (pp. 66–67) Understanding hotel rules and enquiring about facilities Dealing with problems and complaining in a hotel	Imperfect tense (3rd person singular)	Asking questions in the speaking exam

Key language

¿Qué le pasa?
Me duele …
… el brazo/cuello/dedo/diente/estómago/oído/ojo/pie/
tobillo.
… la boca/cabeza/espalda/garganta/mano/nariz/oreja/
pierna/rodilla.

Me duelen …
… los ojos/pies.
… las muelas/orejas.
No me siento bien./Me siento fatal.
Estoy bien/enfermo/mejor.
Tengo catarro/diarrea/fiebre/frío/gripe/sueño/
una insolación/dolor de (cabeza).

(No) tengo calor/hambre/sed/tos/vómitos/la pierna rota.
Estoy mareado/constipado.
¿Desde hace cuánto tiempo?
Desde hace una semana/cuatro días (etc.)
Desde ayer.
Tome este jarabe/estos comprimidos/estas pastillas/
unas aspirinas …

… cuatro veces al día (después de comer).
Ponga esta crema.
Quédese en la cama.
Beba mucha agua.
Llame al médico.

Me he/Se ha …
… cortado (el dedo)/quemado (la boca)/torcido (el tobillo)/
roto (la pierna)/hecho daño en (el ojo).

¿Dígame?
Quisiera reservar una habitación doble/individual/
con dos camas …
… con baño/ducha/balcón/vistas al mar.
¿Para cuántas personas? (Somos) cuatro: dos adultos y dos
niños (etc.)
¿Para cuántas noches? Una semana/tres noches/quince
días (etc.)
Estimado señor …
… Queremos pasar (quince días) en su hotel del (1) al (15)
de (agosto).
Le ruego que me comunique los precios de media pensión/
pensión completa.

¿Hay (un gimnasio) en el hotel?
Vamos a llegar a (las nueve de la noche).
Le saluda atentamente.
¿Tiene una parcela para una tienda/una caravana?
¿Cuánto es por día/noche/persona?
Son (€9) al día los adultos y (€6) los niños.
¿Cuántos son?
¿Hay un supermercado/una lavandería/una
piscina/duchas?
Sí, cerca del bloque sanitario/de la cafetería./Claro que sí.
Sus pasaportes por favor.
¿Quiere firmar aquí?

No se admiten animales.
No se debe lavar la ropa en los lavabos.
Los perros deben estar atados.
Evite ruidos y molestias.
Respete a los otros.
No haga ruido durante la noche.
Limite de velocidad (10 km/h)
¿Tiene la habitación vistas al mar?
¿Dónde está el ascensor? Está (al lado de la cafetería.)
¿Hay un supermercado? Sí, está (cerca de la piscina.)
¿A qué hora se sirve el desayuno? Desde las (siete) hasta
las (diez.)
¿Se puede cambiar dinero/alquilar bicicletas?
¿Vende champú?/Venden pasta de dientes y desodorante?
No hay agua caliente/jabón/papel higiénico/toallas en
la habitación.

El ascensor/la luz/la llave/la televisión no funciona.
Hay muchísimo ruido.
¿Qué habitación es?
Le escribe para quejarme.
Pasé (tres noches) en su hotel y …
… tenía muchos problemas/mucho ruido.
… no había (jabón) en la habitación.
… (la luz) no funcionaba.
… no dormí en (tres noches).
… el servicio estaba malo.
… la comida estaba mala/fría
… la piscina estaba cerrada.
Quiero que me devuelva una parte de mi dinero.

Main topics and objectives

Reporting illness

Grammar

Doler and *tener dolor de*

Key language

¿Qué le pasa?
Me duele …
… el brazo/cuello/dedo/diente/estómago/oído/ojo/pie/
tobillo.
… la boca/cabeza/espalda/garganta/mano/muela/
nariz/oreja/pierna/rodilla.

Me duelen …
… los ojos/pies.
… las muelas/orejas.
No me siento bien./Me siento fatal.
Estoy bien/enfermo/mejor.
Tengo catarro/diarrea/fiebre/frío/gripe/sueño/una
insolación/dolor de (cabeza).

Resources

Cassette B, side 2
CD 2, track 11
Cuaderno pages 28–33
Gramática 7.13, page 176

1a Empareja las letras con los números.

Reading. Parts of the body. Students match the vocabulary to the pictures. Students could work in pairs, identifying first of all the vocabulary which they remember or can guess, and then using a dictionary or the glossary at the back of the Student's Book to look up any unknown words. Teachers may wish to follow this activity with aural/oral practice of the words, to ensure correct pronunciation. Students should be encouraged to learn the vocabulary with the correct definite article.

Answers

a 8	b 10	c 1	d 2	e 3	f 5	g 6	h 7	i 11	j 12	k 13
l 14	m 15	n 17	o 9	p 16	q 4					

1b ¿Qué les pasa a estas personas? (1–8)

Listening. Saying where it hurts. Students listen and note down the letter of the correct word in Spanish from **1a**, above. The speakers use a mix of the verb *doler* (*me duele/n*) and *tener dolor de*. Teachers may wish to pre-teach/revise these expressions, before tackling the listening. The difference between these two ways of saying where it hurts is explained in the *Gramática* feature on the page.

Tapescript

1 – Ay! Me duele la espalda.
2 – Tengo dolor de cabeza.
3 – Me duelen los oídos.
4 – Estoy mal … me duele la pierna.
5 – ¡Ay! Me duele la boca.
6 – Tengo dolor de estómago.
7 – Me duele la mano.
8 – Me duele mucho el pie.

Answers

1 o	2 c	3 e	4 l	5 f	6 k	7 i	8 n

Gramática

Doler and *tener dolor de*. Students' attention should be drawn to the difference in use between *me duele* and *me duelen*, as well as to the fact that *me duele/n* requires the use of the definite article, whereas *tener dolor de* does not.

1c Lee las descripciones. ¿Cómo se sienten – 😀, 😐 o ☹?

Reading. Saying how you feel. Revision of general expressions for saying you feel well, ill, better, etc.

Answers

1 ☹	2 ☹	3 😀	4 😐	5 ☹	6 😀

1d Túrnate con tu compañero/a.

Speaking. Saying how you feel and what is wrong. Students work in pairs to construct mini-dialogues based on the pictures. The example on the page provides a model.

1e Escribe una frase para cada imagen.

Students write a sentence for each of the pictures in **1d**, using the phrases on the previous page for support.

2a Empareja las frases con las imágenes correctas.

Reading. Other expressions for saying what is wrong, using '*tener*'. Students match up the phrases with the pictures. This activity could be done in pairs, groups, or as a whole class. Students should be encouraged to talk through the reading strategies they use to help them do this exercise, such as looking for cognates/near cognates. Dictionaries or the glossary at the back of the book should only be used as a last resort, to look up any words students cannot remember, guess or work out.

Answers

1 B	2 A	3 D	4 E	5 C	6 F

2b Escucha e identifica el problema. Escribe notas breves en español. (1–5)

Listening. Reporting illness and pain. The example shows students how to take simple notes in Spanish.

R Some students might find it easier if teachers provided them with a worksheet on which they join up or underline what each speaker says.

Tapescript

1 – Me siento muy mal. Me duele la cabeza y la garganta. Pienso que tengo gripe.
2 – Me siento fatal. Me duele mucho el estómago y tengo diarrea.
3 – Estoy muy mal. Fui a la playa y ahora tengo una insolación y por eso me duele la cabeza.
4 – Tengo mucho sueño y me duelen los pies.
5 – No estoy bien: tengo fiebre y tengo catarro también.

Answers

1 cabeza/garganta/gripe   **2** estómago/diarrea
3 insolación/cabeza   **4** sueño/pies   **5** fiebre/catarro

2c Inventa un diálogo para cada imagen de **2a**. Tu compañero/a escribe la letra correcta.

Speaking. Reporting illness. Students work in pairs, with one asking the other what is wrong. The other chooses an ailment from those shown in **2a** and his/her partner must note down the letter of the relevant drawing. The example provides a model dialogue for students to follow.

1 Me siento mal

(Student's Book pages 60–61)

Main topics and objectives

Describing symptoms and seeking medical advice

Grammar

Expressions with *tener*
Desde hace
Imperative

Key language

(No) tengo calor/hambre/sed/tos/vómitos/la pierna rota.
Estoy mareado/constipado.
¿Desde hace cuánto tiempo?
Desde hace una semana/cuatro días (etc.)

Desde ayer.
Tome este jarabe/estos comprimidos/estas pastillas/unas aspirinas …
… cuatro veces al día (después de comer).
Ponga esta crema.
Quédese en la cama.
Beba mucha agua.
Llame al médico.

Resources

Cassette B, side 2
CD 2, track 12
Cuaderno pages 28–33

1a Empareja las frases con las imágenes correctas.

Reading. Describing symptoms. This activity introduces more expressions with *tener* and *estar* which are used to describe illness. As before, students could work in pairs to match the phrases to the pictures, first using their reading skills, then a dictionary or the back-of-book glossary to look up any words they cannot work out. The *¡Ojo!* feature, below, draws students attention to the fact that *constipado* is a 'false friend'.

Answers

1 F	2 C	3 D	4 E	5 G	6 H	7 A	8 B

¡Ojo!

The word *constipado/a* is a "false friend", meaning to have a cold.

Gramática

Expressions with *tener*.

1b Escucha los diálogos en la farmacia. Copia y completa la tabla. (1–5)

Listening. Symptoms and how long you have had them. This activity introduces *desde hace* to describe how long you have had symptoms. Students complete the grid in Spanish, noting down the symptom(s) and how long the speaker has had it/them. The *Gramática* feature explains the use of *desde hace* and teachers may prefer to work through the grammar explanation before tackling the listening task.

R Teachers might wish to give some students a partially completed version of the grid, so that they only have to listen for one detail per dialogue, and/or give them a list of the missing words to choose from.

Tapescript

1 – Hola, buenos días. ¿Qué le pasa?
– Tengo tos y tengo gripe.
– Bueno, ¿desde hace cuánto tiempo?
– Desde hace tres días.
– Vamos a ver …

2 – Buenos días. ¿Qué le pasa?
– Me siento enferma.
– ¿Qué es exactamente?
– Tengo vómitos y me duele el estómago.
– ¿Desde hace cuánto tiempo?
– Desde hace cuatro días.

3 – ¿Me puede ayudar?
– ¿Qué le pasa?
– No me siento bien. Estoy mareada y creo que tengo una insolación.
– ¿Y desde cuándo?
– Bueno, fui a la playa el lunes … desde hace dos días.

4 – Buenos días. ¿Tiene algo para el dolor de garganta?
– ¿Le duele mucho?
– Sí, desde hace una semana. Me duele mucho.

5 – Buenas tardes.
– Buenas tardes. ¿En qué puedo servirle?
– Me siento muy mal y tengo diarrea.
– ¿Desde hace cuánto tiempo?
– Desde hace cinco días.
– ¡Ay! ¡Qué pena!
– Sí.

Answers

	¿Problema?	¿Cuánto tiempo?
1	tos/gripe	3 días
2	vómitos/estómago	4 días
3	mareada/insolación	2 días
4	garganta	1 semana
5	diarrea	5 días

Gramática

Desde hace.

1c Traduce estas frases al español.

Writing. Explaining how long you have had symptoms. Translation exercise.

Answers

1 Me duele la cabeza desde hace cuatro días.
2 Estoy constipado desde hace una semana.
3 Tengo tos desde ayer.
4 Tengo frío desde hace dos días.
5 Tengo vómitos desde hace cinco días.

2a Empareja el consejo con la imagen correcta.

Reading. Understanding medical advice. Students match phrases to the pictures. This could be done in pairs, groups or as a whole class. Students should be encouraged to share with others/the rest of the class the reading strategies they used to work out what each expression means.

Answers

| 1 F | 2 G | 3 B | 4 E | 5 A | 6 D | 7 H | 8 C |

2b Escucha los diálogos. Apunta la enfermedade escribe la(s) letra(s) correcta(s) del remedio. (1–5)

Listening. Describing symptoms and receiving medical advice. Students note down the letters of the correct pictures from **2a**, above, and note down in Spanish what is wrong with each patient.

R Some students might require extra support (see **1b**, above, for suggestions).

+ More able students should be encouraged to listen for extra details, such as how long the patient has had the symptoms and any instructions relating to medicines prescribed.

Tapescript

1 – Me siento muy mal.
 – ¿Qué le pasa?
 – Estoy mareada.
 – ¿Desde hace cuánto tiempo?
 – Dos días.
 – Entonces, quédese en la cama y mañana ya veremos. Tome este jarabe cuatro veces al día.
 – Vale.
2 – Me siento fatal.
 – ¿Qué le pasa?
 – Tengo diarrea y me duele el estómago.
 – Bueno, beba mucha agua y quédese en casa.
3 – Tengo gripe. Me siento muy mal. Tengo dolor de cabeza y estoy mareado.
 – ¿Desde cuándo?

– Desde el domingo. Me sentí muy mal el domingo por la mañana.
 – Bueno, quédese en la cama unos días. Tome unas aspirinas cuatro veces al día después de comer.
4 – ¿Qué le pasa?
 – Tengo tos.
 – ¿Le duele la garganta?
 – Sí, mucho.
 – Bueno, tome estas pastillas tres veces al día después de las comidas.
5 – Me siento muy mal.
 – ¿Qué le pasa?
 – Tengo una insolación. Me duele todo.
 – Póngase esta crema y métase en la cama.

Answers

1 – mareada A/E   2 – diarrea/estómago C/A
3 – cabeza/mareado A/H   4 – tos/garganta B
5 – insolación G/A

2c Copia y completa la conversación.

Writing. Describing symptoms and getting medical advice. Gap-filling exercise, from a list of missing words. The completed dialogue could be used for oral work, if teachers wish.

Answers (in bold)

Médico:	¿Qué le **pasa** a usted?
Enfermo:	Me **duele** la cabeza, tengo **tos** y estoy **mareado**. Pienso que **tengo** gripe.
Médico:	¿Desde hace cuánto tiempo?
Enfermo:	Desde **hace** una semana.
Médico:	Sí, tiene gripe. Tome unas **aspirinas** dos veces al día y **quédese** en la cama y beba mucha **agua**.
Enfermo:	Muchas gracias. **Adiós**.

2d Túrnate con tu compañero/a.

Speaking. At the doctor's. Examination-style role-play with multiple options, so that it can be performed several times.

Main topics and objectives

Reporting injuries

Grammar

Perfect tense (first and third person singular)

Key language

Me he/Se ha …

… *cortado (el dedo)/quemado (la boca)/torcido (el tobillo)/roto (la pierna)/hecho daño en (el ojo).*

Resources

Cassette B, side 2
CD 2, track 13
Cuaderno pages 28–33
Gramática 7.10, page 175

1a ¿Qué le pasó a estas personas? Empareja las frases.

Reading. Reporting injuries. Students match up two halves of the same sentence, to create phrases about injuries and how they occurred. Teachers may wish to pre-teach the key language for reporting injuries.

Answers

> 1 Me he cortado el dedo con un cuchillo.
> 2 Me he quemado la boca.
> 3 Me he torcido el tobillo jugando al fútbol.
> 4 Me he roto la pierna en un accidente.
> 5 Me he hecho daño en el ojo.
> 6 Me he hecho daño en los oídos al concierto de rock.

1b Escucha las conversaciones. Identifica el problema en cada caso y escribe notas breves. (1–5)

Listening. Reporting injuries. Students note down the letter of the correct picture for each dialogue.

➕ Able students could note down extra details, such as how the accident occurred and what advice the doctor or receptionist gives.

Tapescript

1 – *¿En qué puedo servirle?*
– *Me he quemado la boca y me duele mucho.*
– *Tome estas pastillas.*
2 – *Consultorio Gómez, ¿dígame?*
– *Tengo un problema muy grave – mi hijo se ha torcido el tobillo jugando al fútbol.*
– *El médico puede verle a las cuatro y media.*
– *Muchas gracias.*
3 – *¿Qué le pasa?*
– *Me he hecho daño en el ojo y me duele mucho.*
– *Vamos a ver … Sí, se ha hecho daño … Aplique esta crema especial dos veces al día.*
4 – *¿En qué puedo servirle?*
– *Es que mi hermana no puede oír bien porque se hizo daño en los oídos en un concierto de rock. ¿Qué puede hacer?*
– *No se preocupe, no es permanente.*

5 – *¿Qué le pasa?*
– *Me he cortado el dedo con un cuchillo.*
– *Lo limpiamos en seguida y se mejorará.*

Answers

> 1 – quernado la boca   2 – torcido el tobillo
> 3 – hecho daño en el ojo   4 – hizo daño en los oídos
> 5 – cortado el dedo con un cuchillo

Gramática

The Perfect tense (first and third person singular). The perfect tense is covered more fully in chapter 10 and in the grammar section at the back of the Student's Book (see page 177).

1c ¿Qué le ha pasado al perro Jesulín? Escribe una frase para cada dibujo.

Writing. An account of an injury. Students write simple captions in Spanish to accompany the cartoon strip. Students could write in either the first or third person singular, using the perfect tense. 'Time marker' expressions are provided, to help students write a simple narrative.

2 Trabaja en grupos.

Speaking. Board game about reporting illness, symptoms and injuries. The board game is explained in English, for simplicity. However, students are required to say a correct phrase in Spanish for each square they land on. Support is given for two key Spanish phrases used in the game: *Vuelve a casilla número …* and *Vuelve (tres) casillas.*

3 Reservas y llegadas

(Student's Book pages 64–65)

Main topics and objectives

Booking hotel rooms and arriving at a campsite

Key language

¿Dígame?
Quisiera reservar una habitación doble/individual/con dos camas …
… con baño/ducha/balcón/vistas al mar.
¿Para cuántas personas?/(Somos) cuatro: dos adultos y dos niños (etc.)
¿Para cuántas noches? Una semana/tres noches/ quince días (etc.)
Estimado señor …
… Queremos pasar (quince días) en su hotel del (1) al (15) de (agosto).
Le ruego que me comunique los precios de media pensión/pensión completa.
¿Hay (un gimnasio) en el hotel?
Vamos a llegar a (las nueve de la noche).
Le saluda atentamente.
¿Tiene una parcela para una tienda/una caravana?
¿Cuánto es por día/noche/persona?
Son (€9) al día los adultos y (€6) los niños.
¿Cuántos son?
¿Hay un supermercado/una lavandería/una piscina/duchas?
Sí, cerca del bloque sanitario/de la cafetería./Claro que sí.
Sus pasaportes por favor.   ¿Quiere firmar aquí?

Resources

Cassette B, side 2   Cuaderno pages 28–33
CD 2, track 14

1a Lee y escucha.

Reading and listening. Booking hotel accommodation. This presents a model dialogue for booking hotel rooms, with pictures to help convey meaning. Teachers should check students have understood all the new vocabulary and phrases before proceeding to the next activity. NB Some words in the dialogue are highlighted in green, as students will be asked to adapt the dialogue in **1c**, below.

Tapescript

– *Hotel Playa de Oro, ¿dígame?*
– *Buenos días. ¿Tiene habitaciones libres para mañana?*
– *Sí, señora. ¿Para cuántas personas?*
– *Somos dos. Quisiera reservar una habitación doble con balcón.*
– *¿Cón baño o ducha?*
– *Ducha.*
– *Muy bien, ¿Para cuántas noches?*
– *Una semana.*

1b Escucha los diálogos. Toma notas en inglés. (1-4)

Listening. Booking hotel accommodation. Students should be able to pick out all the key information about the type of room required, whether it has a bath or shower, the number of people and number of nights.

R Teachers might prefer less able students to focus on picking out one or two details from each dialogue (or play the recording several times, asking them to focus on a different piece of information each time).

Tapescript

1 – *Hotel Miramar, ¿dígame?*
– *Buenas tardes. ¿Tiene habitaciones libres para el sábado?*
– *Sí, señora. ¿Para cuántas personas?*
– *Somos cuatro. Quisiera reservar una habitación doble con ducha y una habitación con dos camas con baño.*
– *Muy bien, ¿Para cuántas noches?*
– *Una semana.*

2 – *Hotel Puente Romano, ¿dígame?*
– *Buenos días. Quisiera reservar dos habitaciones dobles.*
– *Muy bien. ¿Con baño o ducha?*
– *Una habitación con ducha y la otra con baño.*
– *Muy bien.*

3 – *Hotel Ventura, ¿dígame?*
– *Buenos días. ¿Tiene habitaciones libres?*
– *Sí, señor. ¿Para cuántas personas?*
– *Somos cuatro. Quisiera reservar una habitación con dos camas y con ducha y otra habitación con dos camas y con baño.*
– *¿Para cuántas noches?*
– *Tres.*

4 – *Hotel Celimar, ¿dígame?*
– *Buenas tardes. ¿Tiene habitaciones libres para el domingo?*
– *Sí, señorita. ¿Para cuántas personas?*
– *Cuatro. Quisiera una habitación doble con baño y una habitación con dos camas con ducha.*
– *Muy bien.*
– *Gracias. Adiós.*

Answers

1 Saturday, 4 people, double room with a shower and a twin-bedded room with a bath, 1 week
2 2 double rooms (one with a shower, one with a bath)
3 4 people, 1 twin-bedded room with a shower, 1 twin-bedded room with a bath, 3 nights
4 Sunday, 4 people, 1 double-room with a bath, 1 twin-bedded room with a shower.

1c Practica la conversación del ejercicio 1a para reservar una habitación. Cambia las frases en verde.

Speaking. Booking hotel accommodation. Students adapt the dialogue in **1a**, above, changing the highlighted words in the text and using the picture prompts. The activity is supported by a key language grid. Students should practise the model dialogue in **1a** and the language in the support grid, before tackling activity **1c**.

1d Lee la carta. ¿Verdad o mentira?

Reading. Letter booking hotel accommodation. The letter introduces students to the language and conventions of formal letters and teachers may wish to draw students' attention to these, before or after the reading comprehension task. The new expressions *media pensión* and *pensión completa* are explained on the page.

➕ Able students could correct the false statements.

Answers

1 verdad	**2** mentira	**3** mentira	**4** verdad	**5** verdad
6 mentira	**7** mentira			

1e Escribe una carta al hotel, cambiando los detalles de la carta en 1d.

Writing. Booking hotel rooms. Students adapt the letter in **1d**.

🅡 Teachers could give less able students a version of the letter in which the sections to be changed have been highlighted and the new details to be used are provided in a list next to or below the letter. Alternatively, teachers could turn the letter into a gap-filling task (possibly with key words replaced by picture prompts), with a list of the missing words provided.

2a Usa un diccionario. ¿Qué son estas instalaciones del camping en inglés?

Reading. Campsite facilities. Students match the words to the pictures. They could first identify the vocabulary which is familiar to them (such as *cafetería, duchas, piscina* and *supermercado*), then move on to cognates/near cognates (such as *parque infantil* and *consulta médica camping*), and finally guess, then check in a dictionary or the glossary, the meaning of the remaining words.

Answers

1 café	**2** laundry room	**3** hot showers	**4** indoor pool
5 children's play area	**6** wash block		
7 campsite medical centre	**8** camping equipment hire		
9 supermarket	**10** toilets		

2b Escucha el diálogo en el camping y escoge la descripción correcta.

Listening. Booking into a campsite. Students listen and choose the correct description of the family's

requirements. Teachers should first look at the descriptions with students and ensure they understand the key vocabulary: *parcela, caravana, tienda, adulto* and *niño*.

Tapescript

– *Buenos días.*
– *Buenos días. ¿Tiene una parcela para una tienda y una caravana?*
– *Sí, creo que sí.*
– *¿Cuánto es por día y por persona?*
– *Son €9 al día los adultos y €6 los niños.*
– *¿Cuántos son?*
– *Dos adultos y dos niños.*
– *Vale.*
– *¿Hay una lavandería?*
– *Sí, cerca del bloque sanitario. Sus pasaportes por favor y ¿quiere firmar aquí?*

Answer

The correct description is **C**.

2c Lee y completa el diálogo con la información correcta.

Reading. Booking into a campsite. Students are presented with a gapped dialogue similar to the one they heard in **2b**, above, and must fill in the gaps, using the prompts given.

🅡 Teachers might prefer to provide less able students with a list of the missing words.

Answers (in bold)

– Buenos días.
– Buenos días. ¿Tiene una parcela para una **caravana**?
– Sí, creo que sí.
– ¿Cuánto es por día y por persona?
– Son **€10** al día los adultos y **€5** los niños. ¿Cuántos son?
– Dos **adultos** y **tres** niños.
– Vale.
– ¿Hay una **piscina** y un **restaurante**?
– Sí, cerca del servicio de lavandería. Sus pasaportes, por favor, y ¿quiere firmar aquí?

2d Túrnate con tu compañero/a.

Speaking. Booking into a campsite. Students use the flowchart to create dialogues for booking into a campsite. Teachers may wish to give students aural/oral practice of the language in the flowchart, before students work in pairs on a complete dialogue.

➕ More able students could be encouraged to include extra details in their dialogue (such as asking for passports and a signature) and learn it by heart.

4 Al llegar

(Student's Book pages 66–67)

Main topics and objectives

Understanding hotel rules and enquiring about facilities

Dealing with problems and complaining in a hotel

Grammar

Imperfect tense (3rd person singular)

Skills

Asking questions in the speaking exam

Key language

No se admiten animales.
No se debe lavar la ropa en los lavabos.
Los perros deben estar atados.
Evite ruidos y molestias.
Respete a los otros.
No haga ruido durante la noche.
Límite de velocidad (10 km/h)
¿Tiene la habitación vistas al mar?
¿Dónde está el ascensor? Está (al lado de la cafetería).
¿Hay un supermercado? Sí, está (cerca de la piscina).
¿A qué hora se sirve el desayuno? Desde las (siete) hasta las (diez).

¿Se puede cambiar dinero/alquilar bicicletas?
¿Vende champú?/Venden pasta de dientes y desodorante?
No hay agua caliente/jabón/papel higiénico/toallas en la habitación.
El ascensor/la luz/la llave/la televisión no funciona.
Hay muchísimo ruido.
¿Qué habitación es?
No se preocupe. Se arregla/arreglará …/Se lo traigo … … ahora/en seguida.
Le escribo para quejarme.
Pasé (tres noches) en su hotel y …
… tenía muchos problemas/mucho ruido.
… no había (jabón) en la habitación.
… (la luz) no funcionaba.
… no dormí en (tres noches).
… el servicio estaba malo.
… la comida estaba fría.
… la piscina estaba cerrada.
Quiero que me devuelva una parte de mi dinero.

Resources

Cassette B, side 2
CD 2, track 15
Cuaderno pages 28–33
Gramática 7.7, page 174

1a Empareja los dibujos y los letreros.

Reading. Hotel rules. Students match the notices to the pictures. As before, this could be tackled either as a whole-class activity, or in pairs/groups. Students should first look for words they recognise or that remind them of English words and share their thinking processes with other students, only using a dictionary/the glossary at the back of the Student's Book as a last resort.

Answers

1 C	2 F	3 B	4 D	5 A	6 E

1b Empareja las preguntas con las respuestas.

Reading. Enquiring about hotel facilities and services. Students match questions to answers. Much of the vocabulary should be familiar to students and they should be encouraged to use their reading strategies to work out the meaning of new words such as *champú* and *pasta de dientes*. Once students have paired up the questions and answers correctly, they should be given aural/oral practice of both, leading to practice of asking and answering in pairs.

Answers

1 E	2 D	3 H	4 A or F	5 A or F	6 B	7 C	8 G

¡Ojo!

The tip relates to examination-style role-play cards, in which English instructions are often given in indirect speech. Some students find it difficult to transfer indirect speech in English into direct speech in Spanish and teachers may wish to give students practice of doing this, by providing them with a number of exam-style instructions from which they have to work out what to say in Spanish.

1c Haz preguntas para cada dibujo.

Speaking. Asking about facilities and services in a hotel. Students use the picture prompts to adapt the questions in **1b**, above.

➕ Able students could also invent answers to the questions and create mini-dialogues, or even include these questions and answers in longer hotel dialogues.

2a Identifica el problema. Escribe la letra correcta. (1–6)

Listening. Problems and complaints in a hotel. Teachers should first draw students' attention to the labelled pictures of items which might be missing or faulty (key, towel, etc.) and give students aural recognition practice of this new vocabulary. Students then listen to a series of dialogues and note down the letter of the picture which shows the problem referred to in each dialogue.

➕ Able students could also note down extra information, such as the room numbers, what action the hotel employee takes, etc.

Tapescript

1 – *Perdón, señor.*
   – *¿Sí?*
   – *No hay jabón en la habitación.*
   – *¿Qué habitación es?*
   – *504.*
   – *Se lo traigo en seguida, señor.*

2 – *Perdone.*
   – *¿Qué desea?*
   – *Hay un problema en la habitación.*
   – *¿Qué pasa?*
   – *Hay muchísimo ruido.*
   – *¿Qué habitación es?*
   – *101. Está muy cerca de la piscina y la música molesta mucho.*

3 – *Señorita.*
   – *¿Sí? ¿Qué desea?*
   – *La llave no funciona.*
   – *¿Cuál es el número de la habitación?*
   – *339.*
   – *¡Ay! Lo siento. Usted tiene la llave de 239.*
   – *Gracias.*

4 – *Señor. No hay toallas en la habitación.*
   – *Lo siento. ¿Qué número?*
   – *205.*
   – *Vale. Se arregla en seguida.*

5 – *Buenas tardes.*
   – *Muy buenas.*
   – *Hay un problema en mi habitación.*
   – *¿Qué hay?*
   – *La luz no funciona.*
   – *¿Qué habitación es?*
   – *813.*
   – *Se arreglará ahora.*

6 – *Hay un problema.*
   – *¿Sí?*
   – *El ascensor no funciona y tengo tres maletas.*
   – *No se preocupe. Deje las maletas aquí y las llevaremos a su habitación.*

Answers

1 c	2 g	3 e	4 a	5 d	6 f

2b Túrnate con tu compañero/a.

Speaking. Reporting problems in a hotel. Students work in pairs, using the picture prompts and taking it in turns to ask and answer questions about missing or faulty items. Teachers may wish to give students oral practice of the question *¿Qué le pasa?* and the phrases in the language support box, before tackling this activity.

2c Lee la carta. Encuentra el español para estas frases.

Reading. Letter of complaint to a hotel. Students find the Spanish for the phrases listed. They could tackle this in pairs or groups. The letter contains examples of the imperfect tense in the third person singular, which was introduced in module 4 (pages 52–53) and is covered in more detail, with a practice exercise, in the grammar section at the back of the Student's Book (pages 175–176).

Answers

1 Le escribo para quejarme.
2 Tenía muchos problemas.
3 No había jabón.
4 Había mucho ruido de los bares de enfrente.
5 No dormí en tres noches.
6 El servicio en el restaurante estaba muy malo.
7 La piscina estaba cerrada un día.
8 Le saluda atentamente.

2e Escribe una carta similar a un hotel para quejarte, cambiando los detalles.

Writing. Letter of complaint to a hotel. Students adapt the model letter in **2c** to create their own letter of complaint.

🄡 Teachers might wish to give some students a version of the letter in which the sections to be changed are highlighted, or gapped, possibly with a list of the new details to be inserted also provided.

Leer y escribir

(Student's Book pages 154–155)

Leer 1 La familia de Paco está enferma. Completa las frases. Usa las palabras a la derecha.

A series of gapped sentences which students must copy out and complete, using the list of words provided.

Answers (in bold)

1 Lo siento pero no puedo jugar al **tenis** porque me duele **el brazo**.
2 Mi abuela no quiere ver la **televisión** porque le duelen **los ojos**.
3 Mi madre no puede lavar el **coche** porque tiene una **fiebre**.
4 Mi hermana no tiene ganas de **ir al parque** porque está **muy enferma**.
5 Mi hermanastro no puede ir al **partido de fútbol** porque tiene **una insolación**.
6 Mi tío no va a la **fiesta** porque tiene dolor de **estómago**.

Escribir 2 Escribe un mensaje electrónico a tu amigo/a en español.

Students write an e-mail about being ill and unable to go to a party, using the picture and word prompts provided.

Leer 3 Sebastián es un bromista. ¡Pretende que es médico! ¿Estás de acuerdo con sus consejos? Escribe el medicamento correcto y la dosis.

Students correct the medical advice given in the cartoons.

Answers

(Various possibilities)

Leer 4a Lee la carta y contesta a las preguntas en español.

A letter of reservation to a campsite, followed by questions in Spanish.

Answers

1 Va a pasar una semana en Cantabria.
2 Va a estar allí en agosto.
3 Son cinco personas.
4 Prefiere montar la tienda a la sombra.
5 Va a llegar en coche.
6 Le interesa la equitación, el golf, la vela y el windsurf.

Escribir 4b Mira el folleto. Contesta a las preguntas del Señor Isaacs.

Students read a campsite advert and answer the questions asked by the writer of the letter in Leer **4a**.

Answers

1 Sí, tiene una piscina y pistas de tenis.
2 Sí, hay un supermercado y un restaurante.
3 Sí, se puede practicar la equitación y el golf.
4 El camping está cerca de la playa, pero no está cerca de las montañas.
5 No se puede aquilar barcos de pedales, pero se puede aquilar – camas solar y sombrillas.
6 Se puede practicar la vela, pero no se puede practicar el windsurf.

Escribir 4c Tu amigo/a no entiende español. Escribe una carta en español para reservar un camping.

Students adapt the letter in Leer 4, using the prompts in English to write a different letter.

módulo 5

Cuaderno

(Worbook pages 28–33)

page 28

page 29

1a

Answers

1 TOBILLO	ankle
2 ESPALDA	back
3 PIE	foot
4 RODILLA	knee
5 PIERNA	leg
6 ESTOMAGO	stomach
7 CUELLO	neck
8 BOCA	mouth
9 OJO	eye
10 NARIZ	nose
11 DIENTE	tooth
12 OREJA	ear
13 DEDO	finger
14 GARGANTA	throat
15 CABEZA	head

3a

Answers (in bold)

He telefoneado desde hace tres **días** para **reservar** dos habitaciones. Es para dos semanas del **20** de julio al 3 de **agosto**.

Somos tres: dos **adultos** y un niño de 15 años. Quisiera una habitación **doble** con baño y una **habitación** individual con **ducha**.

Si es posible, queremos también **vistas** al mar.

Entiendo que el precio de media **pensión** es €450 para una semana.

Vamos a **llegar** a las siete de la tarde y vamos a cenar en su **restaurante**.

1b

Answers (in bold)

1 Me duele **la** garganta.
2 Me duelen **los** dientes.
3 Me duele **la** cabeza.
4 Me duelen **las** orejas.
5 Me duele **el** dedo.
6 Me duelen **los** pies.

2a

Answer

Dialogue number	What's wrong?	How long ago did it start?	Treatment	Any other information
1	sore throat and cough	1 week	cough mixture and drink a lot of water	fever
2	stomach ache and vomiting	3 days	stay in bed	
3	burnt his/her hand	yesterday	put some cream on	cream 3 times a day
4	toothache	2 days	take some aspirin before each meal	must go to the dentist

page 30

3b

Answers

1 three days ago
2 two weeks
3 his wife and his son
4 two
5 one double with bath and one single with shower, and if possible view of the sea
6 two meals

4a

Answers

A 8   B 4   C 3   D 7   E 10   F 2   G 6   H 9   I 1   J 5

page 31

4b

Answers

¿Tiene una parcela para una tienda?
¿Hay un supermercado?
¿Cuántos son?
¿Hay una lavandería?
¿Cuánto es por día y por persona?
¿Es para cuántas noches?

5a

Answer

1 c   2 a   3 c   4 b   5 a

page 32

Gramática

1

Answers

1 tengo   2 estoy   3 tengo   4 estoy   5 tengo   6 tengo

2

Answers

1 me   2 se   3 me   4 se   5 se

3

Answers

Presente
no hay toallas (there are no towels)
hay mucho ruido (there is a lot of noise)
la sopa está fría (the soup is cold)
el cuchillo está sucio (the knife is dirty)
el ascensor no funciona (the lift does not work)
la luz no funciona (the light does not work)

Imperfecto
no había toallas (there were no towels)
había mucho ruido (there was a lot of noise)
la sopa estaba fría (the soup was cold)
el cuchillo estaba sucio (the knife was dirty)
el ascensor no funcionaba (the lift was not working)
la luz no funcionaba (the light was not working)

En casa y en el trabajo

(Student's Book pages 70–83)

Main topics and objectives	Grammar	Skills
Repaso (pp. 70–71) Discussing film preferences Revising numbers Describing mealtimes	*Gustar, encantar,* etc.	Numbers that sound similar in Spanish
1 Ayudando en casa (pp. 72–73) Discussing what you and others do to help around the house	Present tense and preterite of regular and irregular verbs	
2 El dinero y el trabajo (pp. 74–75) Discussing part-time jobs and how you spend your money Discussing work experience	Direct object pronouns Preterite and imperfect tenses.	
3 La vida sana (pp. 76–77) Discussing healthy living and fitness		
4 Los medios de comunicación (pp. 78–79) Discussing television and cinema	Adjectives	

Key language

¿Qué tipo de película prefieres/no te gusta? ¿Por qué?
Prefiero/(No) me gustan/Me encantan …
… los dibujos animados/las policíacas …
…. las películas de aventura/acción/ciencia ficción/
  terror/del oeste …
… las películas románticas/cómicas …
… porque son fantásticos/as /divertidos/as /graciosos/as
  malos/as /aburridos/as/buenos/as /tontos/as/emocionantes/
  excelentes/interesantes.
… porque tienen muchos efectos especiales.
(Numbers up to 1000.)

Los días de colegio/los fines de semana …
… tomo el desayuno/el almuerzo/la comida/la merienda/la
  cena a la/a las (+ time).
No tengo merienda.
(No) como mucho.
Como en la cantina con mis amigos.
Ceno con mi familia.
Normalmente/siempre tomo pan/mantequilla/ tostadas/un
  bocadillo de jamón (etc.)
Bebo café solo/café con leche (etc.)

¿Ayudas en casa?
Todos los días/a menudo/(dos) veces a la semana/
  a veces/nunca …
… lavo el coche/la ropa/los platos.
… hago la cama/las compras.
… pongo la mesa/plancho la ropa/preparo la comida/
  limpio mi habitación/paso la aspiradora.

¿Quién hace las tareas en tu casa?
¿Qué hace tu madre/padre/hermano (etc.)?
Mi padre prepara la comida./Mi madrasta lava los platos
  (etc.)
¿Qué hiciste la semana pasada?
Lavé la ropa/Limpié mi habitación/Hice las compras/Puse
  la aspiradora (etc.)

¿En qué gastas el dinero?
Me lo gasto en discos compactos/videojuegos/revistas/
  ropa/caramelos.
¿Tienes un trabajo a tiempo parcial?
Sí, tengo un trabajo a tiempo parcial.
Trabajo como/de … camarero/dependiente/recepcionista/
  canguro/repartidor de periódicos/ peluquera.
Trabajo en un garaje/hotel/supermercado (etc.)
¿Cuándo trabajas?
Trabajo los (sábados/fines de semana) de (nueve) a (cinco).
¿Cuánto ganas? Gano € (50).
No tengo trabajo de momento.
Ayudo a mis padres en casa.
Mis padres me dan € (35) al mes.

Hice mis prácticas en (una tienda de discos/
  un polideportivo, etc.)
Me levantaba a las (siete).
Trabajaba de (ocho) a (cuatro) de (lunes) a (viernes).
Tenía (una hora) para comer.
Me llevé bien con los otros empleados.
Mi jefe era muy simpático/severo.
(No) me trataron bien.
(No) me gustó el trabajo porque era muy interesante/
  aburrido (etc.)
Aprendí cosas nuevas.

¿Llevas/tienes una vida sana?
Creo que sí.
Como comida buena/Hago ejercicio.
¿Comes bien?
Para el desayuno/almuerzo como (fruta o cereales/
  una ensalada).
Bebo mucha agua.
Evito la grasa.
No me gustan la fruta y las verduras.
¿Haces bastante ejercicio?
Voy al polideportivo tres veces a la semana.
Me gusta ir al gimnasio/hacer deporte.

Hago ejercicio a menudo/a veces.
Nunca hago ejercicio.
Juego al fútbol/me gusta nadar los (jueves/fines de semana.)
No voy al gimnasio pero voy al colegio en bicicleta.
No me gustan los deportes.
¿Tienes un vicio?
A veces como hamburguesas/perritos calientes/
  las patatas fritas/caramelos.
Fumo tres o cuatro cigarillos al día.
¿Te sientes estresado?
Sí, a veces./No, estoy muy contento/relajado.

¿Qué vamos a ver?/¿Qué ponen?/¿Qué quieres ver en la
  televisión esta tarde?
Hay …
… un documental/concierto/concurso/dibujos animados/
  programa deportivo/programa musical.
… una película/serie/telenovela/comedia.
… las noticias.
¿A qué hora empieza? A las (nueve y treinta).
¿Qué tipo de programa te gusta más/no te gusta en
  la televisión? Por qué?
(No) me gustan/me encantan/odio (los documentales/
  las telenovelas) porque son (tontos/as/ divertidos/as).
Mi programa preferido es …
Creo que la tele(visión) es buena/educativa/peligrosa/
  mala (para la sociedad) porque …

… ofrece muchas cosas interesantes/un servicio de
  información.
… tiene demasiada violencia.
… la gente no habla.
Es una pérdida de tiempo/muy aburrida.
La película se trata de/cuenta la historia de …
Es una película romántica/policíaca/de acción/de ciencia
  ficción/de guerra.
Es una historia triste/cómica/emocionante/de terror/
  divertida/romántica.
(Tom Cruise) juega el papel de …
El héroe/la heroína es alto/a/simpático/a/guapo/a.
Me gustó porque …
… era graciosa/interesante (etc.)
… tenía buenos efectos especiales.

Main topics and objectives

Discussing film preferences
Revising numbers
Describing mealtimes

Grammar

Gustar, encantar etc.

Skills

Numbers that sound similar in Spanish

Key language

¿Qué tipo de película prefieres/no te gusta? ¿Por qué?
Prefiero/(No) me gustan/Me encantan …
… los dibujos animados/las policíacas …
… las películas de aventura/acción/ciencia ficción/
terror/del oeste …
… las películas románticas/cómicas …
… porque son fantásticos/as /divertidos/as /
graciosos/as /malos/as /
aburridos/as /buenos/as /tontos/as /emocionantes/
excelentes/interesantes.
… porque tienen muchos efectos especiales.
(Numbers up to 1000.)
Los días de colegio/los fines de semana …
… tomo el desayuno/el almuerzo/la comida/la
merienda/la cena a la/a las (+ time).
No tengo merienda.
(No) como mucho.
Como en la cantina con mis amigos.
Ceno con mi familia.
Normalmente/siempre tomo pan/mantequilla/
tostadas/un bocadillo de jamón (etc.)
Bebo café solo/café con leche (etc.)

Resources

Cassette B, side 2
CD 2, track 16
Cuaderno pages 34–40
Gramática 10, page 178

1a Empareja las opiniones con las películas apropriadas.

Reading. Film preferences. Matching opinions to titles of films in Spanish. Most of the film titles should be recognisable to students, as they all contain some words which are the same as in English. As well as checking that students understand the titles, teachers may wish to revise the types of films and opinions, before tackling the activity.

Answers

A Scream	**B** Southpark – la película
C Harry Potter y la Piedra Filosofal	**D** Algo Sobre Mary
E Shakespeare Enamorado	**F** Misión Imposible

1b Escribe tu opinión sobre cada tipo de película.

Writing. Opinions about film types. Students use the key language grid to write their opinions of each type of film shown in the picture prompts.

1c Haz las preguntas a tu compañero/a.

Speaking. Opinions about types of films. Students work in pairs to ask each other about their film preferences and dislikes, using the questions provided.

2a ¿Cuánto ganan? (1–8) Túrnate con tu compañero/a. ¿Cómo se dice cada número?

Listening and speaking. Numbers up to 1000. Students firstly listen to people saying how much they earn in euros, choose the correct amount from those listed and note it down. They then work in pairs to ensure

they know how to say each of the numbers. This could be done as a 'partner challenge', with each student taking a turn to point to a number which his/her partner has to say correctly in Spanish. Teachers may wish to revise numbers, aurally and orally (e.g. through number games), before tackling this activity. You may also wish to draw students' attention to the *¡Ojo!* feature on the page, which reminds students about some numbers that sound similar.

Tapescript

1 – *Gano setenta euros.*
2 – *Gano treinta y seis euros.*
3 – *Gano cuarenta y ocho euros.*
4 – *Gano ciento cincuenta euros.*
5 – *Gano veintinueve euros cincuenta.*
6 – *Gano doscientos diez euros.*
7 – *Gano diecisiete euros veinticinco.*
8 – *Gano sesenta y seis euros cincuenta.*

Answers

1 H	**2** A	**3** F	**4** C	**5** D	**6** B	**7** E	**8** G

¡Ojo!
Numbers that sound similar in Spanish.

3a Lee la rutina de Ángel. Lee las expresiones de abajo e identifica si es un día de colegio o un fin de semana.

Reading. Mealtime routines. Students read about Ángel's mealtimes and decide whether the statements which follow refer to his routine on weekdays or at the weekends. Students need to be familiar with the names of the four meals (*desayuno, comida/almuerzo, merienda* and *cena*) as well as the food and drink mentioned, to tackle this activity.

Answers

1 un día de colegio	**2** un fin de semana	**3** un día de colegio
4 un fin de semana	**5** un fin de semana	

3b Mira la rutina. ¿Verdad o mentira? (1–4)

Listening. Mealtimes. A second activity based on the text in **3a**. This time, students listen to Ángel making a series of statements about his mealtime routine and decide whether each is true or false.

Tapescript

1 – *Los fines de semana me levanto más tarde – a las diez. Tomo pan y mantequilla y bebo café con leche.*
2 – *Cuando voy al colegio como en el comedor con mis amigos. Normalmente como bocadillos de queso o jamón.*
3 – *Los sábados y domingos ceno con mi familia a las nueve y media. Siempre comemos flan o fruta para el postre.*
4 – *No bebo vino los días de colegio.*

Answers

1 verdad	**2** mentira	**3** mentira	**4** verdad

3c Escribe tu rutina para el colegio y los fines de semana. Copia y completa la tabla de **3a**.

Writing. Mealtimes. Students adapt the text in **3a** to write a timetable of their own mealtimes and what they eat or drink.

➕ Able students could be encouraged to write a summary of their mealtimes, using full sentences, and transfer this to their *fichero personal* once it has been corrected.

1 Ayudando en casa

(Student's Book pages 72–73)

Main topics and objectives

Discussing what you and others do to help around the house

Grammar

Present tense and preterite of irregular and irregular verbs

Key language

¿Ayudas en casa?
Todos los días/a menudo/(dos) veces a la semana/
a veces/nunca …
… lavo el coche/la ropa/los platos.
… hago la cama/las compras.

… pongo la mesa/plancho la ropa/preparo la comida/limpio mi habitación/paso la aspiradora.
¿Quién hace las tareas en tu casa?
¿Qué hace tu madre/padre/hermano (etc.)?
Mi padre prepara la comida./Mi madrasta lava los platos (etc.)
¿Qué hiciste la semana pasada?
Lavé la ropa/Limpié mi habitación/Hice las compras/Pasé la aspiradora (etc.)

Resources

Cassette B, side 2
CD 2, track 17
Cuaderno pages 34–40
Gramática 7.2, page 171 and 7.6 page 173

1a Empareja los dibujos con las tareas.

Reading. Household chores. Matching phrases to pictures. Teachers may wish to first use the pictures for aural practice of the new language, ensuring that students understand each phrase. Students could then close their books whilst the teacher says the phrases at random, and show they understand by miming each household task.

Answers

| 1 J | 2 G | 3 F | 4 E | 5 B | 6 A | 7 I | 8 C | 9 D | 10 H |

1b Escribe la letra correcta de cada tarea e identifica la frecuencia. (1–5)

Listening. Household chores and expressions of frequency. Teachers should first draw students' attention to the language support box, which lists expressions of frequency, and make sure students understand these. They then listen and note down the letters of the tasks each person does, and write down in Spanish how often they do it.

R Teachers may prefer some students to focus on simply noting the letters of the tasks (and ignore the expressions of frequency, or ask students to only note this at a later stage). Alternatively, less able students could be given a partly-completed grid of the chores mentioned and only have to listen for one chore per speaker.

Tapescript

1 – *Ayudas en casa?*
  – *Paso la aspiradora a veces.*
2 – *¿Ayudas en casa?*
  – *Limpio mi habitación a menudo, a veces friego los platos y paso la aspiradora dos veces a la semana.*
3 – *¿Ayudas en casa?*
  – *Sólo plancho la ropa tres veces a la semana pero nunca lavo la ropa.*

4 – *¿Ayudas en casa?*
  – *Sí. Todos los días pongo la mesa, hago las compras a menudo y a veces lavo la ropa.*
5 – *¿Ayudas en casa?*
  – *¡Hago mucho! Todos los días hago la cama y limpio mi habitación. Lavo el coche de mi padre a menudo porque me da cinco euros y me gusta preparar la comida a veces.*

Answers

1	J – a veces
2	I – a menudo; D – a veces; J – 2 veces a la semana
3	F – 3 veces a la semana/E – nunca
4	G – todos los días/H – a menudo/E – a veces
5	B & I – todos los días/C – a menudo/A – a veces

Gramática

Present tense verbs. A brief reminder that most verbs in the present tense end in 'o' in the first person singular.

1c Escribe una frase para cada tarea.

Writing. Household chores. Students use the key language on the page to write a sentence about each chore, including expressions of frequency.

1d Túrnate con tu compañero/a.

Speaking. Household chores. Students take it in turns to ask one another about what they do to help around the home. They are supported by a model conversation and a list of useful expressions, on the page.

2a Lee la carta y contesta a las preguntas.

Reading. Problem page letter about household chores. This moves students from the first person to third person singular of the key verbs covered in this unit. Students read the text and answer questions in Spanish.

■ Some students might find it easier to answer questions in English, or to complete gapped sentences based on the text.

Answers

1 Tiene 16 años.
2 Porque sus hermanos no hacen nada.
3 Limpia/Tiene que limpiar su habitación.
4 Su madre prepara la comida, lava la ropa, hace las camas y pasa la aspiradora.
5 Su hermano menor escucha música.

Gramática

The third person singular of present tense verbs, contrasted with the first person singular.

2b ¿Quién hace las tareas en tu casa?

Writing. Household chores. Students must write about who does what in their household, using the third person singular to refer to other family members.

2c ¿Qué hizo Paco la semana pasada? Escribe las letras correctas de los dibujos de la página 72.

Listening. Household chores in the past tense. Students listen to Paco describing what he did last week and note down the letters of the household chores in 1a on page 72. This moves students from the present to the preterite tense and teachers may wish to refer students to the *Gramática*, further down the page, which reminds them of verb endings in the preterite, in the first person singular.

✚ Able students could note down extra details, such as at what time of day Paco did each chore.

Tapescript

– ¿Qué hiciste la semana pasada, Paco?
– La semana pasada mi madre estuvo en el hospital e hice mucho para ayudar en casa. Primero, lavé el coche de mi abuela, limpié mi habitación y el cuarto de baño. Después preparé la comida y puse la mesa. Mi hermanastro lavó los platos y yo lavé la ropa de mi Mamá. Por la tarde planché la ropa e hice las camas.

Answers

C, I, [NB he also cleaned the bathroom] **A, G, E, F, B**
[NB His step-brother washed the dishes – **D**]

Gramática

First person singular endings in the preterite tense, contrasted with present tense endings.

2d Túrnate con tu compañero/a. Contesta a las preguntas.

Speaking. Household chores. Students work in pairs to ask and answer three questions about what they and others in their household do to help around the home, plus what they did to help last week. As a follow-up, students could either create an oral presentation about household chores and tape-record it, or write a short piece on the same subject (or do both) and add it/them to their *fichero personal*.

2 El dinero y el trabajo

(Student's Book pages 74–75)

Main topics and objectives

Discussing part-time jobs and and how you spend
your money
Discussing work experience

Grammar

Direct object pronouns
Preterite and imperfect tenses.

Key language

¿En qué gastas el dinero?
*Me lo gasto en discos compactos/videojuegos/revistas/
ropa/caramelos.*
¿Tienes un trabajo a tiempo parcial?
Sí, tengo un trabajo a tiempo parcial.
*Trabajo como/de … camarero/dependiente/
recepcionista/canguro/repartidor de periódicos/
peluquera.*
Trabajo en un garaje/hotel/supermercado (etc.)
¿Cuándo trabajas?
*Trabajo los (sábados/fines de semana) de (nueve)
a (cinco).*

¿Cuánto ganas?
Gano € (50).
No tengo trabajo de momento.
Ayudo a mis padres en casa.
Mis padres me dan € (35) al mes.
*Hice mis prácticas en (una tienda de discos/un
polideportivo, etc.)*
Me levantaba a las (siete).
Trabajaba de (ocho) a (cuatro) de (lunes) a (viernes).
Tenía (una hora) para comer.
Me llevé bien con los otros empleados.
Mi jefe era muy simpático/severo.
(No) me trataron bien.
*(No) me gustó el trabajo porque era muy interesante/
aburrido (etc.)*
Aprendí cosas nuevas.

Resources

Cassette B, side 2
CD 2, track 18
Cuaderno pages 34–40
Gramática 6.2, page 170

1a ¿En qué se gastan el dinero? Identifica las
imágenes correctas. (1–5)

Listening. What young people spend their money on.
Students match what they hear to the pictures. They
need to be familiar with the vocabulary for the items
shown in the pictures and teachers may wish to
precede the listening activity with aural practice of
this key language.

Tapescript

1 – ¿En qué te gastas el dinero?
 – Me lo gasto en videojuegos.
2 – ¿En qué te gastas el dinero?
 – Me lo gasto en caramelos.
3 – ¿En qué te gastas el dinero?
 – Me lo gasto en revistas.
4 – ¿En qué te gastas el dinero?
 – Me lo gasto en ropa.
5 – ¿En qué te gastas el dinero?
 – Me lo gasto en discos compactos.

Answers

1 D	**2** E	**3** B	**4** C	**5** A

Gramática

Direct object pronouns. Following the use of *lo* as an
object pronoun in **1a**, above, the grammar feature
explains briefly how these pronouns work.

1b Haz una encuesta con tu clase. Compara
los resultados.

Speaking. Class survey on spending habits. Students
should prepare a survey grid, with space for the
names of those they ask down the side and a list of
spending items/categories across the top, so that
they can simply tick the boxes to record their
findings. Teachers may wish to encourage students to
use extra vocabulary/categories, such as *cine, vídeos,
partidos de fútbol*, etc.

1c Escribe los resultados de la encuesta.

Writing. Class survey findings. The example shows
students how to present the findings of their survey.
Students could also use ICT to present their findings
in graph or pie-chart form (e.g. using Excel or
PowerPoint software.)

1d Escoge los trabajos correctos. (1–6)

Listening. Part-time jobs. Completing sentences with
job titles, by listening to people describing their work.
Students first need to be familiar with the job titles,
most of which they should either know or be able to
work out from other words they know (e.g. *peluquería/
peluquera.*) If teachers wish, students could first
guess which jobs go in the gaps in the sentences, by
looking for 'clue' words and expressions, such as '*lavo
el pelo*', '*niños pequeños*', etc. Students could then
listen to the recording, to check their answers.

Tapescript

1 – Lavo el pelo de los clientes. Soy peluquera.
2 – Me ocupo de niños pequeños. Trabajo de canguro.
3 – Trabajo en una tienda de deportes. Soy dependiente.
4 – Sirvo comida en un restaurante. Soy camarero.
5 – Trabajo en un hotel. Soy recepcionista.
6 – Voy de casa en casa con periódicos y revistas. Soy repartidor de periódicos.

Answers

1 C	2 E	3 D	4 A	5 B	6 F

2a Lee los textos y completa la tabla.

Reading. Part-time jobs. Students read the texts and complete the table with the name, job, working days/hours and salary of each person.

R Teachers may prefer some students to focus on fewer details, such as just the job title and salary of each person.

+ Able students could note down extra details, such as what the job entails, whether the people like their job and why, etc.

Answers

Nombre	Trabajo	Horario	¿€?
Miguel	dependiente	sábados: 8.00–4.00	€42
Ana	canguro	6.00–8.00, 5 días a la semana	€35

2b Copia la tabla de arriba. Escucha y complétala. (1–5)

Listening. Part-time jobs. Students use the same table from **2a**, above, to listen and note down the details.

Tapescript

1 – ¿Cómo te llamas?
– Me llamo Laura.
– ¿Tienes un trabajo a tiempo parcial?
– Sí. Reparto periódicos.
– ¿Cuándo trabajas?
– Los fines de semana: de nueve a cinco.
– ¿Está bien pagado el trabajo?
– Bastante bien. Gano 63 euros a la semana.
2 – ¿Cómo te llamas?
– Me llamo Jesús.
– ¿Tienes un trabajo a tiempo parcial?
– Sí, soy dependiente en una tienda.
– ¿Cuándo trabajas?
– De ocho a seis los sábados.
– ¿Te pagan bien?
– Bueno, 42 euros
3 – ¿Cómo te llamas?
– Me llamo Julio.
– ¿Tienes un empleo?
– Sí, trabajo como peluquero en la peluquería de mi

hermana.
– ¿Cuándo trabajas?
– Normalmente de cinco a ocho de lunes a viernes.
– Muchas horas.
– Sí.
– ¿Ganas mucho?
– ¡Qué va!
– Recibo 50 euros a la semana. Se gana poco en las peluquerías.
4 – ¿Cómo te llamas?
– Me llamo Juana.
– ¿Tienes un trabajo a tiempo parcial?
– Sí, trabajo en un garaje.
– ¿Trabajas los sábados?
– No, trabajo de ocho a una, de lunes a viernes.
– ¿Cuánto ganas?
– 105 euros.
5 – ¿Cómo te llamas?
– Me llamo Enrique.
– Tienes un trabajo?
– Sí, trabajo como camarero en una cafetería.
– ¿Cuándo trabajas?
– Sábados y domingos por la tarde de una a ocho.
– ¿Ganas mucho?
– No 28 euros.

Nombre	Trabajo	Horario	¿€?
Laura	repartidora de periódicos	fines de semana, 9.00–5.00	€63
Jesús	dependiente	sábados, 8.00–6.00	€42
Julio	peluquero	lunes–viernes, 5.00–8.00	€50
Juana	en un garaje	lunes–viernes, 8.00–1.00	€105
Enrique	camarero	sábados y domingos, 1.00–8.00	€28

2c Túrnate con tu compañero/a. Habla sobre tu trabajo a tiempo parcial. ¡Si no tienes uno, usa tu imaginación!

Speaking. Part-time jobs. Students work in pairs to ask and answer questions about part-time jobs. A model dialogue is provided and students should practise this first, to ensure that they are confident about asking the questions. Students who do not have a part-time job could make one up.

3a Lee las descripciones. ¿Verdad o mentira?

Reading. Work experience. Students read the texts about work experience and do the true/false exercise. Most of the key verbs in the texts are in either the preterite or the imperfect tense and teachers may wish to draw students' attention to these and check understanding, before tackling the exercise.

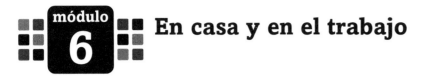

módulo 6 · En casa y en el trabajo

Answers

1 verdad	**2** verdad	**3** mentira	**4** verdad	**5** mentira
6 mentira				

3b Escribe una descripción de tus prácticas.

Writing. Work experience. Students could adapt the texts in **3a**, to write about their own work experience. Further practice of this topic is provided in the coursework section of the Student's Book (see pages 138–139 of the Student's Book and page 113 of this Teacher's Book.) Teachers may prefer to use the coursework section material (even if they do not intend covering work experience as a coursework assignment), to give students further practice of this topic, before asking them to write about their own work experience.

3 La vida sana

(Student's Book pages 76–77)

Main topics and objectives

Discussing healthy living and fitness

Key language

¿Llevas/tienes una vida sana?
Creo que sí.
Como comida buena/Hago ejercicio.
¿Comes bien?
*Para el desayuno/almuerzo como (fruta o cereales/
una ensalada).*
Bebo mucha agua.
Evito la grasa.
No me gustan la fruta y las verduras.
¿Haces bastante ejercicio?
Voy al polideportivo tres veces a la semana.
Me gusta ir al gimnasio/hacer deporte.
*Hago ejercicio a menudo/a veces./Nunca hago
ejercicio.*
*Juego al fútbol/me gusta nadar los (jueves/fines de
semana).*
No voy al gimnasio pero voy al colegio en bicicleta.
No me gustan los deportes.
¿Tienes un vicio?
*A veces como hamburguesas/perritos
calientes/patatas fritas/caramelos.*
Fumo tres o cuatro cigarrillos al día.
¿Te sientes estresado?
Sí, a veces./No, estoy muy contento/relajado.

Resources

Cassette B, side 2
CD 2, track 19
Cuaderno pages 34–40

1a Mira la lista. Copia y completa los diagramas.

Reading. Healthy eating. Students copy and complete
two 'spider' diagrams, categorising the food and
drink listed as either *sano* or *malsano*. All the
vocabulary should be familiar to students, although
teachers may wish to check students' understanding
of the items first.

Answers

Sano:	Malsano:
La ensalada	Las patatas fritas
La fruta	Las hamburguesas
El agua	El café
Los cereales	El chocolate
Las verduras	Los caramelos

1b Decide si llevan una vida sana 😀
o malsana ☹. (1–5)

Listening. Healthy eating and exercise. Students listen
and decide whether each speaker has a healthy or an
unhealthy lifestyle, listing the number of each speaker
under either a smiling face (for healthy living) or a
frowning face (for unhealthy living). Students may
also wish to create a third category (e.g. a neutral face)
for partly healthy/partly unhealthy living.

➕ Depending on students' ability, teachers may wish
to play the recording again and ask students to note
down further details, such as what each speaker
prefers to eat, what type of exercise they take, etc.

Tapescript

1 – Me gusta ir al gimnasio y hacer deporte. Para el desayuno
como fruta o cereales con zumo de naranja y una
ensalada para el almuerzo. También bebo mucha agua.

2 – Como lo que quiero. Prefiero las hamburguesas o los
perritos calientes y me encantan las patatas fritas. No
me gustan los deportes y prefiero viajar en coche.

3 – Nunca desayuno y para el almuerzo sólo tomo algo
pequeño como un café y patatas fritas. No me gustan ni
la fruta ni las verduras. Hago ejercicio a veces pero no
necesito hacer mucho porque voy a la discoteca dos
veces a la semana.

4 – Juego al fútbol los jueves y me gusta nadar los fines de
semana. Me gusta comer un poco de todo: fruta, carne,
verduras, patatas, pollo etc.

5 – A veces como un paquete de patatas fritas o unos
caramelos pero normalmente trato de comer mucha
fruta y verduras. No voy al gimnasio pero voy al colegio
en bicicleta y juego al tenis durante el verano.

Answers

Vida sana: 1/4/5 (or treat 5 as partly healthy)
Vida malsana: 2/3

1c Empareja las preguntas con las respuestas.

Reading. Healthy living. Matching questions and
answers about healthy living. Once students have
completed the matching task, teachers may wish to
practise the questions and answers orally with
students, in preparation for **1d** over the page.

Answers

1 b	2 e	3 d	4 c	5 a

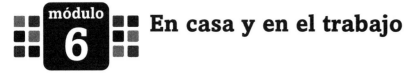

1d Contesta a las preguntas.

Speaking. Healthy living. Examination-style general conversation questions about healthy living. Students should use and adapt answers in **1b** and **1c** to talk about their own lifestyle. They should practise asking and answering in pairs and could tape-record their dialogue as part of their *fichero personal*, if wished.

R Teachers might prefer to give less able students a sentence-building grid on a worksheet or OHT, to help them build answers to the questions.

1e ¿Tienes una vida sana? Escribe unas frases.

Writing. Healthy living. Students write a few sentences about how healthy their lifestyle is. Once corrected, students could add this piece of work to their *fichero personal*.

R Less able students may require a sentence-building grid (see **1d**, above.)

2a Lee el artículo. ¿Verdad o mentira?

Reading. True/false exercise on magazine-style article about celebrity diets. The text is fairly demanding and some vocabulary is given, although teachers may wish to provide further support.

+ Able students could correct the false statements. Teachers will be sensitive to the issue of teenage eating disorders and may wish to preface/follow this item with a discussion about dieting and the obsession with thinness in some quarters of the entertainment industry.

Answers

1 verdad	**2** mentira	**3** verdad	**4** mentira	**5** verdad
6 verdad				

2b Lee el artículo otra vez y completa los espacios con la información correcta.

Writing. Gap-filling activity, based on the text in **2a**, above.

Answers (in bold)

"The Zone" es una dieta muy **popular** con las estrellas de **Hollywood**. Consiste en una forma de comer con dos **consejos** fáciles de cumplir. Hay muchos **actores** que siguen la dieta para perder peso y llevar una vida más **sana**. Se debe comer mucha **fruta** pero evitar el **mango** y las **bananas**.

4 Los medios de comunicación

(Students' Book pages 78–79)

Main topics and objectives

Discussing television and cinema

Grammar

Adjectives

Key language

¿Qué vamos a ver?/¿Qué ponen?/¿Qué quieres ver en la televisión esta tarde?
Hay …
… un documental/concierto/concurso/dibujos animados/programa deportivo/programa musical.
… una película/serie/telenovela/comedia.
… las noticias.
¿A qué hora empieza? A las (nueve y treinta).
¿Qué tipo de programa te gusta más/no te gusta en la televisión? Por qué?
(No) me gustan/me encantan/odio (los documentales/las telenovelas) porque son (tontos/as /divertidos/as).
Mi programa preferido es …
Creo que la tele(visión) es

buena/educativa/peligrosa/mala (para la sociedad) porque …
… ofrece muchas cosas interesantes/un servicio de información.
… tiene demasiada violencia.
… la gente no habla.
Es una pérdida de tiempo/muy aburrida.
La película se trata de/cuenta la historia de …
Es una película romántica/policíaca/de acción/de ciencia ficción/de guerra.
Es una historia …
… triste/cómica/emocionante/de terror/divertida/romántica.
(Tom Cruise) juega el papel de …
El héroe/la heroína es alto/a /simpático/a /guapo/a.
Me gustó porque …
… era graciosa/interesante (etc.)
… tenía buenos efectos especiales.

Resources

Cassette B, side 2
CD 2, track 20
Cuaderno pages 34–40

1a Encuentra un programa para cada categoría.

Reading. Television guide. Students read the Spanish television guide and find types of programmes to match each of the categories in English. The types of programme are also given in Spanish in the TV guide and teachers should check students' understanding of this key vocabulary, once students have completed the activity. This could lead into aural practice of the new Spanish vocabulary, in preparation for **1b**, below.

Answers

Cartoon: Cine Disney/Pokemón de agua.
Series: Lois y Clark.
Sports programme: Estadio 2.
Documentary: Informe semanal/España en Comunidades.
Gameshow: ¿Quiere ser millonario?
Soap opera: Pobre Diabla.
Music programme: Festival de jazz.
Chat show/Magazine programme: Historias de hoy.
News: Telediario.
Film: Sacrificio mortal/Tres hombres y un bebé.

1b Escucha los diálogos. Identifica el canal. ¿TVE1, La2 o TELE5? (1–5)

Listening. Discussing what to watch on TV. Students listen to the dialogues, look again at the TV guide and decide which channel the speakers are going to watch. They should be encouraged to listen for gist and for clues (such as the names or types of programmes and the time at which they are showing), rather than trying to understand every

word. Following the listening activity, teachers could present the key language for asking what someone wants to watch, for asking and saying what is on and at what time it is showing. Students could then create a dialogue, in pairs, along similar lines to those in **1b**, possibly with the support of a key language grid on a worksheet or OHT.

Tapescript

1 – *¿Qué vamos a ver en la televisión?*
   – *Bueno, me gustan los consursos. ¿Te gustan?*
   – *A mí también.*
   – *Hay uno a las nueve.*
   – *Sí, muy bien.*
2 – *¿Qué ponen en la televisión esta tarde?*
   – *¿Te gustan las películas?*
   – *Pues depende de la película pero en general prefiero las películas a las telenovelas.*
   – *Hay una comedia a las once. Es muy divertida.*
   – *¿Cómo se llama?*
   – *Tres hombres y un bebé.*
   – *Vale.*
3 – *¿Qué quieres ver en la televisión esta tarde?*
   – *Bueno, me gusta el deporte.*
   – *¿A qué hora empieza?*
   – *A las seis.*
   – *Vale.*
4 – *¿Qué quieres ver en la televisión?*
   – *Bueno, no me gustan ni los dibujos animados ni los concursos.*
   – *Vamos a ver las noticias a las nueve y el documental a las nueve y treinta y cinco.*
   – *Sí, vamos.*

5 – ¿Qué quieres ver?
– ¿Te gusta la música?
– Depende. No me gusta ver música clásica en la televisión.
– Hay un concierto de jazz a las once.
– Pues, sí. Vamos a verlo.

Answers

1 TELE5	**2** La2	**3** La2	**4** TVE1	**5** TELE 5

1c Lee los textos y completa la tabla con la información correcta.

Reading. Expressing opinions about types of TV programmes. Students read what the four speakers say and complete a grid in Spanish.

R Less able students could focus on completing the first three columns of the grid only.

+ More able students should complete the column for extra information.

Answers

Nombre	Le gustan	No le gustan	Información extra
Felipe	Programas musicales, programas deportivas.	Telenovelas.	Programas musicales y programas deportivas = emocionantes. Telenovelas = tontas y aburridas.
Belén	Concursos.	Documentales.	Concursos = divertidos y graciosos. Documentales = aburridos.
Patricia	Documentales, noticias.	Dibujos animados.	Documentales y noticias = interesantes e informativos. Dibujos animados = estúpidos y para niños pequeños.
Eusebio	Películas.	Concursos.	Películas = emocionantes y efectos especiales. Concursos = tontos y aburridísimos.

1d Túrnate con tu compañero/a. Contesta a las preguntas.

Speaking. Opinions about types of TV programmes. Students answer questions about what type of programmes they like or dislike and why. They could work in pairs or groups, taking turns to ask and answer the questions. They should be encouraged to borrow from and adapt what the four people in **1c** said about their preferences. Teachers may wish to give students oral practice of the questions and the names of types of programmes, before tackling this activity.

Students could then write up their answers. Once corrected, this piece of writing could be added to their *fichero personal*.

R Some students might benefit from being given a language-building grid, from which to create sentences expressing their views.

2a Lee las opiniones. ¿Son positivas (P) o negativas (N)?

Reading. General opinions about television. Students categorise a series of opinions about television according to whether they are positive or negative. They

could work on this in pairs. Although the sentences are quite long, most of the vocabulary is either known or can be guessed fairly easily. However, students could look up any unknown vocabulary in a dictionary or the glossary at the back of the Student's Book.

Answers

> **Positivas:**
> La tele ofrece muchas cosas interesantes y es educativa.
> La televisión ofrece un servicio importante de información.
> **Negativas:**
> Creo que la televisión es una pérdida de tiempo – es muy aburrida.
> La televisión es peligrosa porque tiene demasiada violencia.
> La tele no es buena porque la gente no habla.
> La televisión es mala para la salud y la sociedad.

2b Escribe tu opinión sobre la tele.

Writing. Opinions about TV. Students select from the phrases in **2a**, to write their own views. A language support box is also provided.

+ It is not envisaged that the majority of students will reproduce these statements orally, although able students could be encouraged to do so. They might also be able to adapt the phrases or create different opinions.

3a Identifica la película correcta.

Reading. Descriptions of cinema films. Students read summaries of four well-known films and identify each, from a list of titles in Spanish. Some vocabulary support is given. However, students should be encouraged to look for clues (e.g. words or names they recognise or can guess), rather than trying to understand every word.

Answers

1 C	**2** B	**3** A	**4** D

3b Escribe una descripción de tu película preferida.

Writing. Describing a film. Students should use the model texts in **3a** and the language support grid to write about their favourite film. They should be encouraged to keep it simple. However, it is inevitable that they will require some vocabulary which is not given on the page. They could use dictionaries, but the following *¡Ojo!* tip might be helpful to them:

¡Ojo!

Remember that when you are writing a paragraph in Spanish, start with what you know how to say and with words or phrases you can adapt from texts you have read. Using a dictionary too much, when writing coursework or completing written work, can mean you will score a low grade. This is because some students will look up verbs in the dictionary and not change them to the correct tense or person. For example, if you look up 'go' when you really want to say 'he goes', the dictionary will say '*ir*', which means 'to go'. You could then write something which makes no sense, e.g: *Mi hermano ir al restaurante para trabajar los fines de semana* (My brother to go to the restaurant to work at the weekends).

This should read: *Mi hermano va al restaurante …*

Some dictionaries have verb tables, or you can look at the grammar section at the back of this book, to help you to change verbs correctly.

NB Further material on describing a film is given in the coursework section of the Student's Book (see pages 140–141 of the Student's Book and page 147 of this Teacher's Book.) You may wish to give students access to this material, regardless of whether they are planning to undertake this coursework assignment, before or after they tackle **3b**.

módulo 5/6 *Hablar*

(Student's Book pages 82–83)

Modúlo 5 ¿Qué te ha pasado?

Conversación

General conversation about a past holiday. The suggested areas to cover offer ample opportunity for opinion-giving. A question in the conditional is included, but students are not required to use this tense in their answer, which is mainly related to opinions and reasons. The general guidance at the top of page 82 encourages students to use adverbs and expressions of time, to help boost their performance.

Juegos de rol 1, 2, 3 and 4

Role plays on:

- Reporting illness to a doctor
- Booking hotel accommodation
- Hiring bicycles at a campsite
- Enquiring about hotel facilities

The general guidance at the top of page 82 reminds students not to worry about understanding everything the examiner says in role-play situations, but to concentrate on communicating what is on their role-play card.

Modúlo 6 En casa y en el trabajo

Conversaciones 1, 2, 3 and 4

General conversations on:

- Helping around the house
- Mealtimes, eating habits and healthy eating
- Television and films
- Money and part-time jobs

There are plenty of opportunities here for students to use a range of tenses and give opinions, as well as using adverbs and time expressions.

Juego de rol

A role-play about part-time jobs.

Presentación

Students are offered a choice of two one-minute presentations:

- A film or book
- Your favourite recipe

Trabajo de curso

(Student's Book pages 138–139)

Mis prácticas laborales: A model text about work experience, followed by comprehension exercises and a coursework-style assignment. The *Ayuda* section provides guidance on using the preterite and imperfect tenses, as well as ways of giving opinions about past events.

1 Answers

1 I worked with instructors	trabajé con instructores
2 I would like to continue (with my studies)	me gustaría continuar (con mis estudios)
3 my work experience	mis prácticas laborales
4 before the first day	antes del primer día
5 (Ana) was very friendy	(Ana) era muy amable
6 I worked in (a sports centre)	trabajé en (un centro de deportes)
7 it was very interesting	fue muy interesante
8 I'm good at ICT	se me da bien la informática
9 I used to get up at seven o'clock	me levantaba a las siete
10 I would like to be a footballer	me gustaría ser futbolista
11 I visited (all the departments)	visité (todas las secciones)
12 I learnt a lot	aprendí mucho
13 I used to leave work at five o'clock	salía del trabajo a las cinco
14 I am going to look for work (in a sports centre)	voy a buscar trabajo (en un centro de deportes)

2 Answers

1 B	**2** C	**3** B	**4** C	**5** A	**6** B

Leer y escribir

(Student's Book pages 156–157)

Leer 1 ¿Cuánto cuesta?

An advertisement for fitness equipment. Students note the price next to the picture of each item.

Answers

1 €25	**2** €30	**3** €78	**4** €90	**5** €28	**6** €120

Leer 2 Escoge la imagen correcta para cada resumen.

Guidance on exercising. Students put the correct caption with each picture.

Answers

1 a	**2** e	**3** b	**4** g	**5** c	**6** f	**7** d

Leer 3 Lee el artículo. ¿Verdad o mentira?

A magazine-style article about how young people spend their money, followed by a true/false exercise.

Answers

1 verdad	**2** verdad	**3** mentira	**4** mentira	**5** mentira

Escribir 4 Recibes un mensaje de Miguel. Contesta en español a todas sus preguntas.

Recibes un mensaje de Miguel. Contesta en español a todas sus preguntas.

A writing task in which students must answer questions about a variety of topics from the module: preferred TV programmes, eating habits, helping around the house and exercise.

módulo 6 *Cuaderno*

(Workbook pages 34–40)

page 34

page 36

1a

Answers

1 Pongo la mesa todos los días.
2 Nunca plancho la ropa.
3 Hago las compras dos veces a la semana.
4 Sólo limpio mi habitación a veces.
5 Lavo los platos a menudo.
6 Paso la aspiradora tres veces a la semana.

2b

Answers

1 c, e	**2** d, f	**3** b	**4** a

1b

Answers

	Often	Every day	Twice a week	3 times a week	Sometimes	Never
Cleaning their room					X	
Doing the washing-up	X					
Laying the table		X				
Ironing the clothes						X
Doing the shopping			X			
Hoovering				X		

1c

Answers

1 3 months
2 He is good-looking and funny.
3 He never does the housework.
4 She ironed his clothes, made the bed and did the washing-up.
5 She did the shopping instead.
6 She hoovered, cooked the evening meal and laid the table.
7 He was watching TV and sleeping.

3a

Answers

Name	Place of work	Tasks	Hours	Extra information
Yolanda	hotel in Seville	worked in the reception, answered the phone and e-mails and sent faxes	From 9am to 2pm	It was very interesting and she would like to look for a job in a hotel

page 37

4b

Answers

1 F	2 V	3 V	4 F	5 F	6 V

5a

Answers

a 8	b 9	c 6	d 5	e 3	f 7	g 4	h 1	i 2

page 38

5b

Answers

1 Los Simpsons
2 Estadio 2
3 Al salir de clase
4 Misión Imposible
5 El crimen perfecto
6 Informe semanal

page 39

Gramática

1

Answers (in bold)

1 Mi hermano **prepara** la comida.
2 Yo **lavo** los platos.
3 Mi madre **plancha** la ropa.
4 Yo **pongo** la mesa.
5 Mi hermana **pasa** la aspiradora.
6 Mi padre **lava** el coche.
7 Yo **hago** la compra.
8 Maite **limpia** su habitación.

2

Answers

1 hago
2 voy a lavar
3 limpié, planché
4 pongo, paso
5 voy a hacer, voy a preparar
6 lavé

3

Answers (in bold)

Hice las práticas en una oficina. Todos los días me **leventaba** a las siete. **Iba** al trabajo en autobús. **Trabajaba** de nueve a cinco de lunes a viernes. **Ténia** una hora para comer. **Contestaba** el teléfono, **escribía** correos electrónicos, **preparaba** el café y **mandaba** faxes. Me **llevé** bien con los otros empleados y mi jefe **era** muy simpático. Me **gustó** mucho mis prácticas.

módulo 7 — *De compras*

(Student's Book pages 84–95)

Main topics and objectives	Grammar	Skills
Repaso 1 (pp. 84–85) Shopping for food	Numbers and prices	Giving prices using *Es …* and *Son …*
Repaso 2 (pp. 86–87) Discussing what you are going to wear Shopping for clothes	Immediate future Adjective endings	
1 Comprar comida (pp. 88–89) Buying food in the market and elsewhere	Demonstrative adjectives	
2 Comprar ropa (pp. 90–91) Buying clothes and returning faulty goods	Direct object pronouns	
3 En los grandes almacenes (pp. 92–93) Shopping in a department store Discussing where you prefer to shop and shopping experiences	Ordinal numbers	Different words for shops and departments

Key language

Un estanco/supermercado
Una carnicería/confitería/farmacia/frutería/panadería/
   pastelería/perfumería/tienda de comestibles.
¿Qué desea?/¿En qué puedo servirle?
Quisiera/Déme/Necesito …
… un cartón de leche.
… un kilo de jamón/naranjas.
… un paquete de patatas fritas.
… una barra de pan.

… una botella de cerveza/vino tinto.
… una caja de pasteles.
… una docena de huevos.
… una lata de sardinas.
… una tableta de chocolate.
… 300 gramos de queso.
Aquí tiene.
¿Cuánto es? Es/son € (1,50/9,30).

¿Qué vas a llevar este fin de semana?
El viernes/sábado/domingo voy a llevar …
… un abrigo/chandal/jersey/ sombrero/traje/vestido azul/
   negro/rojo/verde.
… una blusa/camisa/camiseta/chaqueta/corbata/falda/
   gorra azul/negra/verde/roja.
… unos calcetines/guantes/pantalones/vaqueros/zapatos
   azules/negros/rojos/verdes.
… unas botas/zapatillas de deporte azules/negras/
   rojas/verdes.

Quiero comprar un jersey/unos pantalones/unas zapatillas
   de deporte.
¿De qué talla/tamaño/número?
Talla 40 (etc.)/Mediano.
¿De qué color? Blanco/amarillo (etc.)
Lo siento, no tenemos en la talla (40)/en blanco.
¡No me gusta el color!
¡Es demasiado pequeño/grande!

Quisiera un kilo/medio kilo (etc.) de …
… aquellos tomates/melones/aquellas naranjas/ cebollas.
… esos champiñones /esas judías verdes/fresas/peras.
… estos melocotones /estas zanahorias/uvas/ manzanas.
¿Cuánto cuesta (una lata de atún)?

¿Cuánto cuestan (dos botellas de agua mineral)?
Lo siento, no hay (manzanas).
No queda (jamón).
No quedan (zanahorias).
¿Algo más?

¿En qué puedo servirle?
Busco (un chándal).
¿Puedo probármelo?
Claro que sí.
¿Qué tal le queda?
¿Lo tiene en la talla (42)?
Zapatillas/camisas/camisetas/jerseys de …
… cuero/seda/algodón/lana.
Pendientes/anillos de plata/oro.
Quiero cambiar este reloj/esta camiseta/estos
   pantalones (etc.) por favor.

Vale. ¿Por qué quiere cambiarlo/la/los/las?
Porque …
… tiene un(a) agujero/mancha.
… no funciona.
… no me gusta/no le gusta.
… ya tengo uno/a exactamente igual.
¿Tiene usted el recibo?
Sí, tome.
¿Prefieres un reembolso u otro reloj/otra camiseta (etc.)?
Quiero/prefiero un reembolso/otro reloj/otra camiseta (etc.)

Moda joven/caballero/señora.
Agencia de viajes/Aparcamiento/Electrodomésticos/
   Imagen y sonido/Muebles y decoración.
Cafetería/Papelería/Peluquería.
Quisiera comprar un libro/una cámara (máquina
   fotográfica)/una muñeca/unos pendientes (etc.)
¿Dónde está la sección de (libros/fotografía/juguetes)/
   la joyería?
¿(Dónde) se venden (discos)?
(Está) en la planta baja/la primera (segunda/tercera/
   cuarta/quinta/sexta) planta.
En el sótano/En la misma planta que (la peluquería).
Tome el ascensor.
¿Prefieres las tiendas pequeñas o los centros comerciales?
Estoy a favor de los centros comerciales, porque …
… hay mucha variedad/se puede aparcar el coche
   fácilmente/son muy prácticos.

Odio los centros comerciales porque …
… no tienen carácter/hay siempre demasiada gente/son
   aburridos.
(Yo) prefiero las tiendas pequeñas porque …
… los dependientes son muy simpáticos/
los precios son bastante bajos.
¿Adónde vas de compras normalmente?
Normalmente voy al centro comercial.
¿Cuántas veces al mes vas de compras? Dos o tres/Depende.
¿Con quién prefieres ir?
Prefiero ir con mis amigos.
¿La última vez que fuiste de compras, ¿qué compraste?
Compré (un regalo para mi hermano/una camiseta, etc.)
Si ganaras la lotería, ¿qué comprarías?
Compraría (un coche/una casa enorme/mucha ropa, etc.)

módulo 7 — Repaso 1

(Student's Book pages 84–85)

Main topics and objectives

Shopping for food

Grammar

Numbers and prices

Skills

Giving prices using *Es …* and *Son …*

Key language

Un estanco.
Una carnicería/confitería/farmacia/frutería/
panadería/pastelería/perfumería/tienda de
comestibles.
¿Qué desea?/¿En qué puedo servirle?
Quisiera/Déme/Necesito …

… un cartón de leche.
… un kilo de jamón/naranjas.
… un paquete de patatas fritas.
… una barra de pan.
… una botella de cerveza/vino tinto.
… una caja de pasteles.
… una docena de huevos.
… una lata de sardinas.
… una tableta de chocolate.
… 300 gramos de queso.
Aquí tiene.
¿Cuánto es? Es/son €(1,50/9,30).

Resources

Cassette C, side 1
CD 3, track 2
Cuaderno pages 41–47

1a ¿Qué tipo de tienda es?

Reading. Matching names of types of shops to pictures. Students should be encouraged to look for links between the names of the shops and what they sell (e.g. *carne/carnicería, pasteles/pastelería*) and use this information to work out any unknown shop names, as well as to memorise the vocabulary.

Answers

A una perfumería **B** un supermercado **C** una tienda de comestibles **D** una farmacia **E** una pastelería **F** una confitería **G** una panadería **H** un estanco **I** una carnicería **J** una frutería

Información

Where stamps can be bought in Spain.

1b ¿Qué quieren comprar? ¿En qué tienda están? (1–6)

Listening. Buying food and types of shops. Students note down in Spanish what each speaker wants to buy and in which shop it can be bought. Bearing in mind that most things can be bought in a supermarket, you may want to instruct students to ignore that shop and focus on the specialist establishments.

R Teachers may wish to provide some students with a list of the shopping items, on the board or on an OHT, to help them with spelling the items in Spanish. Less able students might find it easier to simply link up the names of the shopping items and the shops on a worksheet.

Tapescript

1 *Necesito unas aspirinas, por favor.*
2 *Quisiera dos limones.*
3 *Quisiera una barra de pan.*
4 *Necesito comprar perfume para mi madre.*
5 *Déme un kilo de patatas.*
6 *Déme cinco sellos, por favor.*

Answers

1 aspirinas – farmacia
2 2 limones – frutería
3 1 barra de pan – panadería
4 perfume – perfumería
5 1 kilo de patatas – tienda de comestibles
6 5 sellos – estanco

¡Ojo!

Using *es* and *son* to give prices.

1c ¿Cuánto es? Escribe el precio correcto. (1–5)

Listening. Prices. Students listen and note down the prices in euros. Students should be shown the convention for writing down prices in euros, using the € and a comma between the number of euros and cents. Bearing in mind the importance of numbers and prices in examinations, teachers may wish to use this opportunity to play a variety of number games, to ensure students are confident in both their understanding and use of numbers.

Tapescript

1 *Son dos euros y treinta.*
2 *Es un euro y veinte.*
3 *Son ocho euros y diez.*
4 *Es un euro y cincuenta.*
5 *Son diez euros y noventa y nueve.*

Answers

1 €2,30	2 €1,20	3 €8,10	4 €1,50	5 €10,99

Answers

	¿Qué?	¿Cantidad?	¿Precio?
1	naranjas	2 kilos	€1,60
2	pan	3 barras	€1,90
3	huevos	1 docena	€1,35
4	vino tinto	2 botellas	€9,55
5	queso	250 gramos	€2,05

2a Completa las frases.

Reading. Quantities and containers. Students complete the sentences about items of food and drink with quantities or containers from the list provided. Teachers may wish first to aurally revise items of shopping and quantities/containers. If teachers wish, they could transfer the gap-filling activity to OHT, with the quantities/containers on individual strips of acetate, so that students can place the items in the correct sentences.

Answers (in bold)

1. una **botella** de Coca-Cola
2. un **kilo** de naranjas
3. una **barra** de pan
4. una **lata** de sardinas
5. una **tableta** de chocolate
6. 300 **gramos** de queso
7. una **caja** de pasteles
8. una **docena** de huevos
9. un **cartón** de leche
10. un **paquete** de patatas fritas

2b ¿Qué necesitan? Copia y completa la tabla. (1–5)

Listening. Shopping for food. Students complete a grid with the item of food each speaker is buying, the quantity/container and the price.

R Teachers could provide less able students with a partially completed version of the grid, so that students only need to listen for one item per speaker.

Tapescript

1 – Buenos días.
– Quisiera dos kilos de naranjas por favor.
– Muy bien.
– ¿Cuánto es?
– Es un euro sesenta.

2 – Buenas tardes, ¿qué desea?
– Quisiera tres barras de pan.
– Es un euro noventa.

3 – Hola, déme una docena de huevos, por favor.
– Aquí tiene.
– ¿Cuánto es?
– Es un euro treinta y cinco.

4 – Buenas tardes, dos botellas de vino tinto por favor.
– Son nueve euros y cincuenta y cinco.
– Muchas gracias.

5 – Buenos días, ¿en qué puedo servirle?
– Necesito 250 gramos de queso por favor.
– Son dos euros cinco.

2c Practica el diálogo. Pues inventa un diálogo para cada producto.

Speaking. Shopping for food. Students first practise the model dialogue, then make up a new dialogue, based on simple adverts.

+ Able students could include a number of items of food in their dialogue, or choose different shopping items from those advertised.

2d a. Inventa cuatro anuncios para productos. Incluye los precios en euros.
   b. Escribe un diálogo para cada producto.

Writing. Students design adverts like the one for lemonade. They could use ICT to create their advertisements, incorporating clip art or scanning in photographs, if possible.

Repaso 2

(Student's Book pages 86–87)

Main topics and objectives

Discussing what you are going to wear
Shopping for clothes

Grammar

Immediate future
Adjective endings

Key language

¿Qué vas a llevar este fin de semana?
El viernes/sábado/domingo voy a llevar …
… un abrigo/chandal/jersey/sombrero/traje/vestido azul/negro/rojo/verde.
… una blusa/camisa/camiseta/chaqueta/corbata/falda/gorra azul/negra/verde/roja.
… unos calcetines/guantes/pantalones/vaqueros/zapatos azules/negros/rojos/verdes.

… unas botas/zapatillas de deporte azules/negras/rojas/verdes.
Quiero comprar un jersey/unos pantalones/unas zapatillas de deporte.
¿De qué talla/tamaño/número?
Talla 40 (etc.)/Mediano.
¿De qué color? Blanco/amarillo (etc.)
Lo siento, no tenemos en la talla (40)/en blanco.
¡No me gusta el color!
¡Es demasiado pequeño/grande!

Resources

Cassette C, side 1
CD 3, track 2
Cuaderno pages 41–47
Gramática 7.8, page 174

1a Escribe la letra correcta. (1–8)

Listening. Saying what you are going to wear. Students match what the speakers say to pictures of clothes. Teachers may wish to revise clothes vocabulary and colours aurally, before tackling this activity.

Tapescript

1 – Voy a llevar unos pantalones negros.
2 – Voy a llevar una camiseta roja.
3 – Voy a llevar una gorra blanca.
4 – Voy a llevar un traje gris.
5 – Voy a llevar una falda morada.
6 – Voy a llevar una chaqueta marrón.
7 – Voy a llevar un chándal azul.
8 – Voy a llevar unos vaqueros.

Answers

1 F	2 D	3 C	4 B	5 A	6 H	7 E	8 G

1b ¿Qué vas a llevar este fin de semana?

Writing. Saying what you are going to wear. Students use the language support grid to write about what clothes they are going to wear at the weekend. Teachers may wish to use this opportunity to revise adjective agreement (covered in Module 1, page 9). As a follow-up, students could ask each other about what they are going to wear at the weekend, or even conduct a class survey on the subject.

Gramática

A brief reminder about the immediate future *ir a +* infinitive (covered in Module 3.)

2a Identifica la talla o número correcto. (1–5)

Listening. Shoe and clothes sizes. Students match what the speakers ask for to the size labels. Before tackling this item, students should be referred to the *Información* feature on this page (see below).

Tapescript

1 – Quiero comprar un jersey.
  – ¿De qué talla?
  – Talla 36.

2 – Quisiera unos pantalones.
  – ¿De qué talla?
  – Talla 42.

3 – Quiero comprar unas zapatillas de deporte.
  – ¿De qué número?
  – Número 40.

4 – Quiero comprar unos zapatos negros.
  – ¿De qué número?
  – Número 39.

5 – Quisiera una falda.
  – ¿De qué talla?
  – Talla 42.

Answers

1 C	2 D	3 B	4 A	5 E

Información

An explanation of continental shoe and clothes sizes, plus the three words for size in Spanish: *talla, tamaño* and *número* and when each is used.

2b Lee y escribe la conversación con la información correcta.

Reading. Shopping for clothes. Students complete the dialogue, by choosing the correct shop assistant's questions/responses from the list. As a follow-up and in preparation for **2c** below, students should then practise the completed model dialogue in pairs.

Answers (in bold)

> – Buenos días.
> – **¿Qué desea?**
> – Quiero comprar una camisa.
> – **¿De qué color?**
> – Blanca.
> – **¿De qué talla?**
> – Mediano, talla 42.
> – **Lo siento, no tenemos más camisas en la talla 42.**

2c Túrnate con tu compañero/a.

Speaking. Shopping for clothes. Students work on the examination-style role-play, in pairs. Multiple options are given, so that students can practise the role-play more than once.

3 ¿Cuál es el problema?

Reading. Problems when shopping for clothes. A brief exercise matching three statements to pictures. This topic is covered in greater depth in unit 2 of this module.

Answers

> **1** B   **2** C   **3** A

1 Comprar comida

(Student's Book pages 88–89)

Main topics and objectives

● Buying food in the market and elsewhere

Grammar

● Demonstrative adjectives

Key language

Quisiera un kilo/medio kilo (etc.) de …
… aquellos tomates/melones /aquellas naranjas/ cebollas.
… esos champiñones /esas judías verdes/fresas/peras.
… estos melocotones /estas zanahorias/uvas/manzanas.

¿Cuánto cuesta (una lata de atún)?
¿Cuánto cuestan (dos botellas de agua mineral)?
Lo siento, no hay (manzanas).
No queda (jamón).
No quedan (zanahorias).
¿Algo más?

Resources

Cassette C, side 1
CD 3, track 3
Cuaderno pages 41–47
Gramática 3.4, page 169

1a Empareja el español con cada cosa en el mercado.

Reading. Pointing out what fruit and vegetables you want. This item introduces both a range of vocabulary for fruit and vegetables (some of it known, some of it new) and the demonstrative adjectives: *aquellos/as*, *estos/as* and *esos/as*. Teachers could first use the picture of the market stall to familiarise students with the vocabulary, then let them tackle the matching task. Students could be asked to guess what they think *aquellos/as*, *estos/as* and *esos/as* mean, before they are directed to the *Gramática*, which explains the demonstrative adjectives and how they work.

Answers

A aquellas naranjas	**B** esas fresas	**C** estos melocotones
D aquellos melones	**E** esos limones	**F** estas manzanas
G aquellas cebollas	**H** esas judías verdes	**I** estas uvas
J aquellas patatas	**K** aquellos champiñones	
L estas zanahorias		

Gramática

Demonstrative adjectives.

1b Usa las listas de compras para pedir lo que necesitas del mercado en 1a.

Speaking. Buying food in the market. Students work in pairs, taking it in turns to ask for the items on the four shopping lists. Teachers may wish to precede this with oral practice, combining different weights with the vocabulary for fruit and vegetables.

1c Mira este recibo del supermercado. Escribe las cantidades y los precios correctos de los errores que hay.

Listening. Shopping for food and drink and understanding prices. Students look at the supermarket price list on the page, listen to the items and prices and spot errors in the prices.

R As this involves numbers and other information

from two different sources, some students may need extra support. Teachers may wish to begin by checking that students understand all the items on the shopping list, then reading out random prices from the list and asking students to say which item they refer to. This could be followed by the teacher reading out the items and the prices on the list and making some deliberate errors; students have to put up their hand as soon as they spot an error and then have to explain what the error consists of.

Tapescript

1 – *Dos kilos de melones son 2 euros 75.*
2 – *Medio kilo de tomates es 1 euro 50.*
3 – *Medio kilo de cebollas es 1 euro 60.*
4 – *Tres kilos de patatas son 3 euros 10.*
5 – *250 gramos de queso es 1 euro 95.*
6 – *500 gramos de jamón son 3 euros 25.*
7 – *1 carton de leche es 1 euro.*
8 – *Dos latas de atún son 3 euros 75.*
9 – *1 lata de sardinas son 2 euros.*
10 – *2 botellas de agua mineral es 1 euro 90.*
11 – *1 botella de fanta naranja es 1 euro 70.*

Answers

(Errors are in bold, with the correct answer in brackets.)

2 Medio kilo de tomates es **1 euro 50**. (1 euro 90)
4 Tres kilos de patatas son **3 euros 10**. (2 euros 10)
5 250 gramos de queso son **1 euro 99**. (1 euro 95)
6 500 gramos de jamón son **3 euros 25**. (2 euros 25)
7 1 carton de leche es **1 euro**. (4 euros 50)
9 1 lata de sardinas son **2 euros**. (1 euro 50)
11 1 botella de fanta naranja es **1 euro 70**. (1 euro 85)

1d ¿Qué compra en el mercado? Escribe una lista breve en español.

Listening. Shopping in the market. Students listen and note down in Spanish what the shopper buys, including quantities. The dialogues include the key shopping phrases listed further down the page. Some of these expressions are new, and teachers should check students' understanding of them before tackling this item. In particular, students need to be forewarned that some of the items the shopper wishes to buy are unavailable. They should listen carefully for *no queda(n)* and only note down what is available.

R Less able students could be given a list of shopping items, which they have to tick if the shopper manages to buy them.

Tapescript

– *Hola buenos días, ¿Qué desea?*
– *Quisiera un kilo de naranjas, por favor.*
– *Aquí tiene. ¿Algo más?*
– *Medio kilo de zanahorias.*
– *Lo siento señor, no quedan zanahorias pero tenemos estas judías verdes muy frescas.*
– *Vale, déme 500 gramos de judías verdes.*
– *¿Algo más?*
– *¿Hay cebollas?*
– *Sí, claro que sí. ¿Cuántos quiere?*
– *Tres, por favor.*
– *¿Algo más?*
– *¿Cuánto cuestan los melocotones?*
– *Son cinco euros y cincuenta el kilo.*
– *Déme medio kilo, por favor. ¿Cuánto es en total?*
– *Son siete euros y diez.*

Answers

> 1 kilo de naranjas
> 500 gramos de judías verdes
> 3 cebollas
> ½ kilo de melocotones

1e Traduce la conversación al español y practícala. Después escribe la conversación y cambia las frases en azul.

Speaking and writing. Buying food in the market. As this pairwork activity involves students playing the roles of both shopper and market stallholder, teachers should ensure that students are confident about saying the stallholder's lines, as well as buying the food and asking prices. In particular, students may need oral practice of the following:

Aquí tiene./¿Algo más?/Lo siento, no quedan (fresas)./ ¿Cuánto cuestan (las manzanas)?/Déme medio kilo, por favor./¿Cuánto es en total?

As a follow-up, students could write their own version of the dialogue, changing the details. They could then practise and perform it for the rest of the class.

1f Vas a tener una fiesta en tu casa. Escribe una lista de lo que necesitas comprar (has invitado a diez personas). Usa un diccionario si es necesario.

Writing. Making a shopping list for a party.

módulo 7

2 Comprar ropa

(Student's Book pages 90–91)

Main topics and objectives

● Buying clothes and returning faulty items

Grammar

● Direct object pronouns

Key language

¿En qué puedo servirle?
Busco (un chándal).
¿Puedo probármelo?
Claro que sí.
¿Qué tal le queda?
¿Lo tiene en la talla (42)?
Zapatillas/camisas/camisetas/jerseys de …
… cuero/seda/algodón/lana.
Pendientes/anillos de plata/oro.
Quiero cambiar este reloj/esta camiseta/estos pantalones (etc.) por favor.

Vale. ¿Por qué quiere cambiarlo/la/los/las?
Porque …
… tiene un(a) agujero/mancha.
… no funciona.
… no me gusta/no le gusta.
… ya tengo uno/a exactamente igual.
¿Tiene usted el recibo?
Sí, tome.
¿Prefieres un reembolso u otro reloj/otra camiseta (etc.)?
Quiero/prefiero un reembolso/otro reloj/otra camiseta (etc.)

Resources

Cassette C, side 1
CD 3, track 4
Cuaderno pages 41–47
Gramática 6.2, page 170

1a Escucha el diálogo y rellena los espacios.

Listening. Buying clothes. Students listen and complete the gapped dialogue. Although the dialogue contains new language, all the missing words should be familiar to students, from *Repaso 2* (page 86). However, to begin with, teachers may wish students to simply listen to the dialogue, without trying to work out the missing words, and then check their understanding.

R Some students could be given a list of the missing words. If necessary, students could simply number these in the order in which they occur in the dialogue.

Tapescript

– *Buenas **tardes**. ¿En qué puedo servirle?*
– *Busco un chándal.*
– *¿De qué **talla**?*
– *Talla **40**.*
– *¿De qué **color**?*
– *Azul o **negro**.*
– *Vale … un momento … Aquí tiene un **chándal** negro muy bonito.*
– *¿Puedo probármelo?*
– *Claro que sí.*

[Diez minutos más tarde]

– *¿Qué tal le queda?*
– *Me gusta mucho el **color** y el estilo pero el problema es que es demasiado **pequeño**.*
  *¿Lo tiene en la talla **42**?*
– *Lo siento. No quedan más chándals de la talla 42. ¿Le gusta esta **camiseta**?*

Answers

(See words in bold in tapescript.)

1b Ahora practica la conversación pero cámbiala por la información siguiente.

Speaking. Buying clothes. Students change the details, using the picture prompts, to create a new dialogue. They should first practise the completed dialogue in 1a. Teachers may then wish to provide students with a version of this dialogue on the board or OHT, in which the details to be changed have been highlighted or taken out. Students' attention should also be drawn to the *Gramática* on the page, which explains the use of the direct object pronoun in questions such as: *¿Puedo probármelo?* and *¿Lo tiene en la talla 42?* Teachers may wish to give students practice of using these phrases, changing the pronoun to refer to different items of clothing, before they tackle the activity in 1b.

+ More able students in particular should be encouraged to use the correct pronoun.

Gramática

Direct object pronouns.

1c Mira la publicidad y haz una lista en inglés de los artículos que se ofrecen.

Reading. Publicity for a special offer in a clothes shop. Students note down in English what articles are being advertised. They could work on this in pairs, using their reading skills and strategies to guess the meaning of new vocabulary, then using a dictionary or the glossary at the back of the Student's Book to check their guesses and find out any remaining unknown words.

Answers

> Leather trainers, silk shirts for men, cotton T-shirts, woollen jumpers, silver earrings, gold rings.

2a Lee el inglés y escribe el español en el orden correcto.

Reading. Returning faulty goods. Students use the English version of the dialogue to rewrite the Spanish in the correct order. They should be encouraged to guess the meaning of the new vocabulary items *el recibo* and *un reembolso* by considering the context and applying logic. Teachers may wish to put the Spanish dialogue onto strips of acetate, which can be assembled on the OHP, or onto strips of paper/card, which the students can assemble themselves on their desk. Students should then practise the completed dialogue in pairs.

Answers

> – Buenos días, ¿en qué puedo servirle?
> – Quiero cambiar esta camiseta por favor.
> – Vale. ¿Por qué quiere cambiarla ?
> – Porque no me gusta el color.
> – ¿Tiene usted el recibo?
> – Sí, tome.
> – Gracias ¿Prefieres un reembolso u otra camiseta?
> – Prefiero otra camiseta.

2b Escucha los diálogos. Copia y completa la tabla. (1–7)

Listening. Returning faulty goods. Students listen to a series of dialogues and note down in a grid the item which is being returned, why it is being returned and whether the customer wants a refund or a replacement. The language support box lists key phrases for explaining why you want to return something.

R Teachers may prefer less able students to listen for only one detail (or only one detail at each playing). Alternatively, these students could be given a version of the grid on a worksheet, with the items already filled in, but in a different order. Students then simply listen and match up the relevant items in the different columns.

Tapescript

1 – ¿Qué desea?
– Mire. Compré estos vaqueros pero tienen un agujero.
– ¡Ay! ¿Tiene el recibo?
– Sí.
– Entonces, lo cambio en seguida.
– Gracias.

2 – Buenos días.
– Buenos días. Quiero cambiar estos guantes. Son demasiado pequeños.
– Sólo tenemos otros en marrón. ¿Los quiere cambiar?

– Sí, gracias.

3 – Buenas tardes. Quisiera cambiar esta caja de bombones.
– ¿Por qué?
– A mi madre no le gustan estos bombones.
– Tiene usted el recibo?
– Sí, tome.
– Sólo te puedo ofrecer un reembolso porque no hay más cajas de bombones.

4 – Quiero cambiar esta chaqueta.
– ¿Qué pasa?
– No me gusta el color.
– Bueno, no tenemos otro color.
– ¿Puede darme un reembolso?
– Si tiene el recibo.
– Sí, tome.
– Vale, el reembolso será posible.

5 – Buenos días. Tengo un problema.
– ¿Qué le pasa?
– Quiero cambiar esta radio.
– ¿Qué le pasa?
– No funciona.
– Vale. ¿Su recibo, por favor?
– Aquí tiene.
– Vale.

6 – Buenos días. Quisiera cambiar esta falda.
– ¿Qué pasa?
– Mire, tiene una mancha aquí.
– ¡Ah! Sí. Lo siento pero no tenemos otra.
– Entonces, quiero un reembolso.
– Vale. ¿Tiene su recibo?
– Sí.

7 – Perdón, señorita.
– Sí.
– Quisiera cambiar esta blusa.
– ¿Por qué?
– Bueno, es demasiado grande.
– Bueno …
– Quiero un reembolso.
– ¿No quiere otra?
– No, quiero un reembolso.
– Vale, en seguida.

Answers

	¿Qué es?	¿Problema?	¿Cambio o reembolso?
1	vaqueros	agujero	cambio
2	guantes	demasiado pequeños	cambio
3	bombones	no le gustan	reembolso
4	chaqueta	no me gusta el color	reembolso
5	radio	no funciona	cambio
6	falda	mancha	reembolso
7	blusa	demasiado grande	reembolso

 **módulo 7** **De compras**

2c Practica la conversación con tu compañero/a.

Speaking. Returning faulty goods. An examination-style role-play, with multiple options. Teachers may wish to give students oral practice of the new language (especially the reasons for returning goods, from the key language box), before tackling the role-play.

3 En los grandes almacenes

(Student's Book pages 92–93)

Main topics and objectives

- Shopping in a department store
- Discussing where you prefer to shop and shopping experiences

Grammar

Ordinal numbers

Skills

Different words for shops and departments

Key language

Moda joven/caballero/señora.
Agencia de viajes/Aparcamiento/Electrodomésticos/
Imagen y sonido/Muebles y decoración.
Cafetería/Papelería/Peluquería.
Quisiera comprar un libro/una cámara (máquina fotográfica)/una muñeca/unos pendientes (etc.)
¿Dónde está la sección de (libros/fotografía/juguetes)/joyería?
¿(Dónde) se venden (discos)?
(Está) en la planta baja/la (primera/segunda/tercera/cuarta/quinta/sexta) planta.
En el sótano/En la misma planta que (la peluquería).
Tome el ascensor.

¿Prefieres las tiendas pequeñas o los centros comerciales?
Estoy a favor de los centros comerciales, porque …
… hay mucha variedad/se puede aparcar el coche fácilmente/son muy prácticos.
Odio los centros comerciales porque …
… no tienen carácter/hay siempre demasiada gente/son aburridos.
(Yo) prefiero las tiendas pequeñas porque …
… los dependientes son muy simpáticos/los precios son bastante bajos.
¿Adónde vas de compras normalmente?
Normalmente voy al centro comercial.
¿Cuántas veces al mes vas de compras? Dos o tres/Depende.
¿Con quién prefieres ir? Prefiero ir con mis amigos.
¿La última vez que fuiste de compras, ¿qué compraste? Compré (un regalo para mi hermano/una camiseta, etc.)
Si ganaras la lotería, ¿qué comprarías? Compraría (un coche/una casa enorme/mucha ropa, etc.)

Resources

Cassette C, side 1
CD 3, track 5
Cuaderno pages 41–47

1a ¿En qué sección pueden comprar lo que quieren?

Reading. Floors and departments in a store. Students read a floor plan for a department store and statements about what people want to buy, then decide which floor each shopper needs to go to. Teachers should first familiarise students with the names of the different floors in a building, which are listed in the key language box on the page. Then students could work in pairs to ensure they understand the names of all the departments in the store plan. The *¡Ojo!* feature on the page offers support with this. As previously, students should be encouraged to use dictionaries/the glossary at the back of the Student's Book as a last resort, first looking for cognates/near-cognates, or words that remind them of other words they already know in Spanish. Finally, they should write their answers to the questions (students could either note down just the name of the relevant department, or the department and the floor, as teachers prefer).

R Teachers might wish to give less able students a simple list of the shopping items in Spanish (with picture clues, if appropriate) on a worksheet, with the store plan alongside, so that students can match up each item to the relevant department.

Answers

> **a** Fotografía (planta baja) **b** Informática (cuarta planta)
> **c** Moda Joven (tercera planta) **d** Deporte/Zapatería (tercera planta) **e** Videojuegos (quinta planta)
> **f** Cafetería (sexta planta)

1b ¿Verdad o mentira? (1–6)

Listening. Directions in a department store. Students look again at the store plan and listen to customers being given directions to different departments. They must decide whether the directions in each case are true or false. Most students should simply listen for the department sought and the floor mentioned.

+ Able students could also note down the directions which are given. Teachers might wish to aurally revise asking the way and giving directions (covered in Module 4, pages 44–45), before tackling this item.

Tapescript

1 – *¿Dónde está la sección de deporte?*
   – *Tome el ascensor, está en la cuarta planta, la primera a la izquierda.*

2 – *Perdón, señor, ¿dónde está la sección de moda caballero?*
   – *Está en la misma planta que la peluquería. Tome el ascensor y bájese en la segunda planta y está a mano derecha.*

3 – *Quisiera comprar unos pendientes. ¿Dónde está la joyería?*

– *Sigue todo recto. Está aquí en la primera planta.*

4 – *¿La sección de zapatos, por favor?*

– *Está en la quinta planta, todo recto.*

5 – *Quisiera comprar una muñeca para mi hermana.*

– *Necesita la sección de juguetes. Tome el ascensor, bájese en la quinta planta y es la segunda sección a la derecha.*

6 – *Perdon, señorita. ¿Dónde se venden muebles?*

– *En la segunda planta al lado de la agencia de viajes.*

Answers

1 mentira	**2** verdad	**3** verdad
4 mentira	**5** verdad	**6** mentira

¡Ojo!

Words for the names of departments or shops.

1c Haz el diálogo con tu compañero/a.

Speaking. Asking for directions in a department store. Examination-style role-play. Students should first practise the model dialogue. Teachers may then wish to give students oral revision of giving directions (covered in Module 4, pages 44–45), before tackling the role-play. Students also need to be familiar with the vocabulary required for saying what they want to buy, as well as being confident about pronouncing the names of the departments and floors.

1d Haz un directorio para unos grandes almacenes. Incluye las secciones que te gustan. Después escribe una descripción para cada planta.

Writing. Students create their own department store floor plan. They could use ICT to design their plan, incorporating different fonts and clip art to make it as clear and attractive as possible.

➕ The second part of the activity – to write a description of each floor of their plan, following the example given – could be used as an extension task for more able students.

2a Lee las opiniones. ¿Prefieren las tiendas pequeñas o los centros comerciales?

Reading. Shopping preferences. Students read the different opinions and decide whether each person prefers shopping centres or individual, small shops. Students should be encouraged to look for 'clue' words, such as *variedad*, *carácter*, *precios*, etc., many of which should either be familiar to them or can be easily guessed.

Answers

Prefieren las tiendas pequeñas: B, C, D.
Prefieren los centros comerciales: A, E.

2b Encuentra el español para estas frases en 2a.

Reading. Shopping preferences. Students find the Spanish for the phrases from the texts in **2a**.

Answers

1 No tienen carácter.
2 Los precios son bastante bajos.
3 Hay siempre demasiada gente.
4 Hay mucha variedad.
5 Los dependientes son muy simpáticos.

2c Escucha la conversación entre Simón y María Teresa. ¿Prefieren las tiendas pequeñas o los centros comerciales? ¿Por qué? Escribe notas en español.

Listening. Shopping preferences. Students listen and note down the two speakers' preferences and reasons.

🆁 Less able students could be given a worksheet with the opinions and reasons written down in Spanish and simply write the initials of each speaker next to the relevant phrases.

Tapescript

Simón: *Yo sé que los centros comerciales son buenos, pero para mí no tienen carácter.*

María Teresa: *Es verdad, pero los precios de los centros comerciales son bastante bajos, entonces no importa si tienen carácter o no.*

Simón: *Sí, … pero en las tiendas pequeñas los dependientes son muy simpáticos.*

María Teresa: *Es verdad, pero para mí es más importante que haya mucha variedad, por eso prefiero los centros comerciales.*

Answers

Simón: Prefiere las tiendas pequeñas – los centros comerciales no tienen carácter; los dependientes en las tiendas pequeñas son muy simpáticos.
María Teresa: Prefiere los centros comerciales – los precios de los centros comerciales son bastante bajos; hay mucha variedad.

2d Empareja las preguntas y las respuestas.

Reading. Shopping habits and experiences. Students match questions and answers. These questions are typical of those that can crop up in the general conversation section of examination speaking tests, and incorporate examples of a range of tenses, including the conditional (covered in more detail in Module 10, page 125, and in the grammar section at the back of the Student's Book). The highlighted sections of the answers can be changed by students, to create their own responses (see **2e**, below).

Answers

1 e	**2** b	**3** a	**4** d	**5** f	**6** c

2e Prepara una entrevista con tu compañero/a. Haz y contesta a las preguntas en 2d pero cambia las frases en azul.

Speaking. Shopping habits and experiences. Students work in pairs to ask and answer the questions from **2d**, adapting the answers by changing the highlighted sections of the phrases. Once it is sufficiently polished, students could tape-record their conversation and keep it, for revision purposes, as part of their *fichero personal*.

2f Escribe tus respuestas en un párrafo con el título "De Compras".

Writing. Shopping habits and experiences. Students use their answers to the questions in **2e** above, to write a paragraph about shopping. Once corrected, they could add this to their *fichero personal*.

Leer y escribir

(Student's Book pages 158–159)

Leer 1 Lee el mensaje electrónico. Escribe la persona en el espacio.

An e-mail about a birthday and what presents were received. Students write next to each present which family member or friend gave it.

Answers

Joyas – abuelo
Ropa – madre
Harry Potter y la piedra filosofal – mejor amigo
Película – tía
Dulces – hermana
Música – padrastro

Escribir 2 Amy está de compras en España. Escoge un regalo para los seis miembros de su familia. Menciona la razón por la que lo comprara.

Students select gifts for Amy's family from a list and write a sentence about each, following the example.

Answers

Various possibilities for the family members. Gifts and reasons should be paired as follows:
1 d   **2** e   **3** a   **4** b   **5** f   **6** c

Leer 3 Contesta a las preguntas del concurso en inglés.

A quiz in the style of TV's 'Who wants to be a millionaire?' In this version, students must answer increasingly difficult questions in English about Spanish shop signs.

Answers

1 Toilets   **2** Pull   **3** Push   **4** No entry
5 Because there is a 35% discount on furniture
6 Because the shop has a sale on
7 From 8.30 in the morning
8 Closed on Monday afternoons
9 Escalators   **10** Bags must be handed in

Leer 4 Contesta a las preguntas en inglés.

An advertisement for the food department of a store, followed by questions in English.

Answers

1 It sells drinks of all flavours, for all tastes, for all occasions and your favourite brands.
2 Fruit and vegetables.
3 Every day.
4 Lamb, turkey, pork, chicken.
5 Bread, rolls, tarts/pies, cakes.

módulo 7 *Cuaderno*

(Workbook pages 41–47)

page 41

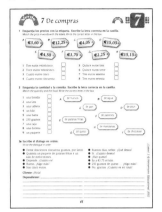

page 42

1

Answers

1 G	**2** B	**3** C	**4** E	**5** D	**6** H	**7** A	**8** F

2

Answers

1 B	**2** D	**3** I	**4** H	**5** C	**6** G	**7** F	**8** A	**9** E

3a

Answers

– Buenos días, señor. ¿Qué desea?
– Quisiera un paquete de patatas fritas y un kilo de melocotones.
– Bueno, ¿Algo más?
– ¿Hay queso?
– Sí. ¿Cuánto desea?
– Depende. ¿Cuánto es?
– Es €3,75 el kilo.
– Déme doscientos cincuenta gramos, por favor.
– 250 gramos de queso. ¿Algo más?
– No, gracias. ¿Cuánto es en total?

3b

Answers

What do they want to buy?	What they bought (including the amount)	The total cost
1 melon pears onions green beans	1 melon 500g onions 500g green beans	€7,20
2 mushrooms strawberries grapes	500g strawberries 1 kg grapes	€4,35

page 43

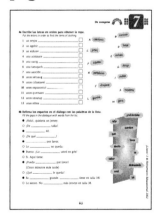

4a

Answers

1 un jersey **C**   **2** un abrigo **G**   **3** un vestido **I**
4 una camiseta **B**   **5** una gorra **M**   **6** una chaqueta **J**
7 una corbata **E**   **8** unos guantes **L**   **9** unos calcetines **A**
10 unos pantalones **H**   **11** unos vaqueros **K**
12 unos zapatos **F**   **13** unas botas **D**

módulo 7

De compras

(Workbook pages 41–47)

4b

Answers (in bold)

- Hola, quisiera un jersey.
- ¿De **qué** talla?
- **Talla** 40.
- ¿De qué **color**?
- **Azul**, por favor.
- Lo **siento**, no queda.
- Bueno. ¿Lo **tiene** usted en gris?
- Sí. Aquí tiene.
- ¿Puedo **probármelo**, por favor?

[Cinco minutos más tarde]

- ¿Qué **tal** le queda?
- Es **demasiado** grande. ¿**Lo** tiene en la talla 38?
- Lo siento. No **quedan** más jerseys en la talla 38.

page 44

5

Answers

1 350
2 First floor
3 Young fashion, toys and video games
4 From 8.30 am to 9.30 pm
5 On the third floor, in the photographic department
6 Hairdresser's and a restaurant
7 True
8 Third floor

page 45

6b

Answers

1 b	2 a	3 c	4 b	5 b

page 46

Gramática

1

Answers

a	Son €5,39.
b	Es €1,25.
c	Son €0,78.
d	Es €1.
e	Son €0,50.
f	Son €3,20.
g	Es €1,99.

2

Answers (in bold)

1 Quisiera **esos** (those) vaqueros.
2 Voy a comprar **esta** (this) camisa.
3 Compré **aquellos** (those over there) pantalones.
4 Compré **estos** (these) pendientes.
5 Mi hermana quiere comprar **aquella** (that over there) falda.
6 Quisiera comprar **ese** (that) anillo.
7 Mi madre compró **esta** (this) botella de perfume.

3

Answers

a los	**b** lo	**c** la	**d** la	**e** las

módulo 8 · *De juerga*

(Student's Book pages 96–109)

Main topics and objectives	Grammar	Skills
Repaso 1 (pp. 96–97) Discussing sports and other leisure activities	*Los* + day of week in plural, *el* + day of week in singular Present tense and present tense plus infinitive	Using time indicators (e.g. *pero, también, sin embargo*)
Repaso 2 (pp. 98–99) Arranging to go out Buying cinema tickets	Prepositions	
1 Una cita (pp. 100–101) Accepting and declining invitations Understanding and leaving telephone messages		
2 Las estrellas hispanohablantes (pp. 102–103) Famous Spanish-speaking people	Interrogatives	Strategies for dealing with long texts and questions in Spanish
3 ¿Cómo fue? (pp. 104–105) Saying what you thought of a film or event Discussing what you did and what it was like	The preterite and the use of different tenses	Using opinions and different tenses in your written work

Key language

¿Qué haces/te gusta hacer en tu tiempo libre?
Los martes/viernes/sábados (etc.) por la mañana/tarde/ noche …
… después de las ocho y media de la noche/desde las seis hasta las siete de la tarde (etc.) …
… bailo en la discoteca/escucho música/juego con el ordenador/leo/toco el piano/voy al cine.
En mi tiempo libre me gusta/encanta bailar en la discoteca/ escuchar música (etc.)
¿Qué deportes practicas?
Juego/Me gusta jugar al baloncesto/fútbol/hockey/rugby/ squash tenis/tenis de mesa …

Practico/Hago/Me gusta practicar (hacer) atletismo/boxeo/ deporte/equitación/gimnasia/monopatín/patinaje/ natación/vela/ muchos deportes …
… todos los días/cada día/cada semana/cada mes/los sábados (etc.)/dos (etc.) veces a la semana/de vez en cuando.
(No) soy muy deportista.
(No) me gustan mucho los deportes.
¿Cuál es tu deporte preferido?
Mi deporte preferido es (el fútbol).

¿Quieres ir …
… al cine/parque/teatro/a la discoteca/piscina (el sábado)?
¿A qué hora? A las (siete y media).
¿Dónde quedamos?
Delante/enfrente/detrás/al lado …
… del cine/café.
… de la parada de autobuses/entrada/taquilla/estación de trenes.

… de mi casa.
De acuerdo. ¡Hasta luego!
Dos entradas para (Parque Jurásico III), por favor.
¿Para qué sesión? Para la sesión de (las ocho).
¿Hay un descuento para estudiantes?
Sí, si tiene su carnet de estudiante.
¿A qué hora termina la película? A (las diez y media).
Días laborales./Día del espectador.
La sesión (de madrugada).

¿Vienes/Quieres venir/Te gustaría ir/Te apetece ir …
… al parque temático/a la fiesta/a un partido de fútbol/a un concierto de jazz …
… el domingo/con nosotros (etc.)?
¡Qué bien!/¡Ay, qué bueno!
Buena idea/Claro que sí.
Me encantaría venir.
No, gracias/No me gusta nada.

Lo siento, pero tengo muchos deberes.
El problema es que no tengo dinero.
Te llamó (Alfredo/Susana). Llámalo/la (esta tarde) al (958 22 38 71).
Estás invitado (al teatro).
Empieza a (las ocho).
Te llamo para saber si quieres ir (a una fiesta).
Te llamaré/Llámame entre 4 y 7/mañana por la tarde.

¿A quién admiras?
Admiro a/La persona a quien más admiro es …
¿Qué hace? Es cantante/actor/actriz/futbolista (etc.)
¿Por qué es famoso/a?
Actuó en (una telenovela/una película).
Su (nuevo/primer) álbum vendió (200.000) copias.
Juega/Jugó para (El Real Madrid).
Ha sido seleccionado para el equipo nacional.
Ha ganado muchas copas.
Ganó una medalla de oro en los Juegos Olímpicos (de Barcelona).

Nació el 2 de febrero en (Colombia).
Cuando era joven (impresionó a sus padres).
Grabó su primer disco (en 1985).
A la edad de (doce años) apareció en anuncios en la televisión.
¿Cómo es?/¿Por qué lo/la admiras?
Lo/La admiro porque es …
… muy guapo/a /honesto/a /inteligente/ambicioso/a (etc.)
… un(a) deportista excepcional/un/a jugador(a) excelente de (tenis).
… su música es muy buena.

¿Cómo fue el partido/la película (etc.)?
¡Fue superfantástico/a /fenomenal/emocionante/estupendo/a!
¡Lo pasé bomba! ¡Lo pasamos bomba!
Fue regular/bastante bien./No estuvo mal.
¡Qué desastre!/¡Fue muy aburrido!
¡Lo pasé fatal!
¿Adónde fuiste? Fui/fuimos al parque/a la discoteca/a una fiesta (etc.)
¿Cuándo? Fui/fuimos el lunes/ayer/la semana pasada (etc.)

¿Con quién fuiste? Fui/salí con mi amigo/mis padres (etc.)
¿Qué hiciste?
Jugué al (tenis)/Leí una revista.
Bailamos/comimos calamares/escuchamos música/vimos una película (etc.)
¿Qué tal fue? (No) me gustó porque la música era muy aburrida/las entradas nos costaron €10 (etc.)

Main topics and objectives

● Discussing sports and other leisure activities

Grammar

● *Los* + day of week in plural, *el* + day of week in singular
● Present tense and present tense plus infinitive

Skills

Using time indicators (e.g. *pero, también, sin embargo*)

Key language

¿Qué haces/te gusta hacer en tu tiempo libre?
Los martes/viernes/sábados (etc.) por la mañana/tarde/noche …
… después de las ocho y media de la noche/desde las seis hasta las siete de la tarde (etc.) …
… bailo en la discoteca/escucho música/juego con el ordenador/leo/toco el piano/voy al cine.
En mi tiempo libre me gusta/encanta bailar en la discoteca/escuchar música (etc.)
¿Qué deportes practicas?
Juego/Me gusta jugar al baloncesto/fútbol/hockey/rugby/squash/tenis/tenis de mesa
Practico/Hago/Me gusta practicar (hacer) atletismo/boxeo/deporte/equitación/gimnasia/monopatín/natación/patinaje/vela/muchos deportes …
… todos los días/cada día/cada semana/cada mes/los sábados (etc.)/dos (etc.) veces a la semana/de vez en cuando.
(No) soy muy deportista.
(No) me gustan mucho los deportes.
¿Cuál es tu deporte preferido?
Mi deporte preferido es (el fútbol).

Resources

Cassette C, side 1
CD 3, track 6
Cuaderno pages 48–52
Gramática 7.2, page 171 and 11.1 page 178

1a Identifica los pasatiempos correctos. ¿En qué día y a qué hora hacen cada actividad? (1–6)

Listening. Hobbies and pastimes. Students match what they hear to the pictures of hobbies and note down the day and time that each person does their hobby. Teachers may wish to revise hobbies, days of the week and times of day, before tackling this activity.

R Teachers may prefer some students to focus on listening for just the hobbies, or the hobbies and the days of the week.

Tapescript

1 – Los sábados por la noche, bailo en la discoteca.
2 – Los martes, escucho música por la tarde.
3 – Los jueves, toco el piano desde las seis hasta las siete de la tarde.
4 – Los domingos por la tarde, voy al cine.
5 – Los miércoles por la mañana, juego con el ordenador.
6 – Los viernes, leo después de las ocho y media de la noche.

Answers

1 C, sábado, por la noche   2 E, martes, por la tarde   3 A, jueves, 6–7 de la tarde   4 B, domingo, por la tarde   5 D, miércoles, por la mañana   6 F, viernes, después de las 8.30 de la noche.

Gramática

Los + day of the week in the plural, contrasted with *el* + day of the week in the singular.

1b ¿Cuáles son sus opiniones sobre las actividades? (1–7)

Listening. Opinions about hobbies. Students write down in Spanish each person's opinion about an activity and any reason given. NB There isn't a reason for every opinion.

Tapescript

1 – Me gusta tocar el piano porque es divertido.
2 – Me encanta escuchar música. Prefiero el rap.
3 – No me gusta leer – es aburridísimo.
4 – Me gusta mucho bailar en la discoteca. ¡Es genial!
5 – Prefiero jugar con el ordenador.
6 – Me encanta ver la televisión porque es informativa.
7 – Odio ir al cine con mis padres.

Answers

1 Le gusta tocar el piano/divertido   2 Le encanta/gusta escuchar música   3 No le gusta leer/aburridísimo   4 Le gusta mucho bailar en la discoteca/genial   5 Prefiere/Le gusta jugar con el ordenador   6 Le encanta/gusta ver la televisión/informativa   7 Odia/No le gusta ir al cine con sus padres

Gramática

The present tense of verbs used to describe pastimes, and the use of the infinitive after *me gusta* (etc.) Activity **1c**, below, provides practice of this.

1c Rellena los espacios con los verbos en el presente o los infinitivos.

Writing. Verbs for pastimes in the present tense or the infinitive. Students copy and complete the text, using the verbs in the *Gramática* box.

➕ As a follow-up, some students could adapt the completed text to write about their own free-time activities.

Answers (in bold)

En mi tiempo libre me gusta hacer muchas cosas. Los sábados siempre **voy** al cine con mi hermano o **bailo** en la discoteca. ¡Me gusta **bailar** en la discoteca porque hay muchas chicas guapas allí! Los domingos prefiero **leer** una novela o **escuchar** música.

2a Identifica los deportes que practica cada persona.

Listening. Sporting activities. Students listen and note down the sports each speaker does. The key language grid provides the names of all the sports mentioned and groups them according to whether they take the verbs *jugar* or *practicar/hacer*.

Tapescript

1 – *Me llamo Rafa y me gustan mucho los deportes. Practico vela y natación cada fin de semana y me gusta jugar al fútbol.*

2 – *Me llamo Soledad y me gustan algunos deportes. Hago monopatín los domingos y a veces juego al baloncesto.*

3 – *Soy Martín y me gusta hacer muchos deportes: juego al tenis, rugby y hockey. También practico boxeo, gimnasia y ciclismo.*

4 – *Me llamo Luisa y me gusta hacer deporte. Hago equitación y juego al tenis de mesa.*

Answers

1 vela, natación, fútbol **2** monopatín, baloncesto
3 tenis, rugby, hockey, boxeo, gimnasia, ciclismo
4 equitación, tenis de mesa

2b Prepara una presentación sobre tu tiempo libre.

Speaking. Sport and other free-time activities. Students prepare an oral presentation about their leisure time. They should include reference to sports and other activities, mentioning how often and when (day of week, time of day) they do each activity. They should use the key language grid about sports (ensuring that they understand when to use *jugar* and when to use *practicar/hacer*), as well as the useful expressions listed in the *¡Ojo!* feature.

¡Ojo!

Time indicators, conjunctions and useful expressions for talking/writing about sport.

2c Escribe la presentación.

Writing. Students write up their presentation. Once corrected, this could be added to their fichero personal.

2d Lee el mensaje electrónico y toma apuntes en inglés. Después escribe una respuesta.

Reading. Hobbies and pastimes. Students read the e-mail and make notes in English. They then write a reply, answering the questions in the message.

Answers

Happy because she's on holiday. Favourite sport is tennis. Plays tennis every day in Valencia with her friends. Her step-brother plays table tennis with his friends, but she thinks it's boring. She asks what sports you play, what your favourite sport is and what you like to do in your spare time.

Main topics and objectives

- Arranging to go out
- Buying cinema tickets

Grammar

Prepositions

Key language

¿Quieres ir …
… al cine/parque/teatro/a la discoteca /piscina (el sábado)?
¿A qué hora? A las (siete y media).
¿Dónde quedamos?
Delante/enfrente/detrás/al lado …
… del cine/café.

… de la parada de autobuses/ entrada/taquilla/estación de trenes.
… de mi casa.
De acuerdo. ¡Hasta luego!
Dos entradas para (Parque Jurásico III), por favor.
¿Para qué sesión? Para la sesión de (las ocho).
¿Hay un descuento para estudiantes?
Sí, si tiene su carnet de estudiante.
¿A qué hora termina la película? A (las diez y media).
Días laborales./Día del espectador.
La sesión (de madrugada).

Resources

Cassette C, side 1
CD 3, track 7
Cuaderno pages 48–52

1a Escucha la conversación y escoge la respuesta correcta.

Listening. Arranging to go out. Students listen to the dialogue and select the correct answers in a multiple-choice exercise.

Tapescript

Mateo: *¿Quieres ir al cine el sábado?*
Elena: *Buena idea. ¿A qué hora?*
Mateo: *A las siete y media.*
Elena: *Vale. ¿Dónde quedamos?*
Mateo: *Delante de la puerta de entrada.*
Elena: *De acuerdo. ¡Hasta luego!*

Answers (in bold)

1 Mateo invita a Elena a ir al cine **el sábado**.
2 Elena **acepta** la invitación.
3 Van a ir a las **siete y media**.
4 Quedan **delante de la entrada**.

1b Escucha las conversaciónes y copia y completa la tabla. (1–5)

Listening. Arranging to go out. Students listen and note details in a grid about where the speakers are planning to go, when, the time at which they are going to meet and the meeting place. The key language grid on the page provides support with prepositions and meeting places. Teachers may want to check students' understanding of this key language and practise it aurally, before tackling the listening comprehension activity.

R Less able students could be given a partially-completed grid, so they listen for only one or two details per dialogue (or per playing). They could also fill in the details in English, if preferred.

Tapescript

1 – *Hola, ¿quieres ir a la discoteca?*
 – *¿Cuándo?*
 – *El sábado.*
 – *Vale. ¿A qué hora?*
 – *A las diez.*
 – *¿Dónde quedamos?*
 – *Enfrente de la parada de autobuses.*

2 – *¿Quieres ir a la piscina el domingo?*
 – *De acuerdo. ¿A qué hora?*
 – *A las tres y cuarto.*
 – *Vale. ¿Dónde quedamos?*
 – *Al lado de la entrada.*

3 – *Hola Simón, ¿quieres ir al parque?*
 – *Vale. ¿Cuándo?*
 – *El lunes, a las cinco.*
 – *Vale.*
 – *¿Dónde quedamos?*
 – *Delante de la estación de trenes?*

4 – *¿Quieres ir al teatro?*
 – *De acuerdo. ¿Cuándo quieres ir?*
 – *El martes.*
 – *¿A qué hora?*
 – *A las seis y media delante de la taquilla.*
 – *Vale. Adiós.*

5 – *¿Quieres ir al cine?*
 – *Buena idea. ¿Quieres ir el viernes?*
 – *Sí, ¿a las nueve y cuarto?*
 – *Vale. ¿Dónde quedamos?*
 – *Delante de mi casa.*
 – *Buena idea. ¡Hasta luego!*

Answers

	¿Actividad?	¿Cuándo?	¿A qué hora?	¿Dónde?
1	discoteca	sábado	10	enfrente de la parada de autobuses
2	piscina	domingo	3.15	al lado de la entrada
3	parque	lunes	5	delante de la estación de trenes
4	teatro	martes	6.30	delante de la taquilla
5	cine	viernes	9.15	delante de mi casa

1c Ahora practica las conversaciones de **1b** con tu compañero/a.

Speaking. Arranging to go out. Students first practise the model dialogue on the page, then use the information they have noted down in **1b** above, to change the details in the model dialogue and create new conversations.

R Teachers might prefer to give some students a version of the model dialogue on a worksheet or OHT, with the sections to be changed highlighted or taken out and the new information alongside.

+ Able students could make up a completely new version of the dialogue, using their imagination to change the details.

2a Escucha la conversación y completa los espacios.

Listening. Buying cinema tickets. Students listen and fill in the missing words in a gapped dialogue. All the missing words should be familiar to them.

R Teachers may wish to provide some students with a list of the missing words.

Tapescript

– Buenas tardes
– **Dos** entradas para Parque Jurásico III, por favor.
– ¿Para qué sesión?
– Para la sesión de las **ocho**.
– Vale.
– ¿Cuánto es?
– **€9**
– ¿Hay un descuento para estudiantes?
– Sí, si tiene su carnet de estudiante son **€7**.
– Aquí tiene. ¿A qué hora termina la película?
– A las **diez** y media.

2b Túrnate con tu compañero/a. Practica las conversaciones.

Speaking. Buying cinema tickets. Students should first practise the completed dialogue in **2a**, then use the prompts on the page to change the details and create different conversations.

2c Contesta a las preguntas en inglés.

Reading. Cinema information. Students read the advertisement and answer questions in English. Although the text includes some new vocabulary, students should be encouraged to infer meaning from context and apply logic to work out the meaning of new words, before using a dictionary or the glossary at the back of the Student's Book to confirm their guesswork.

Answers

1	Three showings.
2	Fridays and Saturdays.
3	€3,50.
4	Mondays.

Main topics and objectives

- Accepting and declining invitations
- Understanding and leaving telephone messages

Key language

¿Vienes/Quieres venir/Te gustaría ir/Te apetece ir …
… al parque temático/a la fiesta/a un partido de fútbol/a un concierto de jazz …
… el domingo/con nosotros (etc.)?
¡Qué bien!/¡Ay, qué bueno!
Buena idea/Claro que sí.
Me encantaría venir.
No, gracias/ No me gusta nada.
Lo siento, pero tengo muchos deberes.

El problema es que no tengo dinero.
Te llamó (Alfredo/Susana). Llámalo/la (esta tarde) al (958 22 38 71).
Estás invitado (al teatro).
Empieza a (las ocho).
Te llamo para saber si quieres ir (a una fiesta).
Te llamaré/Llámame entre 4 y 7/mañana por la tarde.

Resources

Cassette C, side 1
CD 3, track 8
Cuaderno pages 48–52

1a Lee las reacciones a una invitación. ¿Son positivas (P) o negativas (N)?

Reading. Responses to an invitation. Students read the responses and categorise them as positive or negative.

Answers

Positivas	Negativas
A ¡Qué bien!	**B** No, gracias.
H ¡Ay, qué bueno!	**I** No me gusta nada.
F Buena idea.	**C** Lo siento, pero tengo muchos deberes.
E Claro que sí.	**D** El problema es que no tengo dinero.
G Me encantaría venir.	

1b Identifica la invitación ¿Aceptan ✓ o rehusan ✗ las invitaciones? (1–5)

Listening. Responses to invitations. Students listen and note down what each person is invited to and whether they accept or decline.

R Less able students could be given a list of the places, in jumbled order, so that students can simply number each one and put a tick (for acceptance) or a cross (for refusal) next to each.

+ More able students could note down the reasons people give for accepting or declining.

Tapescript

1 – Oye, Fede, ¿vienes al polideportivo con nosotros?
– ¿Qué vais a hacer?
– Vamos a jugar al tenis.
– Sí, vale, me gusta el tenis.

2 – Mariluz, ¿quieres venir al cine?
– ¿Qué ponen?
– Parque Jurásico III.
– No, gracias. Vi Parque Jurásico II y no me gustó.

3 – ¿Vienes al partido el domingo?
– ¡Fenomenal! Juega el Barcelona, ¿verdad? ¡Qué bien!

4 – ¿Quieres venir a la fiesta el sábado?
– ¿Quién va a estar?
– Teo, Rafa, Carlos.
– ¡Sí! Me gusta mucho Carlos.

5 – ¿Vienes a la discoteca el viernes?
– No sé. Creo que no. Voy a salir con Martín y no le gustan las discotecas.

Answers

1 polideportivo ✓	**2** cine ✗	**3** partido ✓
4 fiesta ✓	**5** discoteca ✗	

1c Túrnate con tu compañero/a.

Speaking. Role-play on inviting someone out and arranging to meet. The first line of the activity offers multiple options, so that students can do the task more than once, and they should be encouraged to vary the other information (including how they accept the invitation) each time they tackle it. Parts of the activity are open-ended (e.g. the meeting time and place) and teachers may wish to brainstorm for ideas with students first. It is also important to clarify the meaning of instructions such as 'agree the arrangement' and how students should do this.

1d Escribe tu reacción a cada invitación.

Writing. Responses to invitations. Students write down how they would respond to each invitation, according to their own preferences.

2a Lee los recados y toma apuntes breves en inglés.

Reading. Telephone messages. Note-taking in English. Most of the language in the messages should be familiar. Students should be encouraged to work out the meaning of *llámalo/llámala* and when you would use each of these.

Answers

A Alfredo – invitation to a football match. Starts at 6pm. Call him this evening on 93 22 38 710.
B Susana – needs to know where concert on Saturday is and when it starts.
C Ana – invitation to a party at 9 on Friday.
D Pili – have you got the theatre tickets? Call her between 4 and 7.
E Rafa – can't go to park this afternoon because he has a lot of work.

2b ¿Quién dejó cada mensaje en el contestador automático? (1–5)

Listening. Answerphone messages. Students listen and match the speakers to the written messages in **2a,** noting down the name of each caller.

+ Some students could note down extra information, which does not appear in the written messages.

Tapescript

1 – Quiero invitarte a una fiesta el viernes. Todos nuestros amigos van a ir. Te llamaré mañana por la tarde. Adiós.
2 – Hola. Quiero dejar un recado. No puedo salir esta tarde. Es imposible. Tengo muchísimo trabajo. Lo siento mucho. Pero me gustaría salir mañana. Adiós.
3 – Hay un partido muy bueno. ¡Barcelona y Real Madrid! Empieza a las seis. ¿Me llamas esta tarde si puedes? El número es 93 22 38 710. Repito 93 22 38 710.
4 – Quiero saber si tienes las entradas para el teatro y dónde quedamos – ¿delante de la taquilla? ¿Llámame entre 4 y 7? Gracias. Hasta ahora.
5 – Te llamo para saber si sabes dónde es el concierto el sábado y a qué hora empieza. ¿Llámanos, por favor? El número es 987 16 39 45. Hasta luego.

Answers

| **1** Ana | **2** Rafa | **3** Alfredo | **4** Pili | **5** Susana |

2c Inventa un recado para cada situación con tu compañero/a.

Speaking. Leaving answerphone messages. Students work with a partner, using the picture and word prompts, to create new messages, similar to those in **2b** and following the model on the page. Teachers may wish to provide students with key phrases from the tapescript in **2b** above, on the board or an OHT.

2d Ahora escribe los mensajes de arriba.

Writing. Telephone messages. Students note down their answerphone messages from **2c** above, as written messages, similar to those in **2a**.

2 Las estrellas hispanohablantes

(Student's Book pages 102–103)

Main topics and objectives

● Famous Spanish-speaking people

Grammar

Interrogatives

Skills

Strategies for dealing with long texts and questions in Spanish

Key language

¿A quién admiras?
Admiro a/La persona a quien más admiro es …
¿Que hace? Es cantante/actor/actriz /futbolista (etc.)
¿Por qué es famoso/a?
Actuó en (una telenovela/una película).
Su (nuevo/primer) album vendió (200.000) copias.
Juega/Jugó para (El Real Madrid).
Ha sido seleccionado para el equipo nacional.
Ha ganado muchas copas.
Ganó una medalla de oro en los Juegos Olímpicos (de Barcelona).
Nació el (2 de febrero) en (Colombia).
Cuando era joven (impresionó a sus padres).
Grabó su primer disco (en 1985).
A la edad de (doce años) apareció en anuncios en la televisión.
¿Cómo es?/¿Por qué lo/la admiras?
Lo/La admiro porque es …
… muy guapo/a /honesto/a /inteligente/ambicioso/a (etc.)
… un(a) deportista excepcional/un(a) jugador(a) excelente de (tenis).
… su música es muy buena.

Resources

Cassette C, side 1
CD 3, track 9
Cuaderno pages 48–52

1a Lee el artículo y escoge las respuestas correctas.

Reading. Famous people. A magazine article about the Colombian pop singer Shakira, followed by a multiple-choice activity. Although the text contains some unknown language, students should be encouraged to use reading skills and strategies, such as looking for cognates/near-cognates, inferring from context and predicting, to work out meanings. Here and in the texts in **2b** below, dictionaries or the glossary at the back of the Student's Book should be used only as a last resort, in order to build up the skills students will need to apply in the reading test section of their examination.

Answers

1 b	2 c	3 a	4 a	5 a

1b Rellena los espacios sobre Shakira.

Writing. Famous people. Students copy and complete a gapped text about Shakira, using the list of words provided. In line with the conventions of some examinations boards when using this type of task, the list contains some 'distractor' words, which are not needed for the gap-filling.

Answers (in bold)

Shakira es una cantante **colombiana**. Nació en **Barranquilla** en 1977. Siempre ha sido muy **creativa** y escribió su primera **canción** cuando tenía ocho **años**. Shakira es famosa también en la **televisión** colombiana. Actuó en una **telenovela** que se llama "El Oasis". Ahora Shakira es muy **popular** en los Estados Unidos y en Europa.

2a ¿A quién admiran y por qué? (1–6)

Listening. Saying who you admire and why. Students listen and take notes in Spanish.

R Less able students could be given a worksheet with a list of the famous people mentioned and reasons why the speakers admire them. Students listen and match up to link the people to the reasons.

Tapescript

1 *Admiro a John Lennon porque era muy honesto.*
2 *Admiro a David Beckham porque es muy ambicioso.*
3 *La persona que más admiro es Ricky Martín porque es muy guapo y su música es muy buena.*
4 *La persona que más admiro es el futbolista Raúl porque es un deportista excepcional.*
5 *Admiro mucho a Arantxa Sanchéz Vicario porque es una jugadora excelente de tenis.*
6 *La persona a quien más admiro es la princesa Diana porque era muy simpática y ayudó a muchas personas.*

Answers

(See tapescript.)

2b Lee el texto y busca el español para las frases de abajo.

Reading. Famous people. Three texts about Cristina Aguilera, Luís Enrique Martínez and Ricky Martin. Students find the Spanish equivalents of the phrases in English. Once again, students should use reading strategies, rather than look up too many words (see notes under **1a**, above).

Answers

> **1a** la banda sonora de Pokémon   **1b** canta en inglés
> **1c** viaja por todo el mundo   **2a** ha sido seleccionado
> muchas veces para el equipo nacional   **2b** Ganó una
> medalla de oro   **3a** apareció en anuncios en la televisión
> **3b** obtuvo ocho discos de oro en …   **3c** es una
> superestrella y le amo.

2c Contesta a las preguntas.

Reading. Famous people. A follow-up task to 2b. Students answer questions in Spanish about the texts in **2b**. The *¡Ojo!* feature give students tips on tackling longer texts and questions in Spanish.

✚ Teachers may wish to use this as an extension activity for able students.

Answers

> **1** Habla dos idiomas.   **2** Se llama 'Don't make me love you'.   **3** Ganó una medalla de oro.   **4** Jugó para El Real Madrid entre 1991 y 1996.   **5** Nació en Puerto Rico.
> **6** Obtuvo ocho discos de oro.

2d Prepara una descripción sobre una persona hispánica famosa.

Writing. Famous Spanish-speaking people. Students should draw on the key phrases used in the texts about famous people on this double-page spread to write about another famous Spanish-speaking person. Four names are suggested on the page, but students might prefer to choose another celebrity. The questions help to guide their writing.

2e Encuentra información sobre una estrella hispanohablante y prepara una presentación sobre él/ella.

Speaking. Famous people. Students research information about other famous Spanish-speaking people (using the Internet, if possible) and prepare an oral presentation.

Note: Teachers seeking further material and guidance for students on writing about famous people may wish to refer to pages 142–143 of the *Trabajo de curso* section and page 146 of the *Leer y escribir* section, at the back of the Student's Book, where the film director Pedro Almodóvar and the actor Brad Pitt are profiled. See also pages 147 (for Pedro Almodóvar) and 32 (for Brad Pitt) of these Teacher's Notes for more information and answers to exercises.

módulo 8

3 ¿Cómo fue?

(Student's Book pages 104–105)

Main topics and objectives

- Saying what you thought of a film or event
- Discussing what you did and what it was like

Grammar

- The preterite and the use of different tenses

Skills

Using opinions and different tenses in your written work

Key language

¿Cómo fue el partido/la película (etc.)?
¡Fue superfantástico/a /fenomenal/emocionante/
estupendo/a!
¡Lo pasé bomba! ¡Lo pasamos bomba!
Fue regular/bastante bien/No estuvo mal.
¡Qué desastre!/¡Fue muy aburrido!

¡Lo pasé fatal!
¿Adónde fuiste? Fui/fuimos al parque/a la discoteca/a una fiesta (etc.)
¿Cuándo? Fui/fuimos el lunes/ayer/la semana pasada (etc.)
¿Con quién fuiste? Fui/salí con mi amigo/mis padres (etc.)
¿Qué hiciste?
Jugué al (tenis)/Leí una revista.
Bailamos/comimos calamares/escuchamos música/vimos una película (etc.)
¿Qué tal fue? (No) me gustó porque la música era muy aburrida/las entradas nos costaron €10 (etc.)

Resources

Cassette C, side 1
CD 3, track 10
Cuaderno pages 48–52
Gramática 7.6, page 173

1a Lee las reacciones. ¿Son , o ?

Reading. Reactions to recent social events. Students categorise the reactions under three headings, according to whether they are positive, negative or neutral.

Answers

😃	🙁	😐
¡Fue superfantástico!	¡Qué desastre!	Fue regular.
¡Lo pasé bomba!	¡Fue muy aburrido!	No estuvo mal.
¡Fue fenomenal!	Lo pasé muy mal	Fue bastante bien.
¡Fue emocionante!		

1b Escucha las opiniones de la gente. Copia y completa la tabla. (1–6)

Listening. Reactions to recent social events. Students copy the grid. They then listen and note down the activity or event each speaker refers to and categorise the reactions under the same three headings as in **1a**. Teachers may wish to give students aural practice of the reactions in **1a**, before tackling **1b**.

➕ Able students complete the 'extra information' column of the grid with any other details they spot.

Tapescript

1 – Fue regular la película. Tom Cruise es bueno pero no fue una de sus mejores películas.

2 – Gabrielle fue fantástica. El concierto fue fenomenal. Lo pasé bomba.

3 – Lo pasé fatal. El Barça perdió dos goles a cero. La entrada me costó €40. €40 ¡Qué desastre!

4 – El ballet fue muy emocionante. Me gustó muchísimo la música.

5 – La comedia no fue muy divertida. Pero fue bastante bien.
6 – Me encantó la fiesta. ¡Fue superfantástica!

Answers

¿Actividad?	😃	🙁	😐	Información extra
Película			✓	Tom Cruise es bueno pero no fue una de sus mejores películas.
Concierto	✓			Gabrielle fue fantástica.
Partido de fútbol		✓		El Barça perdió dos goles a cero. La entrada costó €40.
Ballet	✓			Me gustó muschísimo la música.
Comedia			✓	No fue muy divertida pero fue bastante bien.
Fiesta	✓			

1c Haz un diálogo con tu compañero/a.

Speaking. Reactions to recent social events. Students use the picture prompts to ask and answer questions about what events were like. Teachers may wish to give students oral practice of the key phrases in **1a**, before tackling the pairwork activity.

2a Empareja las actividades con las frases correctas. ¿Puedes traducir las frases al inglés?

Reading. Discussing what you did. Students match the phrases to the pictures, then translate them into English.

Answers

1 C	**2** A	**3** E	**4** D	**5** B

1 I went to the cinema with my parents. **2** My friends and I went to a football match. **3** I played tennis in the afternoon. **4** I listened to music in my bedroom. **5** I read a magazine about cars.

Gramática

A brief reminder about which page to go to to revise the preterite.

2b Lee el texto y contesta a las preguntas.

Reading. An account of an event. Students read the e-mail and answer questions in Spanish.

Answers

1 Fue a un concierto. **2** Fue con su hermano. **3** Le gustó el concierto – ¡fue estupendo! **4** Después fueron a cenar en una hamburguesería. **5** Van a ir a otro concierto.

¡Ojo!

This draws students' attention to the opinions and range of tenses used in the text in **2b** and why this makes it a good model piece of examination written work.

2c Usa el modelo para escribir una descripción de un espectáculo.

Writing. An account of a past event. Students use the writing frame to describe a past event and give their opinion of it. Once corrected, this piece of work could be added to student's *fichero personal*.

Topics revised:

- Giving opinions about shopping
- Shopping for clothes and food
- Asking for information in a department store
- Discussing free-time activities
- Discussing famous people
- Buying tickets
- Arranging to go out

Modúlo 7 De compras

Conversación

A general conversation about shopping experiences, giving opportunities for the use of a range of tenses and giving opinions. The general advice at the top of page 108 encourages students to use expressions such as *lo bueno/malo/importante es que …*

Juegos de rol 1, 2 and 3

Three shopping role-plays, one on buying clothes, one on getting information in a department store and one on buying food in a market. The general guidance at the top of page 108 encourages students to find alternative ways of saying things, if they cannot say exactly what is on the role-play card.

Modúlo 8 De juerga

Conversaciones 1 and 2

Two general conversations, the first about free-time activities, the second about a famous person. The first requires using a range of tenses, and both require students to give opinions and back them up with reasons.

Juegos de rol 1 and 2

Two role-plays, the first on buying cinema tickets and the second on arranging to go to a concert with a friend.

Presentación

A choice of two presentations:
A concert or sporting event
Preferred weekend activities

The guidance at the top of page 108 encourages students to use a range of vocabulary and structures and to always back up opinions with reasons.

Trabajo de curso
(Student's Book pages 140–143)

There are two tasks linked to this module. (i) *Crítica de una película:* A model text reviewing a film, followed by comprehension exercises and a coursework-style assignment. The *Ayuda* section offers guidance on using a variety of tenses (including the conditional – covered more fully in Module 10), as well as on how students can use conjunctions to enhance their coursework.

1 Traduce al inglés las palabras en verde del texto.
Answers

películas	films
dirigida por	directed by
basada en	based on
escrito por	written by
demasiada violencia	too much violence
cuenta la historia de	tells the story of
interpretado por	played by
los actores son muy buenos	the actors are very good
lo mejor de la película es la banda sonora	the best thing about the film is the soundtrack

2 ¿Verdad o mentira?
Answers

1 verdad
2 mentira – en vídeo en casa con su hermana
3 mentira – es una película de acción y de aventuras
4 verdad
5 mentira – no le gusta ver demasiada violencia
6 mentira – visita una isla en Tailandia
7 mentira – cuenta la historia de un grupo de turistas de varias nacionalidades
8 mentira – los actores son muy buenos, especialmente Leonardo Di Caprio
9 verdad
10 mentira – compré el CD
11 mentira – va a ver *Trainspotting* en DVD

3 Empareja las frases españolas con las inglesas.
Answers

1 c	2 j	3 h	4 i	5 n	6 a	7 m	8 d	9 e
10 k	11 b	12 f	13 g	14 l				

(ii) A text about a famous Spanish-speaking person (Pedro Almodóvar), followed by comprehension questions and a coursework-style assignment to write about another famous Spanish speaker. The *Ayuda* section includes guidance for students on using time markers and conjunctions to enhance their coursework, and how to incorporate the use of different tenses in their writing.

1 Empareja el español con el inglés.
Answers

1 c	2 a	3 f	4 h	5 e	6 b	7 i	8 d	9 g

2 Lee el texto a la página 143 y busca estas expresiones en español:
Answers

1 una persona que me gusta mucho   2 desde hace más de veinte años   3 nació   4 tiene (los ojos castaños)   5 llevaba el pelo largo   6 cuando tenía treinta y un años   7 hizo (su primera película)   8 ganó   9 continuará   10 escribirá

3 Contesta a las preguntas en español.
Answers

1 Es director de cine.   2 Es famoso desde hace más de veinte años.   3 Nació el 24 de septiembre en Calzada de Calatrava.   4 Hay cinco personas en su familia.   5 Vive en Madrid.   6 (To be worked out from his date of birth – 24/9/1951)   7 Es trabajador, ambicioso y alegre.

Leer y escribir
(Student's Book pages 160–161)

Leer 1 Empareja las frases con los dibujos.

Students match a series of sentences about what people did to the pictures.

Answers

1 B	2 F	3 A	4 E	5 C	6 D

Escribir 2 Escribe seis frases sobre el tiempo libre. Usa el pretérito y anoche/ayer etc.

Students write six sentences about leisure events in the past.

Leer 3 Lee los anuncios. Copia la frase correcta.

Advertisements for four leisure facilities or events in Spain, followed by a multiple-choice exercise.

Answers (in bold)

1 Aquópolis está abierto **durante el verano**.
2 Para ir al polideportivo **no es obligatorio ser miembro**.
3 Los Multicines ofrecen descuento **cada lunes**.
4 La fiesta es **a principio de mayo**.

Escribir 4 Imagina que fuiste al polideportivo La Ermita. Escribe un anuncio para atraer jugadores.

Students design an advertisement for La Ermita, using ICT if possible, following the prompts in Spanish.

page 48

page 49

1a

Answers

1 Los sábados por la noche bailo en la discoteca.
2 Me encanta escuchar música: prefiero el R & B.
3 Voy al cine con mio amigos.
4 Juego con el ordenador por la tarde.
5 Leo mucho porque es informativo y divertido.
6 En mi tiempo libre me gusta hacer deporte: el ciclismo y el monopatín.

1b

Answers

Juego/Me gusta jugar al …	Practico/Hago/Me gusta practicar/Me gusta hacer el/la …
fútbol	deporte
tenis	boxeo
tenis de mesa	natación
baloncesto	gimnasia
rugby	atletismo
hockey	equitación
squash	vela
	patinaje
	monopatín

2

Answers

a a la una y cuarto	la piscina
b a las cinco menos cuarto	del cine
c al mediodía	del restaurante
d a las seis y media	en mi casa

3a

Answers

● Vienes al cine con nosotros?
○ Depende. ¿Qué quieres ver?
● Vamos a ver una película de acción.
○ Sí vale, me gustan las películas de acción.

3b

Answers

Caller's name	Invitation to do what?	Meet where?	Meet when?
1 Alfonso	football match	in front of the stadium ticket office	2.45
2 Manuela	to see an adventure film	next to the cinema	3.30

4a

Answers

a 3	**b** 7	**c** 4	**d** 6	**e** 8	**f** 1	**g** 5	**h** 2

page 50

4b

Answers

- ● Buenas tardes.
- ○ Quisiera tres **entradas** para Monsters, Inc.
- ● ¿Para qué sesión?
- ○ Para la **sesión** de las ocho.
- ● Vale
- ○ ¿Cuánto es?
- ● €24.
- ○ ¿Hay **descuento** para estudiantes?
- ● Sí, si tiene un **carné** de estudiante son €18 en total.
- ○ Aquí tiene. ¿A quí hora **termina** la película?
- ● A las **siete**.

5a

Answers

a V	b F	c F	d V	e F	f F	g V	h V

page 51

Gramática

1

Answers

- **a** **El** lunes pasado fui a la discoteca.
- **b** Todo **los** martes vamos a jugar al fútbol.
- **c** **Los** miércoles voy a la piscina con mi hermana.
- **d** **El** primer jueves del mes compro una revista de moda.
- **e** Este año mi cumpleaños es **el** viernes.
- **f** **Los** sábados mis padres van de compras.
- **g** **Los** domingos vemos los deportes en la tele.

2

Answers (in bold)

- **a** **Bailo** cuando voy a la discoteca con mis amigos.
- **b** Me gusta **escuchar** música.
- **c** **Practico** natación pero prefiero **jugar** al tenis.
- **d** **Hago** muchas cosas durante la semana pero durante los domingos me encanta **leer**.
- **e** Odio **ver** la tele. Normalmente **salgo** con mis amigos.

3

Answers (in bold)

Presente	Pretérito
El lunes **juego** al balonmano. (On Mondays I play handball.)	El lunes **jugué** al balonmano. (On Monday I played handball.)
Voy al cine con mi familia. (I go to the cinema with my family.)	**Fui** al cine con mi familia. (I went to the cinema with my family.)
Por la noche, **como** con mi amiga. (In the evening, I eat with my friend.)	Por la noche, **comí** con mi amiga. (In the evening, I ate with my friend.)
Viajo por avión. (I travel by plane.)	**Viajé** por avión. (I travelled by plane.)
Tengo que ir de compras con mi madre. (I have to go shopping with my mother.)	**Tuve** que ir de compras con mi madre. (I had to go shopping with my mother.)
Después del colegio, **hago** muchos deberes. (After school I do a lot of homework.)	Después del colegio, **hice** muchos deberes. (After school I did a lot of homework.)
Bailo durante toda la noche en una discoteca. (I dance all night in a club.)	**Bailé** durante toda la noche en una discoteca. (I danced all night in a club.)
Veo la tele para relajarme. (I watch TV to relax.)	**Vi** la tele para relajarme. (I watched TV to relax.)

módulo 9 — *Yo*

(Student's Book pages 110–121)

Main topics and objectives	Grammar	Skills
Repaso (pp. 110–111) Describing and comparing people's personality	The comparative Adjective endings	Adjectival agreement
1 ¿Cómo eres? (pp. 112–113) Describing yourself, family and teachers Discussing the qualities of a good friend	Adjectives	Similarities between Spanish and English adjectives
2 Problemas (pp. 114–115) Discussing family relationships and problems at home	*Deber* Negatives	
3 La dependencia (pp. 116–117) Discussing attitudes towards smoking Discussing the dangers of drug dependency		
4 La calidad de vida (pp.118–119) Talking about environmental issues	*Se debe* + infinitive	

Key language

¿Cómo es tu mejor amigo/a /tu hermano/a /tu primo/a (etc.)? ¿Cómo eres? Es/soy (muy/bastante) ambicioso/a estúpido/a /feo/a gracioso/a/guapo/a /inteligente/serio/a /simpático/a tímido/a/trabajador(a).	(Antonio Banderas/mi profesor(a) de inglés) es más/menos (serio/a) que (Brad Pitt/mi profesor(a) de español). ¿Prefieres a (Britney) o a (Jennifer López)? Prefiero a (Britney) porque es más (inteligente) que (Jennifer López).
En general/creo que soy/es (honesto/a) pero un poco (hablador(a)). Soy siempre (generoso/a). De vez en cuando soy (perezoso/a). No soy nunca (agresivo/a). Mi defecto más importante es que soy egoísta. Activo/a /agradable/alegre/amable/antipático/a /cariñoso/a celoso/a /comprensivo/a /contento/a /cruel/desagradable/ extrovertido/a /leal/maleducado/a /nervioso/a /popular/ responsable/sensible/serio/a /sincero/a /tonto/a.	¿Cuáles son las características de un buen amigo? Un buen amigo debe ser (leal y comprensivo). Chico/a de (17 años) busca a un/a chico/a (guapo/a e inteligente). Busco a un amigo/a (sincero/a y paciente).
Tengo un problema. No me llevo bien con (mis padres) porque … … no me dejan fumar en casa/salir (durante la semana/ por la noche)/usar su coche. … no me entienden/no me dan mucho dinero. Estoy estresado/a /triste porque … … no tengo novio/novia/ muchos amigos/dinero.	… tengo que estudiar demasiado. … tengo muchos deberes. … no tengo tiempo para relajarme. … soy gordo/a. No sé que hacer. ¿Me puede ayudar? Debes tratar de hablar con tus padres/pensar en el futuro (etc.)
¿Estás a favor de/ en contra de fumar y por qué? No fumo porque es muy peligroso. Es dañino para la salud. Puede causar cáncer de pulmón y otras enfermedades. Causa mucha contaminación ambiental. Odio los cigarrillos – es un vicio terrible/muy malo No me gusta el olor, ni el aliento de los fumadores. Creo que cada persona tiene derecho a fumar. Pienso que debemos respetar las preferencias de los demás. Es genial fumar con tus amigos.	Tomar drogas (no) es … … una dependencia seria/una pérdida de dinero/una pérdida de tiempo. … peligroso/tonto y no se saben los efectos. … bueno para escaparse del estrés de la vida. … una manera de prolongar la noche y bailar mucho. Las drogas legales/ilegales/socialmente aceptadas. La droga más peligrosa es el alcohol. Provoca accidentes/peleas/robos/daños a propiedades públicas.
El problema más importante con el medio ambiente (en mi región/el mundo) es … … el desperdicio de energía/la basura del hogar/la contaminación acústica/la polución ambiental. ¿Qué se debe hacer para proteger al medio ambiente? Se debe …	… apagar las luces/comprar productos orgánicos/duchar en vez de tomar un baño/hacerse miembro de un grupo ecologista/reciclar (botellas/latas/papel)/viajar en (autobús/bicicleta). ¿Qué haces para mejorar el medio ambiente? Reciclo papel/Voy al colegio a pie (etc.)

Main topics and objectives

● Describing and comparing people's personality

Grammar

● The comparative
● Adjective endings

Skills

Adjectival agreement

Key language

¿Cómo es tu mejor amigo/a /tu hermano/a /tu primo/a (etc.)?
¿Cómo eres?
Es/soy (muy/bastante) ambicioso/a /estúpido/a /feo/a
/gracioso/a /guapo/a / inteligente/serio/a /simpático/a /tímido/a /trabajador(a).
(Antonio Banderas/mi profesor(a) de inglés) es más/menos (serio/a) que (Brad Pitt/mi profesor(a) de español).
¿Prefieres a (Britney) o a (Jennifer López)?
Prefiero a (Britney) porque es más (inteligente) que (Jennifer López.)

Resources

Cassette C, side 2
CD 3, track 10
Cuaderno pages 53–58
Gramática 3.3, page 168 and 3 page 167

1a Empareja el español con el inglés.

Reading. Adjectives. Matching exercise.

Answers

serio/a – serious   simpático/a – nice
inteligente – intelligent   estúpido/a – stupid
guapo/a – good-looking   feo/a – ugly
gracioso/a – funny   ambicioso/a – ambitious
tímido/a – shy   trabajador(a) – hard-working

1b Escucha las descripciones. ¿Cómo son las personas? (1–5)

Listening. Describing people. Most students should listen and note down both the person/people referred to and the relevant adjectives. This could be done in Spanish or in English.

R Teachers could provide less able students with a worksheet which has the people listed in one column and the adjectives in another, so that they can listen and match the person to the adjectives, to show comprehension.

Tapescript

1 – *¿Cómo es tu mejor amigo?*
   – *Es muy guapo y simpático también.*
2 – *¿Cómo es tu mejor amiga?*
   – *Mi amiga es inteligente y trabajadora.*
3 – *¿Cómo son tus primos?*
   – *No me gustan mis primos – son feos y estúpidos.*
4 – *¿Cómo eres?*
   – *Soy bastante tímido pero muy simpático.*
5 – *¿Cómo es tu hermana?*
   – *Es muy seria y ambiciosa.*

Answers

1 mejor amigo – guapo y simpático
2 mejor amiga – inteligente y trabajadora
3 primos – feos y estúpidos
4 tú – bastante tímido pero muy simpático
5 hermana – muy seria y ambiciosa

Ojo!
A reminder about adjective endings/agreement.

1c Túrnate con tu compañero/a. Describe a tu familia y a tus amigos.

Speaking. Describing people. Students work in pairs to ask and answer questions about what they, their friends and family members are like.

1d Escribe las descripciones de **1c**.

Writing. Describing people. Students create written descriptions of the people they talked about in **1c**. Once corrected, this could be added to students' *fichero personal*.

2a Lee las frases. En tu opinion, ¿son verdaderas ✓ o falsas ✗?

Reading. Comparing people. Students read a series of comparisons between their teachers and famous people and decide whether they agree with each one. Teachers may wish to refer students to the *Gramática* on the comparative, before tackling this activity.

Gramática

The comparative.

2b ¿A quién prefieren? ¿Por qué? (1–6)

Listening. Comparing people. Students listen to the speakers and must note down in Spanish whom each one prefers and why.

R Less able students could be given a worksheet with the information in four columns, as follows, and simply link up the information to demonstrate comprehension:

Brad Pitt	es	más	guapo/a	que	Antonio Banderas
Britney		menos	seria		Madonna

Tapescript

1 – Prefiero a mi profesor de español porque es más simpático que mi profesor de geografía.
2 – Prefiero a mi hermana porque es más graciosa que mi hermano.
3 – Prefiero a Brad Pitt porque es más guapo que Antonio Banderas.
4 – Prefiero a Britney porque es menos seria que Madonna.
5 – Prefiero a mi primo porque es menos tímido que mi prima.
6 – Prefiero a Penélope Cruz porque es más guapa que Buffy.

Answers

1 Profesor de español, más simpático
2 Hermana, más graciosa
3 Brad Pitt, más guapo
4 Britney, menos seria
5 Primo, menos tímido
6 Penélope Cruz, más guapa

2c Haz diálogos con tu compañero/a.

Speaking. Saying who you prefer and why. Students work in pairs to ask one another questions about which celebrities they prefer and why, following the model on the page.

2d Escribe unas comparaciones de dos profesores, dos estrellas de pop, dos actores, dos deportistas y dos miembros de tu familia.

Writing. Comparing people. Students write comparisons between pairs of people, using the categories given and following the example on the page.

1 ¿Cómo eres?

(Student's Book pages 112–113)

Main topics and objectives

- Describing yourself, family and teachers
- Discussing the qualities of a good friend

Grammar

Adjectives

Skills

Similarities between Spanish and English adjectives

Key language

En general/creo que soy/es (honesto/a) pero un poco (hablador(a)).
Soy siempre (generoso/a).
De vez en cuando soy (perezoso/a).
No soy nunca (agresivo/a).

Mi defecto más importante es que soy egoísta.
Activo/a /agradable/alegre/amable/antipático/a /cariñoso/a /celoso/a/ comprensivo/a /contento/a /cruel/desagradable/extrovertido/a /leal/ maleducado/a /nervioso/a /popular/responsable /sensible/serio/a /sincero/a /tonto/a.
¿Cuáles son las características de un buen amigo?
Un buen amigo debe ser (leal y comprensivo).
Chico/a de (17 años) busca a un(a) chico/a (guapo/a e inteligente).
Busco a un amigo/a (sincero/a y paciente).

Resources

Cassette C, side 2
CD 3, track 11
Cuaderno pages 53–58

1a Identifica si los adjetivos son positivos o negativos. Haz dos listas. Escribe el inglés con la ayuda de un diccionario.

Reading. Adjectives. Students could work on the list of adjectives in pairs or groups. They should first try to work out the meaning of as many as possible, without referring to a dictionary or the glossary at the back of the Student's Book. Many are cognates or near-cognates, but before they begin, teachers should draw students' attention to the *Ojo!* feature, which lists some 'false friends'. Once they have established all the meanings, students should categorise the adjectives under two lists – positive and negative. If, as anticipated, students feel that some adjectives (such as *serio*) could fall into either category, they could draw up a third column, labelled *Depende*.

Answers

Positivo	Negativo	Depende (answers may vary)
activo/a	agresivo/a	extrovertido/a
agradable	antipático/a	hablador(a)
alegre	celoso/a	sensible
amable	cruel	serio/a
cariñoso/a	desagradable	
comprensivo/a	egoísta	
generoso/a	maleducado/a	
honesto/a	nervioso/a	
leal	perezoso/a	
popular	tonto/a	
responsable		
sincero/a		

1b Pablo describe a seis miembros de su familia. Apunta los adjetivos.

Listening. Describing the personality of family members. Students note down the adjectives used to describe each family member. Depending on students' ability, they could be expected to listen to all, a few, or just one of the adjectives for each person.

R Teachers could give students a partially completed list (on the board, an OHT or worksheet), so that the activity becomes a gap-filling exercise. A list of the missing words could be provided for extra support.

+ Able students could listen out for and note down any extra information about Pablo's family members, such as age, marital status, etc.

Tapescript

– *Bueno, empezando con mi hermanito, Paco. Paco tiene diez años y habla todo el tiempo. Es tan hablador que no se puede ver la televisión. Es simpático y alegre pero a veces tonto.*
Mi hermana mayor Merche – Mercedes – tiene veinte años y me entiendo bien con ella. Es muy cariñosa e inteligente. Va a la universidad y estudia medicina. Es muy trabajadora y comprensiva.
Mi hermana menor se llama Ana. Tiene catorce años. Ésta celosa de mi hermana mayor. Es perezosa y no trabaja en el instituto. Es un poco egoísta. No me entiendo bien con ella en este momento.
Mi abuelo Fede es un caso. Es muy popular. Es gracioso, sensible y generoso. Tiene sesenta y dos años pero su carácter es muy atractivo.
Mi padre, Gabriel, es muy activo y bastante inteligente. Es responsable pero a veces un poco agresivo.
Mi madre se llama Pepita. Es tímida y muy nerviosa. Es seria todo el tiempo.
Mi abuela María tiene sesenta años y es muy extrovertida. Le amo mucho.

Answers

> Paco – hablador, simpático, alegre, tonto.
> Merche – cariñosa, inteligente, trabajadora, comprensiva.
> Ana – celosa, perezosa, egoísta.
> Fede – popular, gracioso, sensible, generoso.
> Gabriel – activo, inteligente, responsable, agresivo.
> Pepe – tímido, nervioso, seria.
> María – extrovertida

1c Escoge un profesor. Haz una descripción y tu compañero/a tiene que adivinar quién es.

Speaking. Describing teachers. Pairwork. One student describes a teacher and the other must guess who it is. Teachers may wish to remind students about adjective agreement before they tackle this activity, and ensure students know how irregular adjectives such as *egoísta* and *cruel* work.

1d Completa las siguientes frases con tus características.

Writing. Describing yourself. The useful phrases provided give students a framework for describing themselves and show them how to enhance their writing. Once corrected, this piece of work could be added to students' *fichero personal*.

2a Lee las descripciones de una revista. Contesta a las preguntas.

Reading. The characteristics of a best friend. Students read two texts about people's best friends and answer questions in Spanish.

Answers

> **1** Se llama Ángela. **2** Se llama Pedro. **3** Debe ser honesto, leal y sensible. **4** Debe ser generoso, honesto y nunca cruel. **5** Es simpática, graciosa y nunca es tonta. **6** Es comprensivo, amable, extrovertido. No es nunca egoísta ni agresivo.

2b Túrnate con tu compañero/a. Contesta a las preguntas.

Speaking. Describing your best friend. Students work in pairs to answer questions about their best friends and the qualities of a best friend. The prompts on the page show them how to start their answers.

2c Escribe una descripción de tu mejor amigo/a.

Writing. Describing your best friend. Students use the texts in **2a** as a model for writing about their own best friend.

R Less able students could be given a version of one of the texts in **2a**, with the sections to be changed highlighted or gapped.

3a Lee los anuncios a la derecha. ¿A quién prefieres?

Reading. Adverts for friends. Students read the four adverts and decide who they prefer and why. They should be familiar with the verb *buscar* from instructions for activities throughout the Student's Book, but teachers should ensure that students do understand this word, as it is used in all the adverts.

3b Escribe un anuncio para ti y para tu amigo/a.

Writing. Adverts for friends. Students use the adverts in **3a** as models for writing an advert for themselves and for one of their friends.

R Less able students might benefit from being given a framework, in the form of a partially completed advert to complete (e.g. with just the adjectives to be added by students).

Main topics and objectives

● Discussing family relationships and problems at home

Grammar

Deber
Negatives

Key language

Tengo un problema.
No me llevo bien con (mis padres) porque …
… no me dejan fumar en casa/salir (durante la semana/por la noche)/usar su coche.
… no me entienden/no me dan mucho dinero.

Estoy estresado/a /triste porque …
… no tengo novio/novia/ muchos amigos/dinero.
… tengo que estudiar demasiado.
… tengo muchos deberes.
… no tengo tiempo para relajarme.
… soy gordo/a.
No sé que hacer.
¿Me puede ayudar?
Debes tratar de hablar con tus padres/pensar en el futuro (etc.)

Resources

Cassette C, side 2
CD 3, track 12
Cuaderno pages 53–58

1a Lee la carta y encuentra el español para estas frases.

Reading. Problem page letter. Students read the letter about a teenager's problems with his parents and find the Spanish for the key phrases listed.

R The text is quite demanding and teachers might prefer to give less able students a version of the text with the phrases to be found highlighted and numbered, so that students can simply select the correct phrase and note down letters and numbers.

Answers

> **a** No me llevo bien con mis padres.   **b** Tengo que estudiar demasiado.   **c** No tengo tiempo para relajarme.
> **d** Mis padres no me dejan salir durante la semana.
> **e** No sé qué hacer.   **f** ¿Me puede ayudar?

1b Contesta a las preguntas en inglés.

Reading. Problem page letter. A follow-up exercise to 1a, in which students have to demonstrate more in-depth understanding of the text, by answering questions in English.

Answers

> **1** Because he doesn't get on with his parents and he has to study too much.
> **2** He does his homework.
> **3** He has to study after school.
> **4** No.
> **5** When he goes to university.
> **6** Because he doesn't have any/he is an only child.

1c Escribe una respuesta a Pablo. Escoge tres frases apropiadas.

Writing. Answering a problem page letter. Students choose three phrases from the list provided, to write an answer to Pablo's letter. Students obviously need to fully understand all the phrases given before

tackling the writing task. They could spend a few minutes, in pairs, working out what each one means, then report back to the class.

1d Escucha los problemas de estos tres jóvenes y escoge la imagen correcta. ¿Puedes apuntar información extra?

Listening. Describing problems at home. Students listen to each speaker describing a problem at home and find the correct picture.

✛ Able students could note down any extra information that they hear.

Tapescript

1 – Me llamo Rosa y el problema es que mis padres no me dan mucho dinero. No hay mucho empleo en el pueblo y no tengo trabajo. Mis padres me dan €20 al mes que no es suficiente. Me compran la ropa y otras cosas pero quiero ser más independiente. Ayudo en casa: preparo las comidas, pongo la mesa, paso la aspiradora … No es que sea perezosa yo.

2 – Me llamo Ángel y no estoy contento. Mis padres no me dejan fumar en casa. Tengo mi dormitorio y abro las ventanas, pero no me dejan. Dicen que afecta mi salud y que es tonto. Yo fumo en la calle y con mis amigos. ¿Por qué no me dejan fumar en casa?

3 – Me llamo Sebastián y me encantan los coches y tengo ganas de conducir. Pero mis padres no me dejan usar su coche. Mis amigos saben conducir pero yo no puedo. Es injusto.

Answers

> **1** C   **2** B   **3** A

1e Escribe una carta a Tía Dolores.

Writing. Describing problems at home. Students use the key language grid to write their own problem page letter.

3 La dependencia

(Student's Book pages 116–117)

Main topics and objectives

- Discussing attitudes towards smoking
- Discussing the dangers of drug dependency

Key language

¿Estás a favor de/en contra de fumar y por qué?
No fumo porque es muy peligroso.
Es dañino para la salud.
Puede causar cáncer de pulmón y otras
enfermedades.
Causa mucha contaminación ambiental.
Odio los cigarrillos – es un vicio terrible/muy malo.
No me gusta el olor, ni el aliento de los fumadores.
Creo que cada persona tiene derecho a fumar.
Pienso que debemos respetar las preferencias de los
demás.

Es genial fumar con tus amigos.
Tomar drogas (no) es …
… una dependencia seria/una pérdida de dinero/una
pérdida de tiempo.
… peligroso/tonto y no se saben los efectos.
… bueno para escaparse del estrés de la vida.
… una manera de prolongar la noche y bailar mucho.
Las drogas legales/ilegales/socialmente aceptadas.
La droga más peligrosa es el alcohol.
Provoca accidentes/peleas/robos/daños a propiedades
públicas.

Resources

Cassette C, side 2
CD 3, track 13
Cuaderno pages 53–58

1a Lee las opiniones de los jóvenes. ¿Están a favor, en contra de o sólo toleran fumar?

Reading. Attitudes towards smoking. Students can either write a sentence summarising each person's view (as in the example), or categorise each person's attitude under one of three headings (*a favor, en contra, toleran*). Students could work in pairs or groups to establish the meaning of each phrase, using dictionaries or the glossary at the back of the Student's Book as a last resort.

Answers

A favor: Alejandro.
En contra: Santiago, Sarah, Paco, Pili, Josefa.
Toleran: Julia, Antonio.

1b ¿Quién habla? (1–8)

Listening. Attitudes towards smoking. Students must relate what they hear to the attitudes expressed in **1a** and work out who each speaker is.

Tapescript

1 – *No fumo porque es muy peligroso. Hay el riesgo de cáncer de pulmón y otras enfermedades.*
2 – *Odio los cigarrillos – es un vicio terrible.*
3 – *Yo no fumo porque es malo para la salud.*
4 – *Fumo. Me gusta fumar porque es una actividad social – lo hago con mis amigos.*
5 – *Creo que cada persona puede fumar si quiere hacerlo. Es su derecho.*
6 – *El problema es que huele muy mal y el aliento de los fumadores es asqueroso.*
7 – *No fumo, pero pienso que debemos respetar a otros si quieren hacerlo. Cada uno tiene sus preferencias.*
8 – *No fumo porque causa mucha contaminación ambiental.*

Answers

1 Josefa	**2** Santiago	**3** Paco	**4** Alejandro	**5** Julia
6 Pili	**7** Antonio	**8** Sarah		

1c Haz una encuesta para saber si los miembros de tu clase están a favor de o en contra de fumar y por qué?

Speaking. Class survey on attitudes towards smoking. The example on the page shows students how to prepare a grid to record the findings of their survey. Students could include a *toleran* column, if they wish. Teachers may wish to give students oral practice of the questions in **1c** and the key language from **1a**, before tackling the survey. Students could use ICT to present the findings of their survey in graph or pie chart form.

1d Escribe un artículo sobre fumar.

Writing. Smoking. Students write a short piece in response to three questions about smoking. They should be encouraged to borrow and adapt key phrases from **1a**, above.

2a Lee este artículo sobre la droga. Contesta a las preguntas en inglés.

Reading. The problems of drug dependency. Students read the article and answer questions in English. Much of the vocabulary consists of cognates or near-cognates, and other key vocabulary is listed on the page.

Answers

1 Tea, coffee, chocolate, some fizzy drinks, tobacco, alcohol and medicines such as aspirin.
2 Marijuana, cocaine, heroin, LSD and ecstasy.
3 Alcohol.
4 It can cause death, accidents, fights, robberies and damage to public property.
5 At the age of 16.
6 At the age of 18½.

2b Diseña un póster para prevenir a los jóvenes contra las drogas.

Writing. The dangers of drug dependency. Students design an anti-drugs poster, using the key language grid for support and ideas. They could use ICT to make their poster eye-catching, incorporating different fonts, colours and clipart.

Main topics and objectives

● Talking about environmental issues

Grammar

● *Se debe* + infinitive

Key language

El problema más importante con el medio ambiente (en mi región/el mundo) es …
… el desperdicio de energía/la basura del hogar/la contaminación acústica/la polución ambiental.
¿Qué se debe hacer para proteger al medio ambiente?

Se debe …
… apagar las luces/comprar productos orgánicos/ducharse en vez de tomar un baño/hacerse miembro de un grupo ecologista/reciclar (botellas/latas/papel)/viajar en (autobús/bicicleta).
¿Qué haces para mejorar el medio ambiente?
Reciclo papel/Voy al colegio a pie. (etc.)

Resources

Cassette C, side 2
CD 3, track 14
Cuaderno pages 53–58

1a Empareja las imágenes con las frases correctas.

Reading. Environmental issues. Students match the pictures to the phrases. Although the language is new, they should look for 'clue' words which they recognise or can guess, such as *polución, energía, contaminación* and *acústica*. This should enable them to work out which phrase goes with at least three of the pictures and to work the fourth one out by a process of elimination.

Answers

A La polución ambiental.	**B** La basura del hogar
C El desperdicio de energía	**D** La contaminación acústica

1b Lee los consejos sobre la protección del medio ambiente. Escucha y escribe la letra correcta. (1–6)

Listening. Tackling environmental problems. Students note down the letter of the picture which matches what each speaker says they do for the environment. Each picture is also labelled with a phrase using *se debe …* This construction is explained in the *Gramática* on the opposite page.

Tapescript

1 – ¿Qué hace usted para el medio ambiente?
– Yo voy en bicicleta cuando puedo o voy andando.
2 – ¿Le importa el medio ambiente?
– Sí, mucho. Soy miembro de Greenpeace. Creo que es muy importante protestar.
3 – ¿Qué hace usted para el medio ambiente?
– Yo hago la compra en el mercado. Prefiero los productos orgánicos.
4 – Hablando del medio ambiente, ¿qué haces tú para mejorarlo?
– No hago mucho pero yo me ducho por la mañana porque se usa menos agua.
5 – ¿Haces algo para mejorar el medio ambiente?
– Cuando salgo de casa, apago las luces para usar menos electricidad.
6 – ¿Qué hace usted para el medio ambiente?
– Pues, no tiramos las botellas a la basura. Las reciclamos.

Answers

1 C	2 F	3 E	4 B	5 D	6 A

1c Túrnate con tu compañero/a. Contesta a la pregunta.

Speaking. Saying what you do to improve the environment. Teachers may wish to give students oral practice of key phrases used by the speakers in **1b** above, before students ask and answer the question.

1d Lee el mensaje electrónico y escribe una respuesta.

Writing. Environmental issues. Students read the e-mail from Paco and write a reply, answering his questions.

Gramática

Se debe + infinitive.

1e Lee y haz la encuesta de una revista española. ¿Haces lo que debes para proteger al medio ambiente?

Reading. Magazine-style quiz about helping the environment. Students do the quiz and look at the results, to find out how environmentally friendly they are.

Teachers may be interested to know that further material on discussing environmental issues is available on pages 144–145 of the *Trabajo de curso* section, at the back of the Student's Book. (See below, in these Teacher's Notes).

A formal letter about protecting the environment, followed by comprehension exercises and a coursework-style assignment to write a similar letter.

Trabajo de curso

(Student's Book pages 144–145)

The *Ayuda* section explains how to set out, begin and end a formal letter, as well as how to incorporate different tenses and helpful expressions for enhancing a piece of coursework.

1 Lee el texto y traduce al inglés las expresiones en verde.

Answers

miembro	member
basura	rubbish
botellas	bottles
latas	cans/tins
contaminación	pollution
afortunadamente	fortunately
crueldad	cruelty
perros maltratados	ill-treated dogs
gatos abandonados	abandoned cats
reciclar	recycle
comprar	buy
usar	use
trabajar	work
continuar	continue
controlar el tráfico	control the traffic
un programa de publicidad	a publicity campaign

2 Empareja las frases españolas con las inglesas.

Answers

1 b	**2** f	**3** a	**4** j	**5** g	**6** c	**7** h
8 d	**9** i	**10** e				

3 Busca las respuestas a las preguntas.

Answers

1 El grupo se llama GURELUR.
2 Está basado en Pamplona.
3 Basura en las calles, demasiado tráfico en el centro, contaminación del aire, la polución atmosférica.
4 El asma y otros problemas respiratorios.
5 Reciclar más, comprar productos reciclados, usar más el transporte público y la bicicleta y usar menos el coche, trabajar con el público y en los colegios.
6 La educación sobre el medio ambiente es esencial para futuras generaciones y la protección del planeta.
7 Controlar el tráfico en Pamplona y organizar un programa de publicidad contra abusos de animales domésticos; campañas de reciclaje.

módulo 9 · Leer y escribir

(Student's Book pages 162–163)

Leer 1 ¿A quién admiran? Empareja la calidad con la persona.

A series of statements about which celebrity people admire and why. Students match each quality to one of the texts.

Answers

Calidad	Persona
a does a lot for young people	Chris Eubanks
b quite ambitious	Britney
c always very friendly	Denise Lewis
d never lazy	David Beckham
e very talented	Britney
f hard-working	Denise Lewis
g serious and honest	Chris Eubanks
h modest	David Beckham

Escribir 2 Escribe sobre la persona a quien más admiras.

Students use the prompts to write about someone they admire.

Leer 3 Haz la encuesta.

A magazine-style quiz on the laws about alcohol. Students score points for each answer and then look at the results to see how much they knew.

Leer 4 Lee el anuncio y contesta a las preguntas en inglés.

An advertisement for a centre which young people can go to for help in giving up smoking. Students answer questions in English.

Answers

> **1** It is aimed at young people.
> **2** It says it will help you to give up smoking in five sessions of 30 minutes.
> **3** There are no injections or medicines; it doesn't make you put on weight; it takes away your dependence on tobacco; it has no side effects; you do not suffer any stress, bad temper, anxiety or discomfort.
> **4** Call 417 07 04 76 (the number at the bottom of the advertisement) or Guillerno de Lyon 71 6-5 34105 Toledo

Escribir 5 Escribe seis inconvenientes de fumar durante la adolescencia.

Students write six disadvantages of teenage smoking. They are referred back to the Student's Book page on smoking, for help, and encouraged to use a dictionary.

Cuaderno

(Workbook pages 53–58)

page 53

1

Answers

simpático	antipático
trabajador	perezoso
tímido	hablador
guapo	feo
serio	gracioso
egoísta	generoso
inteligente	estúpido
contento	triste

2b

Answers

1 Marco	**2** Cristina	**3** Rosa
4 Sofía	**5** Carlos	**6** Ronaldo

page 54

3

Answers

a 5	**b** 3	**c** 2	**d** 4	**e** 6	**f** 1

4a

Answers

años	amigos	ordenador	padres	dejan	feo
debe	colegio	más	estresado	exámenes	que

4b

Answers

a mentira	**b** mentira	**c** verdad	**d** mentira
e verdad	**f** verdad		

page 55

5b

Answers

1 c	**2** a	**3** c	**4** b

6a

Answers

a Se debe reciclar botellas.
b Se debe ducharse en vez de tomar un baño.
c Se debe usar menos el coche.
d Se debe apagar las luces.
e Se debe comprar productos verdes.
f Se debe hacerse miembro de un grupo ecológico.

6b

Answers

a You should recycle bottles.
b You should have a shower instead of having a bath.
c You should use the car less.
d You should switch off the lights.
e You should buy green products.
f You should become a member of an ecological group.

page 56

6c

Answers

1 She likes it a lot.
2 Her geography teacher.
3 They have been collecting rubbish.
4 They have to separate the plastic from the glass.
5 Because they are using organic products.
6 Around the district.
7 They are planning to become members of an ecological group.

Gramática

page 57

1

Answers

Masculine singular	Feminine singular	Masculine plural	Feminine plural
celoso	celosa	celosos	celosas
inteligente	inteligente	inteligentes	inteligentes
trabajador	trabajadora	trabajadores	trabajadoras
simpático	simpática	simpáticos	simpáticas
maleducado	maleducada	maleducados	maleducadas
contento	contenta	contentos	contentas
leal	leal	leales	leales
honesto	honesta	honestos	honestas
egoísta	egoísta	egoístas	egoístas
responsable	responsable	responsables	responsables
gracioso	graciosa	graciosos	graciosas
cariñoso	cariñosa	cariñosos	cariñosas

2

Answers

1 más rica que
2 más trabajadora que
3 menos activa que
4 menos deportista que
5 mayor que

3

Answers

1 se debe hacer
2 no se debe fumar
3 se debe hablar
4 se debe usar
5 no se debe tomar
6 se debe comer

El futuro

(Student's Book pages 122–135)

Main topics and objectives	Grammar	Skills
Repaso (pp. 122–123) The jobs people do and the good or bad points of different jobs Discussing strengths, weaknesses and preferences at school	Masculine and feminine versions of nouns	
1 Después de los exámenes (pp. 124–125) Discussing plans for further study, work or travel	The conditional tense	Answering all questions when replying to letters, emails or postcards
2 ¿Qué carrera? (pp. 126–127) Discussing career choices Understanding job adverts and drawing up a CV	The future tense	
3 Buscando un empleo (pp. 128–129) Applying for a job	The perfect tense	
4 La comunicación (pp.130–131) Making telephone calls.	Numbers Imperative	

Key language

Trabajo en una comisaría/un consultorio dental/un hospital/
   una empresa (grande)/obra/oficina/tienda (de modas).
Soy … actor/actriz/ama de casa/basurero/a/camarero/a/
   carnicero/a/cantante/carpintero/a/cartero/a/cocinero/a/
   comerciante/dentista/dependiente/a/electricista/enfermero/a/
   futbolista/granjero/a/ingeniero/a/mecánico/a/médico/a/
   obrero/a/peluquero/a/periodista/profesor(a)/policía/
   recepcionista/secretario/a.
Es un trabajo aburrido/bien pagado/difícil/interesante/
   que vale la pena.
¿En qué trabaja tu (hermana)?
Mi (hermana) trabaja en una oficina – es secretaria.
No trabaja. Está en paro.

Se me dan bien (las ciencias).
No se me dan bien (las asignaturas artísticas).
Tengo buenas/malas notas en (informática).
(No) me gusta (el colegio/el deporte).
(No) me gustan (todas las asignaturas/las asignaturas
   académicas/los ordenadores).
Me encantan (las asignaturas prácticas).
Estudio (diseño y tecnología).
En el futuro quiero/me gustaría ser
   (actor/actriz/enfermera/mecánico) porque …
… me parece un trabajo interesante/es bien pagado/paga
   bien/quiero ayudar a la gente/me gustan los coches (etc.)

¿Qué quieres hacer después de los exámenes?
Depués de los exámenes quiero/quisiera/me gustaría …
… buscar un empleo/continuar con mis estudios/
descansar/ir a la universidad/no hacer nada/
   tomar un año libre/viajar.
¿Cómo sería tu futuro ideal?

Iría a (los Estados Unidos).
Trabajaría (en una hamburguesería).
Compraría (mucha ropa).
Haría (los cursos de AS).
Estudiaría (español) en la universidad.
Quiero ser arquitecto/científico (etc.)

¿En el futuro en qué trabajarás y por qué?
¿En qué trabajarás durante las vacaciones?
Trabajaré como (mecánico/a/camionero/a/au-pair/niñera)
Quiero/me apetecería/encantaría/gustaría ser (deportista/
   secretaria/profesor(a) /policía), porque …
… quiero trabajar al aire libre/en una oficina.
… quiero ayudar a la gente.
… me gustaría/me interesa tener un trabajo con mucha
   variedad/responsabilidad.
… me gusta viajar.
… me gustan las cosas técnicas.
… me gustaría hacer algo útil en la vida.

Se busca/se necesita chico/a para (restaurante/trabajar los
   sábados).
Dominio de (francés).
Experiencia (no) es necesaria/Se valora experiencia
   (con coches).
Buena presencia e informes.
Interesados preséntense a …/escribir al apartado …
Nombres/Apellidos/Dirección/Fecha de nacimiento/
   Lugar de nacimiento/Educación/Experiencia laboral/
   Pasatiempos.
¿Cuando podrás trabajar?
Podré trabajar (en agosto).

Me gusta/prefiero …
… aceptar responsabilidades/trabajar solo/a/trabajar
   en equipo/la compañía de otra gente.
Me importa más el dinero que el trabajo.
Soy ambicioso/a/entusiasta/dinámico/a/una persona
   independiente.
Aprendo rápidamente.
En relación a su anuncio publicado en el (Diario Montañés) …
… del día 15 de (este mes/julio) …
… le escribo para solicitar el puesto de (recepcionista).
Tengo experiencia en este tipo de trabajo.
He trabajado (en una oficina) como (recepcionista) durante
   el verano pasado.

He hecho unas prácticas de (diez semanas) en
   (el Hotel Francia).
Adjunto mi currículum vitae.
Le saludo atentamente.
¿Qué asignaturas ha estudiado usted en el colegio? He
   estudiado (matemáticas, inglés …).
¿Le gustó el colegio?
Sí, mucho. Tengo muchos amigos y me gusta estar con
   gente.
¿Por qué quiere ser (au-pair)?
Porque me encantan (los niños).
¿Tiene experiencia?
Sí. Me ocupo de mis hermanos cuando trabaja mi madre.

¿Puedo hablar con (name)/el director?
(Name) no se encuentra. ¿Quiere dejar un mensaje?
¿De la parte de quién?
Por favor, que me llame al (number) lo más pronto posible.
Descuelgue el aurícular.
Espere el tono.
Utilice monedas de (5 céntimos).

Marque el código/el número.
Coloque las monedas en la ranura.
Quisiera información sobre el puesto de….
Es un trabajo a tiempo completo.
Mande su currículum vitae/una carta de presentación al…
¿Puede venir (mañana) para una entrevista?

Main topics and objectives

- The jobs people do and the good or bad points of different jobs
- Discussing strengths, weaknesses and preferences at school

Grammar

Masculine and feminine versions of nouns

Key language

Trabajo en una comisaría/un consultorio dental/un hospital/una empresa (grande)/obra/oficina/tienda (de modas).
Soy ... actor (actriz)/ama de casa/basurero/a /camarero/a /carnicero/a /cantante/carpintero/a /cartero/a /cocinero/a /comerciante/dentista/ dependiente/a /electricista/enfermero/a /futbolista/ granjero/a /ingeniero/a /mecánico/a /médico/a/ obrero/a /peluquero/a /periodista/profesor(a)/policía/ recepcionista/secretario/a.
Es un trabajo aburrido/bien pagado/difícil/
interesante/que vale la pena.
¿En qué trabaja tu (hermana)?
Mi (hermana) trabaja en una oficina – es secretaria.
No trabaja. Está en paro.
Se me dan bien (las ciencias).
No se me dan bien (las asignaturas artísticas).
Tengo buenas/malas notas en (informática).
(No) me gusta (el colegio/el deporte).
(No) me gustan (todas las asignaturas/las asignaturas académicas/los ordenadores).
Me encantan (las asignaturas prácticas).
Estudio (diseño y tecnología).
En el futuro quiero/me gustaría ser (actor/actriz /enfermera/mecánico) porque ...
... me parece un trabajo interesante/es bien pagado/paga bien/quiero ayudar a la gente/me gustan los coches (etc.)

Resources

Cassette C, side 2
CD 3, track 15
Cuaderno pages 59–63

1a Categoriza los trabajos, según tu opinión.

Reading. Jobs. Students categorise the list of jobs under five headings, according to their own opinion. Although the list is a substantial one, much of the vocabulary will already be familiar to students or can be easily guessed. Teachers could place students in groups and set them a challenge – to find out which group needs to look up the smallest number of words from the list in a dictionary or in the glossary at the back of the Student's Book. After students have completed the categorisation activity, the results could be pooled in a class survey, to find out, for example, which job most students consider interesting, which they think is the most worthwhile, etc.

1b ¿En qué trabajan? Escribe la letra correcta. (1–8)

Listening. Jobs. Students listen to people saying where they work and what job they do and note down the letter of the correct picture.

Tapescript

1 – *Trabajo en un hospital y ayudo a las personas. Soy enfermera.*
2 – *También trabajo en un hospital y trabajo con los enfermos. Soy médica.*
3 – *Trabajo en una tienda de modas. Soy dependienta.*
4 – *Trabajo en un colegio. Soy profesor.*
5 – *Trabajo en una empresa grande. Soy comerciante.*
6 – *Trabajo en un consultorio dental. Soy dentista.*
7 – *Trabajo en una comisaría. Soy policía.*

Answers

1 E	2 F	3 K	4 H	5 I	6 B	7 A

1c Rellena los espacios con el trabajo correcto.

Reading. Jobs. Students read the definitions and copy the sentences, filling each gap with the correct job.

Answers

1 mecánico/a   2 obrero/a   3 peluquero/a
4 secretario/a or comerciante
5 cocinero/a or camarero/a

1d Haz preguntas a tu compañero/a.

Speaking. Family members and jobs. Students work in pairs to ask and answer questions about family members' jobs. The key language box gives some useful phrases.

2a Lee las preferencias de los alumnos. ¿Cuál sería el trabajo más apropiado para cada persona?

Reading. Strengths, weaknesses and preferences at school. Students read what each person says and choose an appropriate career for them, from a list. Students should be encouraged to guess the meaning of new expressions such as *se me dan bien ...* and *tengo buenas notas en ...* Teachers may wish to revise school subjects (see Module 2) before beginning this activity, or before **2b**.

Answers

1 b	2 f	3 c	4 d	5 e	6 a

2b Prepara una presentación sobre tus preferencias.

Speaking. Strengths, weaknesses and preferences at school. Students adapt the phrases from **2a** to prepare a presentation about themselves.

2c Escribe sobre tus preferencias.

Writing. Students write about their strengths, weaknesses and preferences at school, using the key language support. They should be encouraged to use conjunctions and adjectives, to enhance their writing. Once corrected, this piece of work could be added to students' *fichero personal*.

2d ¿Qué van a hacer en el futuro y por qué? Toma apuntes en inglés. (1–6)

Listening. Future jobs. Students listen to people describing the jobs they would like to do in the future, and take notes in English.

R ✚ Some students could focus on simply noting down the jobs, whilst others could also note down the reasons the speakers give. NB The theme of career choices is extended in unit 2 of this module.

Tapescript

1 – *En el futuro quiero ser dentista porque me parece un trabajo interesante.*
2 – *En el futuro quisiera ser médico porque está bien pagado.*
3 – *En el futuro me gustaría ser futbolista porque me encanta el fútbol.*
4 – *En el futuro quiero ser enfermera porque quiero ayudar a la gente.*
5 – *En el futuro quiero ser mecánico porque me gustan los coches.*
6 – *En el futuro quisiera ser actor porque paga bien.*

Answers

1 Dentist, because it seems an interesting job.
2 Doctor, because it's well paid.
3 Footballer, because loves football.
4 Nurse, because wants to help people.
5 Mechanic, because loves cars.
6 Actor, because it's well paid.

1 Después de los exámenes

(Student's Book pages 124–125)

Main topics and objectives

● Discussing plans for further study, work or travel

Grammar

● The conditional tense

Skills

Answering all questions when replying to letters, emails or postcards

Key language

¿Qué quieres hacer después de los exámenes?
Depués de los exámenes quiero/quisiera/me gustaría …
… buscar un empleo/continuar con mis

estudios/descansar/ir a la universidad/no hacer nada/tomar un año libre/viajar.
¿Cómo sería tu futuro ideal?
Iría a (los Estados Unidos).
Trabajaría (en una hamburguesería).
Compraría (mucha ropa).
Haría (los cursos de AS).
Estudiaría (español) en la universidad.
Quiero ser arquitecto/científico (etc.)

Resources

Cassette C, side 2
CD 3, track 16
Cuaderno pages 59–63
Gramática 7.9, page 175

1a Empareja las opiniones con las imágenes correctas.

Reading. Plans for further study, work or travel. Students match the phrases to the pictures. Most of the phrases contain 'clue' words which students should recognise.

Answers

1 C	2 A	3 E	4 B	5 F	6 D

1b Escucha a los jóvenes y escribe la letra correcta. (1–6)

Listening. Plans for further study, work or travel. Students match what each speaker says to the pictures in 1a.

➕ Some students should be able to note down extra details from what each speaker says.

Answers

1 F	2 C	3 A	4 D	5 E	6 B

Tapescript

1 – *No me gusta en absoluto estudiar. Quiero salir del colegio a los 16 años y encontrar un trabajo.*

2 – *Tengo ganas de conocer a otros países. Quisiera ir a África.*

3 – *Me gustaría tomar un año de descanso antes de hacer otra cosa.*

4 – *No quiero estudiar ni viajar ni nada. Sólo quiero relajarme.*

5 – *Quiero ser dentista y por eso voy a vivir en Manchester para ir a la universidad.*

6 – *En realidad, me gusta mucho el colegio y he decidido hacer mis cursos de AS y A2.*

1c Haz una encuesta a los alumnos de tu clase. Muestra los resultados en un gráfico.

Speaking. Plans for the future. Students conduct a class survey on what their classmates are planning to do next year and beyond. The grid on the page shows them how to record their findings and the key language box gives them support in answering the question. Afterwards, students could use ICT to present their findings in graph or pie-chart form.

2a Lee el texto y después inventa un texto parecido.

Writing. Ideal future plans. The text uses a number of verbs in the conditional, which are highlighted. Students have come across *quisiera* and *me gustaría* previously and now the *Gramática* offers a summary of how this new tense works. Teachers could first work through the *Gramática* with students, then ask them to give the meaning of each of the highlighted verbs in the text, as well as checking their understanding of the detail of the writer's ideal future plans. Students then adapt the text to write about themselves. Teachers may wish to put a version of the text on the board or an OHT, with the sections to be changed highlighted or gapped, and work with the class to brainstorm for ideas, before students write their own text.

2b Lee el mensaje electrónico de Nestor. Contesta a las preguntas.

Reading. Future plans. Students read the e-mail and answer questions in Spanish. Students may need some guidance on answering the third question in the third person singular.

Answers

1 Se llama Nestor.
2 Vive en Almería.
3 Le gustaría tomar un año libre y viajar a Cuba. Después quisiera continuar sus estudios.
4 Quiere ser arquitecto.

2c Escribe una respuesta al mensaje electrónico.

Writing. Future plans. Students write a reply to the e-mail, answering Nestor's questions. The *¡Ojo!* feature reminds them that, in a similar task in an examination, they must answer all the questions to gain full marks.

módulo 10

2 ¿Qué carrera?

(Student's Book pages 126–127)

Main topics and objectives

- Discussing career choices
- Understanding job adverts and drawing up a CV

Grammar

- The future tense

Key language

¿En el futuro en qué trabajarás y por qué?
¿En qué trabajarás durante las vacaciones?
Trabajaré como (mecánico/a/camionero/a/
au-pair/niñera) …
Quiero/me apetecería/encantaría/gustaría ser
(deportista/secretaria/profesor(a)/policía),
porque …
… quiero trabajar al aire libre/en una oficina.
… quiero ayudar a la gente.
… me gustaría/me interesa tener un trabajo con
mucha variedad/responsabilidad.
… me gusta viajar.
… me gustan las cosas técnicas.
… me gustaría hacer algo útil en la vida.
Se busca/se necesita chico/a para
(restaurante/trabajar los sábados).
Dominio de (francés).
Experiencia (no) es necesaria/Se valora experiencia
(con coches).
Buena presencia e informes.
Interesados preséntense a …/escribir al apartado …
Nombres/Apellidos/Dirección/Fecha de
nacimiento/Lugar de nacimiento/Educación/
Experiencia laboral/Pasatiempos.
¿Cuando podrás trabajar?
Podré trabajar (en agosto).

Resources

Cassette C, side 2
CD 3, track 17
Cuaderno pages 59–63
Gramática 7.9, page 175

1a Empareja las dos partes de las frases. Hay varias posibilidades.

Writing. Career plans and reasons. Students match up sentence halves. The phrases use a mixture of the conditional and future tenses. The conditional was explained in unit 1 and the future tense is explained in the *Gramática* on this page. Teachers may wish to work through the *Gramática* with students, before tackling 1a. Once they have completed the matching exercise, students could be asked to identify which verbs are in the conditional and which are in the future and to explain how they would translate each one.

Answers

Various possibilities.

1b Escucha el texto y rellena los espacios con las palabras correctas.

Listening. Future career plans. Gap-filling task.

R Teachers may wish to provide students with a list of the missing words (with one or two 'distractors' if wished) on the board or an OHT.

Tapescript

– En el futuro trabajaré como **profesora** porque me **gustan** los niños. Yo sé que no ganaré **mucho** dinero pero no importa porque conoceré a gente **interesante** y es un trabajo **útil** que vale la pena. Mi hermano trabajará como piloto porque le gusta **viajar** y continuará sus estudios en la **universidad**.

Answers

(In bold in tapescript).

Gramática

The future tense.

1c Túrnate con tu compañero/a.

Speaking. Future career plans. Students work in pairs, asking and answering questions about what job they will do and why. They should draw on the key phrases in 1a above, adapting them if necessary.

2a Empareja los trabajos con los anuncios. ¿Cuál es el trabajo?

Reading. Job advertisements. Students match jobs to advertisements, using 'clue' words in the adverts to complete the task. Afterwards, students could look at the advertisements in more detail. They should be encouraged to use reading strategies such as predicting and inferring from context, to work out the meaning of expressions such as *Buena presencia e informes/Interesadas preséntense a …/Dominio de francés e inglés/Interesados escribir al apartado …/ Se valora experiencia.*

Answers

| **A** Peluquero/a | **B** Camarero/a | **C** Au-pair/niñera |
| **D** Mecánico/a | | |

2b Copia la ficha y pon los detalles en el orden correcto.

Reading. CV. Students copy out and complete the CV, using the details given.

Answers

Nombres: Francisco
Apellidos: San Giménez
Dirección: Calle Valencia, 23, 28025 Madrid, España
Fecha de nacimiento: 05/06/85
Lugar de nacimiento: Madrid
Educación: Español, inglés, matemáticas, ciencias, historia, tecnología, dibujo, informática
Experiencia laboral: Camarero en un restaurante chino, dependiente en una zapatería
Pasatiempos: Fútbol, lectura, música rock

2c Escribe tu propio currículum vitae.

Writing. CV. Students copy out the form in **2b** and write their own CV.

2d Escoge uno de los anuncios de **2a** e inventa un diálogo con tu compañero/a.

Speaking. Plans for holiday jobs. Students choose one of the jobs advertised in **2a** and work in pairs to ask and answer questions about what holiday job they will do, why and when they will do it.

2e Escribe sobre tus ideas para el futuro.

Writing. Students use and adapt the key phrases in **1a** to write about what job they will do in the future and why. Once corrected, this piece of work could be added to students' *fichero personal*.

3 Buscando un empleo

(Student's Book pages 128–129)

Main topics and objectives

● Applying for a job

Grammar

● The perfect tense

Key language

Me gusta/prefiero …
… aceptar responsabilidades/trabajar solo/a
/trabajar en equipo/la compañía de otra gente.
Me importa más el dinero que el trabajo.
Soy ambicioso/a /entusiasta/dinámico/a /una persona independiente.
Aprendo rápidamente.
En relación a su anuncio publicado en el (Diario Montañés) …
… del día (15) de (este mes/julio) …
… le escribo para solicitar el puesto de (recepcionista).
Tengo experiencia en este tipo de trabajo.
He trabajado (en una oficina) como (recepcionista)
durante el verano pasado.
He hecho unas prácticas de (diez semanas) en (el Hotel Francia).
Adjunto mi currículum vitae.
Le saludo atentamente.
¿Qué asignaturas ha estudiado usted en el colegio?
He estudiado (matemáticas, inglés …)
¿Le gustó el colegio?
Sí, mucho. Tengo muchos amigos y me gusta estar con gente.
¿Por qué quiere ser (au-pair)?
Porque me encantan (los niños).
¿Tiene experiencia?
Sí. Me ocupo de mis hermanos cuando trabaja mi madre.

Resources

Cassette C, side 2
CD 3, track 18
Cuaderno pages 59–63
Gramática 7.10, page 175

1a Lee las frases. Decide si son verdaderas o falsas para ti.

Reading. What you enjoy or look for in a job. Students decide whether each of the statements is true or false for them. After completing the exercise for themselves, students could then try to guess their partner's responses, write them down and compare notes, to see how well they know each other.

1b Lee la carta y encuentra las expresiones en español necesarias para estas frases.

Reading. Letter of application for a job. Students find the Spanish for key phrases in the letter. The letter includes several examples of the perfect tense, which is explained in the *Gramática* on the page.

Answers

a En relación a su anuncio publicado en …
b Le saludo atentamente.
c Estimado señor
d Tengo experiencia en este tipo de trabajo.
e Le escribo para solicitar el puesto de …

Gramática

The perfect tense. Teachers may wish to point out to students that they have met this tense before, in expressions such as *me he/se ha cortado el dedo* (Module 5, unit 2).

1c Escribe una carta para solicitar un puesto de trabajo en el hotel Sol y Sombra.

Writing. Applying for a job. Students use the advertisement and adapt the letter in **1b**, to write an application of their own.

R Some students might find this task easier if they were given a worksheet with a writing frame or sentence-building grid for creating the letter. The support sheet could include multiple options for such details as where the advert was seen and when, the type of job in question, whether or not the applicant has experience, where and when any such experience was gained, the qualities they would bring to the job, etc.

2a Escucha las dos entrevistas. ¿Quién es, Laura o Felipe? (1–7)

Listening. Job interviews. Students listen to two separate interviews for the same job and decide to which interviewee each of the statements on the page applies. Afterwards, students could be asked how well they thought each interviewee performed, which candidate should be given the job and why.

Tapescript

1 – ¿Cómo te llamas?
– Me llamo Laura.
– ¿Qué asignaturas ha estudiado usted en el colegio?
– Matemáticas, inglés, lengua, ciencias y educación física.
– ¿Le gustó el colegio?
– No mucho.
– ¿Por qué no?
– Porque los profesores no eran simpáticos. Había muchas reglas.

– *¿Por qué quiere ser au-pair?*
– *Porque quiero viajar.*
– *¿Tiene experiencia?*
– *No.*
– *¿Le gusta trabajar solo o en equipo?*
– *No lo sé. Depende.*
– *¿Le importa más el dinero o el trabajo?*
– *Bueno, el dinero es importante porque sin dinero no se puede hacer nada.*
– *¿Le importa la responsabilidad?*
– *Soy bastante responsable, creo yo.*
– *Gracias.*

2 – *¿Cómo te llamas?*
– *Me llamo Felipe.*
– *¿Qué asignaturas ha estudiado usted en el colegio?*
– *Muchas: matemáticas, inglés, ciencias – me gustó la biología, cocina – me gusta cocinar.*
– *¿Le gustó el colegio?*
– *Sí, mucho. Tengo muchos amigos y me gusta estar con gente.*
– *¿Por qué quiere ser au-pair?*
– *Porque me encantan los niños de todas las edades.*
– *¿Tiene experiencia?*
– *No, pero tengo hermanos y hermanas menores y me ocupo de ellos cuando trabaja mi madre.*
– *¿Le gusta trabajar solo o en equipo?*
– *De las dos maneras. Puedo trabajar sola pero también me gusta estar con otros.*
– *¿Le importa más el dinero o el trabajo?*
– *El trabajo. Si no te gusta el trabajo, el dinero no es importante.*
– *¿Le importa la responsibilidad?*
– *Soy responsable.*

Answers

1 Laura	**2** Felipe	**3** Felipe	**4** Laura	**5** Felipe
6 Laura	**7** Felipe			

2b Imagina que tienes una entrevista para un trabajo. Túrnate con tu compañero/a.

Speaking. Job interviews. Students work with a partner to create a job interview dialogue, using the model and prompts provided. If teachers wish, students could be given different attitudes or backgrounds for the interview (e.g. bored or unsympathetic interviewer, apathetic, overenthusiastic or negative interviewee.)

2c Escribe una entrevista parecida.

Writing. Students write a job interview dialogue, using the framework from **2b**.

4 La comunicación

(Student's Book pages 130–131)

Main topics and objectives

● Making telephone calls

Grammar

Numbers
Imperative

Key language

¿Puedo hablar con (name)/el director?
(Name) no se encuentra. ¿Quiere dejar un mensaje?
¿De la parte de quién?
Por favor, que me llame al (number) lo más pronto posible.
Descuelgue el aurícular.

Espere el tono.
Utilice monedas de (5 céntimos).
Marque el código/el número.
Coloque las monedas en la ranura.
Quisiera información sobre el puesto de....
Es un trabajo a tiempo completo.
Mande su currículum vitae/una carta de presentación al...
¿Puede venir (mañana) para una entrevista?

Resources

Cassette C, side 2
CD 3, track 19
Cuaderno pages 59–63
Gramática 7.11, page 177 and 10, page 180

1a Escucha los números de teléfonos españoles. ¿Son correctos? Cambia los errores.

Listening. Telephone numbers. Students listen and correct any mistakes in the phone numbers on the page. Before tackling this item, teachers should refer students to the *Información* feature, which explains how telephone numbers are given in Spanish. Teachers may also wish to precede this item with aural revision and practice of numbers up to 999 in Spanish.

Tapescript

1 – *Buenos días, Hotel Buenavista 957 43 22 04*
2 – *Buenas noches, Restaurante Caracol 954 14 65*
3 – *Buenos días, el Corte Inglés 952 78 45 51*
4 – *Buenas tardes, Bar La Bodega, 914 20 29 19*

Answers

Incorrect digits in the telephone numbers on the page are highlighted below. The correct numbers appear in the tapescript, above.
1 – Hotel Buenavista, 957 43 22 0**1**
2 – Restaurante Caracol 954 14 65 (number correct)
3 – El Corte Inglés 952 **7**7 45 5**0**
4 – Bar La Bodega 914 20 29 19 (number correct)

1b Lee y escucha la conversación. Encuentra las expresiones en español necesarias para estas frases.

Listening and reading. Telephone calls. Students listen to and read the telephone conversation and find the Spanish for key phrases.

Tapescript

– *Buenos días, Empresas Micanor.*
– *Buenos días, ¿puedo hablar con el señor Martínez?*
– *Lo siento. El señor Martínez no se encuentra aquí.*
  ¿Quiere dejar un mensaje?
– *Sí.*
– *¿De parte de quién?*

– *Me llamo señorita Grieve. Se escribe G-R-I-E-V-E. Por favor, que me llame al 913 21 30 64 lo más pronto posible.*
– *De acuerdo. Gracias. Adiós.*
– *Adiós.*

Answers

a Por favor, que me llame al ...   **b** Lo más pronto posible.
c ¿De parte de quién?   **d** ¿Puedo hablar con ...?
e El señor Martínez no se encuentra aquí.
f ¿Quiere dejar un mensaje?

1c Túrnate con tu compañero/a y practica la conversación. Ahora cambia la información en azul.

Speaking. Making a telephone call. Students first work with a partner to practise the conversation in **1b.** Then they change the details in bold in the conversation (the name of the person they wish to speak to and their own telephone number). They are given four sets of prompts so that they can do the conversation several times, if teachers wish.

2a Mira el teléfono de una cabina telefónica. Pon las frases en el orden correcto.

Reading. Instructions on a telephone box. Students look at the picture and put the instructions in the correct order.

Answers

E	F	A	C	B	D

2b Escucha los diálogos por teléfono. ¿Verdad ✓ o mentira ✗? (1–2)

Listening. Telephone calls about a job. Students listen to the two telephone conversations and do a true/false exercise.

■ ■

Tapescript

1 – *Hola, buenos días.*

– *Buenos días. ¿Puedo hablar con el director, por favor?*

– *Un momento. ¿De parte de quién?*

– *Me llamo Sara Gutiérrez López.*

– *Sí, ¿en qué puedo servirle?*

– *Quisiera información sobre el puesto de peluquera.*

– *Bueno, es un trabajo a tiempo completo y no se necesita experiencia.*

– *¿Qué debo hacer?*

– *Mande su currículum vitae y una carta de presentación al salón de belleza.*

– *Muchas gracias.*

2 – *Hola, buenas tardes.*

– *Buenas tardes. ¿Puedo hablar con el director, por favor?*

– *Un momento. ¿De parte de quién?*

– *Me llamo Javier García Martín.*

– *Sí, ¿en qué puedo servirle?*

– *Quisiera información sobre el puesto de cocinero.*

– *¿Tiene usted experiencia en este tipo de trabajo?*

– *Sí, trabajé en un restaurante durante las vacaciones pasadas.*

– *¡Perfecto! ¿Puede venir mañana para una entrevista?*

– *Claro que sí. ¿A qué hora?*

– *A las diez.*

– *Vale. ¡Hasta luego!*

Answers

1 verdad	**2** mentira	**3** verdad	**4** mentira
5 mentira	**6** mentira	**7** verdad	**8** mentira

2c Practica la conversación con tu compañero/a.

Speaking. Making a telephone call about a job. Students practise the role-play in pairs.

➕ Some students could then create a different version of the conversation, changing the details.

módulo 9/10 *Hablar*

(Student's Book pages 134–135)

Topics revised:

- Describing your character, friends and relationships
- Discussing environmental issues
- Talking about smoking, alcohol and drug dependency
- Talking about your education, future study and careers
- Job interviews

Modúlo 9 Yo

Conversaciones 1, 2 and 3

Three conversations about:
Your character, friends and relationships
Environmental issues
Smoking, alcohol and drug dependency

The general advice at the top of page 134 encourages students to ask questions of the examiner, as part of the general conversation section of their speaking test.

Juego de rol

A role-play on discussing a family disagreement with a friend.

The guidance at the top of page 134 advises students to try to get into character in role-play situations, to stay calm and to practise the role-play conversations in the book as much as possible.

Módulo 10 El futuro

Conversaciones 1 and 2

Two conversations: the first about education and plans for further study; the second about ideal jobs and key criteria for future work.

Juego de rol

A role-play about being interviewed for a job in Spain.

Presentación

A choice of three presentations:
How to be more environmentally friendly
The dangers of smoking
How to have a good work experience

Leer 1 Empareja los anuncios con las calidades que se necesitan.

Students match a series of statements to job adverts.

Answers

1 f	**2** d	**3** a	**4** e	**5** c	**6** b

Escribir 2 Elige uno de los puestos y escribe tu propia carta. Escribe de manera formal.

Writing a letter of application for one of the job advertisements above. Key phrases are given for support.

Leer 3 Lee el anuncio para un teléfono móvil. ¿Verdad (V), mentira (F) o no se sabe (¿)?

An advertisement for mobile telephones, followed by a true/false exercise.

Answers

a V	**b** V	**c** F	**d** ¿	**e** F

Leer 4 Lee el artículo y contesta en inglés.

A magazine article about the possible health hazards of mobile telephones, followed by questions in English.

Answers

> **1** The parents of young people with mobile phones.
> **2** Tiredness, headaches, dizziness/sickness, nervousness, insomnia, cancer, Alzheimer's disease.
> **3** Mobile phones, most domestic electrical appliances.
> **4** Frequency of absorption/proximity to the source.
> **5** Use mobiles sensibly/carefully.

Escribir 5 Tus padres han leído el artículo sobre los peligros de los móviles.
Escribe cinco razones por las que deben comprarte uno para Navidad.

Writing reasons why your parents should buy you a mobile. Students are encouraged to use and adapt language from the advertisement in 3 and the key phrases provided.

Cuaderno

(Workbook pages 59–63)

page 59

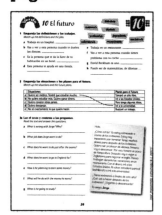

1

Answers

a enfermero	**b** dentista	**c** recepcionista
d dependiente	**e** cocinero	**f** mecánico
g futbolista	**h** profesor	

2

Answers

a Iré a la universidad   **b** Buscaré un trabajo
c Iré a las Estados Unidos   **d** Tomaré un año libre
e Pero tengo algunas ideas

3a

Answers

a He is stressed because of the exams
b Language teacher
c Rest and take some time off
d To improve his English
e He is planning to work in a restaurant during the holidays
f He will go to the USA
g A levels

page 60

4a

Answers

futuro/de/porque/idiomas/trabajado/gustó/ganar/
importante/gente/ingeniera/universidad

4b

Answers

1 D	**2** B	**3** A	**4** C

page 61

5

Answers

1 b	**2** a	**3** a	**4** c

6

Answers

1 F	**2** E	**3** D	**4** A	**5** B	**6** G	**7** C

page 62

Gramática

1

Answers (in bold)

> **a** Mañana **iré** a la piscina.
> **b** Mi hermano **estudiará** en la universidad para ser profesor.
> **c** En el futuro ideal **estudiaría** en la universidad para ser profesor.
> **d** Quisiera ser actriz de cine. **Ganaría** mucho y **viajaría** por el mundo.
> **e** El próximo verano, mis padres **viajarán** por Italia.
> **f** Me gustaría ganar mucho dinero. **Compraría** un coche grande y **llevaría** ropa cara.

2

Answers

> **a** he escrito
> **b** he visitado
> **c** he ganado
> **d** he ido
> **e** he comido

3

Answers

> **1** Future   **2** Present   **3** Conditional   **4** Perfect
> **5** Preterite   **6** Future   **7** Present   **8** Perfect
>
> **1** In August I will be on holiday.
> **2** I go to school by car.
> **3** In my ideal school we would not wear uniform.
> **4** I have written a letter to the hotel this morning.
> **5** Did you have lunch with your boss on the first day?
> **6** If you win the lottery will you buy a luxury car?
> **7** I put on a tie for the interview.
> **8** I (have) played tennis with the secretary.

Answers to Gramática exercises

Exercise 1

1 los dependientes
2 los conciertos
3 los balcones
4 las fotos
5 las cafeterías

Exercise 2

1 el vino
2 la abuela
3 los zapatos
4 el gato
5 las ciencias

Exercise 3

1 La chica es simpática.
2 Normalmente, en una casa hay una cocina.
3 El hermano de María tiene 8 años.
4 Estudio la historia y las matemáticas.

Exercise 4

1 Mis padres son ingleses.
2 La sección de ropa está en la tercera planta.
3 La falda es gris.
4 El país es pequeño.
5 Buenas noches.

Exercise 5

1 No me gusta su primo.
2 Mi perro se llama Ron.
3 No sé donde están tus libros.
4 Nuestro amigo vive en Madrid.
5 Su novio es alto.

Exercise 6

1 I am taller than my friend.
2 My brother is as friendly as you.
3 My mother is less strict than my father.
4 Pedro is the oldest/biggest of all the cousins.
5 Crisps are better than vegetables!

Exercise 7

1 Esta película es aburrida.
2 Aquellos caramelos son deliciosos.
3 Este chico es muy guapo.
4 Esas botas están muy de moda.
5 Ese libro es interesante.

Exercise 8

1 How is your brother?
2 When does the train leave?
3 What is your mother called?
4 Where do you live?
5 How many brothers/siblings do you have?

1 ¿Cuánto es?
2 ¿A qué hora sale el autobús?
3 ¿Cómo se llama tu tío?
4 ¿Dónde está tu colegio?
5 ¿Cuántas asignaturas estudias?

Exercise 9

1 Juega bien al baloncesto.
2 El tren va lentamente por el campo.
3 Escucha silenciosamente.
4 Los alumnos van rápidamente a clase.
5 Trabaja tranquilamente los sábados.
(Or any other sensible answers).

Exercise 10

1 Yo no tengo deberes.
2 El es muy simpático pero ella no.
3 ¿Tiene usted un mapa?
4 Tu estudias mucho.
5 Nosotros vivimos en Inglaterra.

Exercise 11

1 Quieres ir al cine esta tarde?
2 ¿Tiene aspirinas? Tengo dolor de cabeza.
3 ¿Prefiere un té o un café?
4 ¿Trabajas en una tienda los sábados?
5 ¿Le gusta ser profesor?

Exercise 12

1 Where is the ice-cream? I ate it.
2 Have you got your homework? No, I left it at home.
3 Do you want to try on the jacket? Yes, I would like to try it on.
4 Have you seen my rucksack? I'm sorry, I haven't seen it.
5 I have lost my purse. Where did you lose it?

Exercise 13

1 Me gusta jugar al fútbol con ellos.
2 El regalo es para ella.
3 Va al instituto conmigo.
4 Vive detrás de nosotros.

Exercise 14

1 hacer   2 ir   3 comer   4 escribir   5 escuchar
6 saltar   7 pensar   8 conducir   9 viajar   10 cantar

Answers to Gramática exercises

Exercise 15

1 bebes – you drink
2 practicamos – we practise
3 compran – they buy
4 toco – I play (an instrument)
5 estudias – you study
6 sale – he/she goes out

Exercise 16

1 Estoy fatal.
2 El libro es interesante.
3 Mi tío es un hombre de negocios.
4 Los alumnos son muy simpáticos.
5 Mi hermano es joven.
6 Los coches están en el garaje.
7 ¿Estás bien? No, no estoy bien. Tengo gripe.
8 ¿Eres de Barcelona? No, soy de Málaga.

Exercise 17

1 Lo siento, estoy haciendo los deberes.
2 Lo siento, estoy jugando con mi hermano menor.
3 Los siento, estoy arreglando mi dormitorio.
4 Lo siento, estoy limpiando la cocina.
5 Lo siento, estoy preparando la comida.

Exercise 18

1 I went out at eight o'clock.
2 You ate a lot!
3 My friend bought a T-shirt for his birthday.
4 I studied art last year.
5 We played basketball.

1 Jugaron al rugby.
2 Mi primo compró un reloj.
3 Comí patatas fritas.
4 Bebo limonada.
5 Escuchamos música.

Exercise 19

1 Ayer fui al cine.
2 El año pasado compré un walkman.
3 Practiqué la equitación con mi hermana.
4 Tuvo mucha suerte.
5 Hice deportes acuáticos.

Exercise 20

1 We went to an excellent concert.
2 María had a very serious accident.
3 I did my homework on Sunday.
4 They drank a bottle of lemonade.
5 Did you buy a present for your mother?

Exercise 21

1 It was sunny.
2 We went to the shops every day.
3 The sky was clear.
4 I watched television.
5 We ate at the cafeteria.
6 There were a lot of people at the swimming-pool.
7 The boy was fair and had curly hair.

Exercise 22

1 Voy a ir a la discoteca.
2 Vamos a comer paella.
3 Va a comprar un ordenador.
4 Va a vivir con su tía.
5 Van a trabajar en un hospital.

Exercise 23

1 People won't work during the day.
2 Schools will not exist.
3 There will be lots of different types of food.
4 Cars will be electric.
5 We will go to other planets for our holidays.

Exercise 24

(Accept any answer that is sensible).

Exercise 25

1 I have lost my suitcase.
2 Have you seen the new Star Wars film?
3 They wrote a letter.
4 Have you lost your passport?
5 They haven't done their homework.

Exercise 26

1 Tome la segunda calle a la derecha.
2 Escriba con bolígrafo.
3 Abra el cuaderno.
4 Escuche la cinta.
5 Pase el puente.

Exercise 27

1 Me despierto a las seis.
2 ¿A qué hora te levantas?
3 Normalmente mi hermano se ducha antes de desayunar.
4 Mis padres se acuestan muy tarde.
5 Me lavo los dientes dos veces al día.

Exercise 28

1 No trabaja nunca/nada en Madrid.
2 No entiendo nunca/nada el francés.
3 No voy nunca a Colombia.
4 Mis padres no se levantan nunca tarde.
5 No quisiera nada un helado de chocolate.

Exercise 29

(Accept any sensible answers).